MAIMONIDES AND THE BOOK
THAT CHANGED JUDAISM

The Jewish Publication Society
expresses its gratitude for the generosity
of the following sponsors of this book:

GAYLE AND DAVID SMITH

In memory of our parents.

UNIVERSITY OF NEBRASKA PRESS

Lincoln

MAIMONIDES AND THE BOOK THAT CHANGED JUDAISM

Secrets of *The Guide for the Perplexed*

MICAH GOODMAN

THE JEWISH PUBLICATION SOCIETY
Philadelphia

English-language edition © 2015 by Micah Goodman
Hebrew-language edition, *Sodotav shel Moreh ha-Nevukhim*,
© 2010 by Kinneret Zmora-Bitan, Dvir—Publishing House, Ltd.
Excerpts from *The Guide of the Perplexed*, by Moses Maimonides,
trans. Shlomo Pines, are reprinted by permission of the University
of Chicago Press, © 1963 by the University of Chicago.

Library of Congress Cataloging-in-Publication Data
Goodman, Micah, author.
[Sodotav shel Moreh ha-nevukhim. English]
Maimonides and the book that changed Judaism: secrets of "The
Guide for the Perplexed" / Micah Goodman.
pages cm
Includes bibliographical references and index.
ISBN 978-0-8276-1210-5 (cloth: alk. paper)
ISBN 978-0-8276-1198-6 (epub)
ISBN 978-0-8276-1199-3 (mobi)
ISBN 978-0-8276-1197-9 (pdf)
1. Maimonides, Moses, 1135–1204. Dalalat al-ha'irin.
2. Jewish philosophy. 3. Philosophy, Medieval. I. Title.
BM545.D35G6613 2015
181'.06—dc23
2014042653

Designed and set in Adobe Garamond Pro by Rachel Gould.

For Tzipi

CONTENTS

PART 3. PERPLEXITY

ACKNOWLEDGMENTS

I wish to thank my good friend Yedidya Sinclair for his fine, fluent, and intelligent English translation of this book.

My teacher Ze'ev Harvey gave me precious keys to the gates of *The Guide for the Perplexed*. I am extremely grateful to him for years of philosophical conversation, intellectual guidance, and friendly encouragement.

This book has been enriched by good advice from teachers and friends: Moshe Halbertal, Ran Baratz, Yair Loeberbaum, Ben Reis, Yuval Kahan, Rani Alon, and Shraga Bar-On, whose fingerprints are discernible all over the book. Boaz Lifschitz, Batya Huri, Yochai Ofran, and David Dishon read different sections of the Hebrew manuscript and contributed to it greatly. My thanks go to all of you.

The manuscript of this book was written at the Shalom Hartman Institute in Jerusalem. I am grateful to the institute's director, Donniel Hartman, for creating a meeting place of Torah scholars that enabled the book's birth.

Shmuel Rosner invested much time and notable effort in editing the Hebrew book. I am grateful to him for the artistry, wise advice, and profound conversations that clarified the structure of the book and brought it to its present form; the critical thinking, intelligence and refinement of Galia Graver improved the book very much. I am grateful.

Thanks to Tirza Eisenberg and everyone at the Kinneret Zemora Betan Dvir publishing house who worked on the Hebrew book with dedication and love. Thanks also to my agent, Deborah Harris, whose great wisdom and experience in publishing helped find the right home for the English version. George Eltman's meticulous and insightful editing improved the text considerably; Yaffa Aranoff contributed much to the final stages of the editing process. I am grateful to my publishers, Rabbi Barry Schwartz and Carol Hupping at the Jewish Publication Society, for their enthusiastic embrace of the book and their perceptive reading and comments. Many thanks also to Sabrina Stellrecht and Jonathan Lawrence for their painstaking proofing and editing. I am grateful to Lynn Schusterman for believing that the thoughts in this book could interest readers in English as much as they appear to have done so in Hebrew. And my thanks to her for the generosity that made this translation possible.

Many years ago, my teacher David Hartman goaded me to dive into the perplexity of the perplexed. Avi Ravitsky revealed to me many facets of the secrets of the *Guide*; Hertz Makov provoked and encouraged me to write this book. My heartfelt thanks to you all.

This book could not have been written without many years of conversations with my students at Midreshet Ein Prat and the Hebrew University of Jerusalem. This rich and enriching discussion sharpened the thoughts that went into the book. I feel fortunate to have been blessed with such excellent students, who listened to me and challenged my claims. To all of you, my students over the years, through whom I have learned more than from anyone else, my very deep thanks.

For sixteen years, the *Guide* has preoccupied my thoughts. Throughout most of that journey, my beloved life partner has walked at my side. This book is dedicated to my best friend, to my wife, to Tzipi.

INTRODUCTION TO THE
ENGLISH-LANGUAGE EDITION

I first encountered *The Guide for the Perplexed* when I was nine years old. It was at Yehuda Halevy Synagogue in Jerusalem's Katamon neighborhood where my parents prayed. After the services one Shabbat morning, while waiting for the bustling committee members to bring out the *kiddush*—whisky and pickled herring for the grownups, potato chips and ice pops for the children—I wandered over to the expansive pine-wood bookcases at the back of the sanctuary and stopped at a shelf marked "Jewish Philosophy." I did not know then what philosophy was, but I had a vague notion that it was something important and that I would learn more about it someday.

The book's cover was plain, with dark blue letters on the spine: *The Guide for the Perplexed.* I took it down and began to turn the pages, my eyes lighting here and there on words and phrases that I couldn't understand: "physics . . . metaphysics . . . homonyms . . ." My interest was piqued, and I turned, meaning to sit down with the book in one of the back pews, but found myself instead facing a rabbi in the synagogue, who was towering over me.

The rabbi looked at the book and then at me, a mixture of pride and concern in his kind gray eyes. He gently removed the book from my hands, replaced it on the shelf, and murmured, "Not yet, Micah," and then guided me by the arm to the Kiddush tables, by now laden with goodies. As I tore the wrapper off an ice pop I wondered, what could be in this book that would make the rabbi take it away from me?

In my early teens, I saw the book again, in the library of a small town in the south of Israel. There were several shelves in the Jewish philosophy section, and I saw that they were divided between shelves marked "Up to Maimonides" and "After Maimonides." Once again my curiosity was aroused. Why was Maimonides so important that Jewish philosophy was not the same after him? Why didn't books written before *The Guide for the Perplexed* even sit on the same shelf as books that had been written afterward?

I was born in Israel into an American family. Growing up in Jerusalem, I felt that my American home was in a different universe from Israeli society. It wasn't just a language gap; there was also a huge gap in culture, and even in body language. As a kid who wanted to fit in, I decided, at a very early age, "I am Israeli." I spoke English with an affected Israeli accent and tried to hide from my friends the secret of my American-ness, wanting desperately to broadcast the message, "I am one of you."

But there was an even bigger secret that I was hiding; my background was not just American, it was also part Christian. My mother had become a Jew by choice, but her amazing family, including a beloved grandmother who talked to Jesus all day long, and cousins who were priests, were also part of my life. I was torn, but I also yearned to just submerge myself utterly in one world—the Israeli world.

Early on, I sensed that Maimonides—who is also known as the Rambam, an acronym for the name Rabbi Moses Ben Maimon— would be my guide. Later, as an academic, I discovered that the Rambam wasn't just a teacher to Jews but also a major influence on Christian thought. I began to understand that he was a teacher to the different worlds that had formed me. The Rambam did not just change the face of Jewish philosophy; he also transformed Western thought.

Philosophy was not the only area that occupied Maimonides. In addition to *The Guide for the Perplexed*, the Rambam also wrote the

Mishneh Torah, the most important book on *halakhah*, or Jewish law. The fourteen volumes of the *Mishneh Torah* include minute details about sacrifices, kashrut, the Jewish holidays, and family law. The Rambam deduces from the Talmud and Rabbinic literature clear halakhic decisions, reorganizes them, and creates an almost perfect order out of the apparent talmudic disarray. No one since has achieved anything like it.

In the eighteenth century, the great Torah scholar Jacob Emden concluded that the Rambam could not have authored *The Guide for the Perplexed*; someone else must have written it and attributed it to Maimonides. Emden was wrong, but his underlying question was on the mark: How was it possible that the author of the *Mishneh Torah* also wrote the *Guide*? The two books are so profoundly unlike one another. The *Mishneh Torah* is all law, whereas the *Guide* is entirely a world of thought. The *Mishneh Torah* deals with matters such as how one separates meat from milk. The *Guide* asks questions such as "Is there a God?" The Jew nourished by the *Mishneh Torah* is an obedient Jew. The Jew who springs from the *Guide* is a thinking Jew.

Much of my life experience has been characterized by a sense of being caught between worlds. Maimonides did not live between worlds, but rather was able to fully inhabit each of the worlds that he lived in. He was neither a philosopher who dabbled in *halakhah* nor a halakhic man with an interest in philosophy. He was a philosopher *and* a halakhist in the fullest sense of both words.

THE PERPLEXED ISRAELI AND THE PERPLEXED AMERICAN

I initially wrote this book for Israelis. Over the past decade, a hunger for Jewish cultural identity has emerged, particularly among the secular. Israeli rock stars perform arrangements of verses from Psalms. Popular Israeli television shows feature Jewish themes. The Israeli film *Footnote*, nominated for an Oscar as Best Foreign Film of 2012, was about Talmud scholars. Today there is a profound and exciting awakening in Israel. But this is not a return to traditional

Judaism; there is no great wave of secular Israelis suddenly becoming religious. Rather, more and more Israelis are becoming Jews. Back in the generation of the founders—of Israel and of Israeli-ness—the dominant sense was of the emergence, in the words of one of them, of "a new psychological strain of Jewishness." Zionism attempted to do more than just establish a new state; it also sought to establish a new kind of person.

The "new Jew" would be different from the old Jew of the exile, because he would shake off the restraints of exilic Judaism, including, in particular, obedience to *halakhah*. The new Jew would be a free man. He would not be constrained by the force of any higher authority—neither the nation-states of Europe nor the books of Rabbinic law. Secularization was an essential part of the revolution wrought by Israel's founders, whose mission was not merely to defend Jews but also to replace Judaism. The secular did not press any claim to ownership of Judaism (in particular, the halakhic variety); on the contrary, they wanted to shake themselves free of it. They left Judaism to the *haredim*, the punctiliously orthodox, who felt that it really belonged to them. And so now in Israel there is one group of Jews who tend to be doctrinaire about Judaism living alongside another group who are inclined to be apathetic about it. This combination of dogmatism and ignorance has come to be a distinguishing mark of Israeli culture.

But the atmosphere is changing. The young, secular community in Israel is beginning to embrace its Judaism again. Whereas for the founding generation Judaism was a burden to be cast off, today, for more and more Israelis, Judaism is a no longer a threat but is instead a source of inspiration and enrichment.

The book in your hands seeks to explain another book, *The Guide for the Perplexed*. Apparently, tens of thousands of Israelis were hungry to know what Maimonides said, because my book, in its original Hebrew, became a best-seller in Israel almost from the day it was published.

The big questions about God, existence, and the universe are not, of course, just Jewish or Israeli questions. They are questions that most of us start to ask from the time we are able to ask questions at all. The Rambam attempted to prove God's existence; he also asked how God could be interested in people. Maimonides considered whether there are any limits to reason and also explained how people can satisfy their thirst to know God. The questions he asked are eternal and the answers original.

Modernity suspends us between worlds. In the tension between worlds, perplexity is born. For American Jews, characteristic perplexities include the gaps between their secular and Jewish lives, between involvement in contemporary intellectual life and commitment to Jewish tradition, or between the arguments of universal ethics and the moral claims of Israel and the Jewish people. Maimonides addressed earlier versions of these perennial perplexities in the *Guide*, and his seminal solutions still illuminate the contemporary incarnations of these issues that we face today. Studying the *Guide* can help us to have an enriched and nuanced religious awareness that is also in tune with how we live in the modern world.

The Rambam believed that the great truths transformed a person only if one reached them through genuine effort. Therefore he buried his central ideas deep within *The Guide for the Perplexed*. And that is why the difficulties that readers face in understanding the *Guide* are typically the result of deliberate decisions by the author. For seekers of insight, the *Guide* is no shortcut. Maimonides does not supply his readers with easily accessible answers to the central questions of existence. Rather, he leads his readers toward discovering the answers for themselves.

The Secret

In the world of *kohanim*, or priests, proximity to the inner sancta of the Temple—the Holy and the Holy of Holies—reflected one's place in the social hierarchy. In the intellectual world of Maimonides, it is access to *knowledge* that determines who is important. According to Maimonides, in the ancient world there was a small group of people who held a monopoly on true knowledge, but following a series of historical catastrophes, the possessors of the secret were lost, and the secret along with them. Only hundreds of years later did Maimonides succeed, according to his own testimony, in recovering the lost true knowledge.

Maimonides believed that his historical role was to decipher this secret, to transmit it and yet, paradoxically, to keep it hidden. This is why he wrote *The Guide for the Perplexed*, in which the exalted knowledge is withheld. The book, which draws together his main philosophical ideas, was written between 1187 and 1191, when Maimonides was in his early fifties. By means of a complex, esoteric system, Maimonides conceals beneath many layers the great philosophical secrets of Judaism. The book transformed Jewish philosophy.

It was not just Jewish philosophy that changed in the wake of the *Guide*, but kabbalistic teachings too. There are those who claim that the phenomenon of committing kabbalistic wisdom to writing, which had not previously been widespread and which gathered momentum in the thirteenth century, was a reaction to the *Guide*. This was a book that simultaneously awakened the two major strains of Jewish thought: philosophy and Kabbalah. But, the impact of the *Guide* was not limited to Jewish thought. The revival of Christian philosophy that began in the thirteenth century and reached maturity in the writings of Thomas Aquinas and his followers was also influenced by the *Guide*.

For more than eight hundred years, scholars, philosophers, and commentators have been trying to unravel this text. A work that deals with the great riddles of existence has, down through the ages, become a riddle itself.

At the end of the introduction to the *Guide*, where we become acquainted with the techniques of concealment that are deployed throughout the book, Maimonides makes a surprising move.[1] He begs the reader who believes that he has successfully deciphered the secrets and reached the transformative truth to swear that he will not share with anyone else what he has uncovered. Maimonides asks that his own unmediated teaching be the sole instructor. He wished there to be no courses on the *Guide*, nor any commentaries, articles, or books. Maimonides wanted anyone who sought to penetrate his secret to do so by means of a direct, personal encounter with his text. But the hundreds of books and thousands of scholarly articles and lectures written about the *Guide* are evidence that Maimonides failed in his effort to restrain his readers. The author lost control over his book.

The oath Maimonides adjured his readers to swear has been broken in every generation. Some have argued that an oath without the agreement of both sides has no force or effect. Others have claimed that since books had already been written explaining the secrets of the *Guide*, the wall has been breached and the oath already broken. Perhaps an intellectual passion burning inside readers of the *Guide* moved them to break the chains of this prohibition and interpret hidden matters. The book that is in your hands, which addresses the secrets of the *Guide*, continues the venerable tradition of the breakers of the oath.

In recent years there have been a number of books on Maimonidean philosophy, and considerable academic research on many and diverse subjects that are covered in *The Guide for the Perplexed*, including politics, mysticism, and *halakhah*.[2] There have also been several important biographies of Maimonides within which the *Guide* is discussed. (I am a product of the Israeli academy, and ask forgiveness of my English-speaking readers from the outset if this book does not cite much of the excellent scholarship on Maimonides produced in North America over recent decades.) However, it is remarkable that there has not been a single work written originally in Hebrew that deals exclusively with the *Guide*, the most important work of Jewish philosophy ever written.

This book does not presume to reveal all the secrets; many will remain unresolved. Nevertheless, I hope that my book will enrich the discussion around *The Guide for the Perplexed* and awaken curiosity about it and about the message enfolded within it.

The Structure of This Book

Maimonides was a virtuoso of organization and structure. His *Mishneh Torah* established an astonishing order out of the halakhic unruliness of talmudic literature. *The Guide for the Perplexed*, on the other hand, often appears to be an almost chaotic work. There are chapters that appear to be unrelated to other chapters, and within a chapter, the author may digress to discuss seemingly peripheral issues. It is a demanding read. Maimonides's words on a particular subject sometimes are fragmented into half-utterances, and these may be dispersed throughout the *Guide* in a way that seems very far from any sort of orderly, all-encompassing system. A lightning bolt of truth may appear from unexpected places throughout, but afterward the reader may be back in darkness. Entering the chambers of the *Guide* is like coming into a room where no object is in its proper place. It is as if a storm has passed and utterly upended the normal order of things. But it is a deliberate disorder. All of the disarrangements in the *Guide* are carefully planned.

Maimonides spent ten years writing the fourteen books of the *Mishneh Torah*. It took him five years to complete the *Guide*: five years dedicated to the *dis*organization of just one book. So the reader of the *Guide* must first and foremost be its organizer. As Maimonides recommends, in order to understand the *Guide*, we must order it anew.

There have been numerous attempts to reorder the book, and this book is one more effort to organize the thoughts of the *Guide* for the curious, confused, or skeptical contemporary reader. Two kinds of readers are likely to be interested in my book: those who want to understand what Maimonides has to say in the *Guide*, and those who are involved in the big questions of human existence and want to know what the *Guide* has to offer them on their journey. And so this book is organized as such:

Part 1 considers the existence of God.
Part 2 addresses questions about who wrote the Torah and the reasons for the commandments it contains.

Part 3 deals with the issue of perplexity and with the role and therapeutic purpose of doubt.

The conclusion to part 3 offers a midrash that brings the *Guide* into dialogue with the post-ideological, doubt-ridden sensibility of the twenty-first century. It takes the skeptical questioning of postmodernism seriously, while arguing that the Rambam provides us with intellectual resources that can help us to avoid postmodernism's skeptical answers.

Two central questions infuse these discussions. One is the issue of the ideal life: What is the right kind of life to live? The second is political and of two parts: What are the conditions for creating an ideal society, and what sort of society should we strive to establish?

PART 1
GOD

God is the greatest threat to religion. This paradoxical idea is central to *The Guide for the Perplexed*.

The absolute perfection of God voids religion of meaning, in the sense that the greatness of God renders absurd the thought that God needs our worship. Many eighteenth-century European philosophers were deists, and deism—the belief in God without religion—pervades much of the Western world today. Surveys show more than 60 percent of secular Israelis believe in God.[1] They are not atheists; they believe in God, but not in religion. Their preference not to commit to a religion isn't *despite* belief in God; rather it is *because* of belief in God.

Rejection of religion is not necessarily rejection of God. Sometimes it is a deeper expression of belief in God. The *Guide* seeks to grapple with this profound theological problem.

1

THE GOD OF MAIMONIDES

Proving the Existence of God

Many of us are conditioned during childhood to think of God as a reflection of ourselves. We imagine God as being like a person. It may be an image of a wise old man, or a glowing, celestial figure, full of light, but often it is some enhanced and ennobled version of the human form. Moses led a vigorous, even violent assault against idolatry, against physical representations of God. He enjoined future generations to continue waging war on idolatry until it was obliterated. In Maimonides's world, the worship of statues and images had all but disappeared, but the inner statues and images of God in the human imagination still stood firm. Maimonides, who saw himself as heir to the biblical struggle against idolatry, sought to explode our inner pictures of God.[2]

He understood the enormity of the challenge. Ideas that are formed in childhood are particularly hard to uproot. Images from the early, formative stages of cognitive development are deeply influential. In Maimonides's view, the greatest enemies of the educator and the theologian are those who plant false ideas in the minds of children.[3]

How does one break into human consciousness and smash the idols that are found there?

The tool that Maimonides deploys to uproot our internal images of God is reason. The battle against idolatry is a struggle of reason

3

against the imagination. And it is Maimonides's other great work, the *Mishneh Torah*, a book all about law and reason, that we turn to first to begin to understand his argument for the proof of God. Arguments that the Rambam develops at length in the *Guide* are stated with unparalleled clarity and conciseness in the *Mishneh Torah*, making this a good place to begin our study.

In the seminal first chapter of the *Mishneh Torah*, Maimonides uses pure intellect to shatter our pictures of the imagined God. He demonstrates the existence of God, and the God whose existence he demonstrates is a divinity that is not physical. When, through the power of reason, the reader internalizes the idea of the abstract God, the corporeal God will disappear.

Proving the Unity of God

The Foundation of Foundations and the Pillar of all Wisdom is to know that there is a First Cause, that He brought everything else into existence, and that everything that exists, from the heavens to the earth and everything that is in them would not exist, were not His existence true. (*Mishneh Torah* [hereafter *MT*], *Hilkhot Yesodei HaTorah*, 1:1)

The opening section of the *Mishneh Torah* is called *Hilkhot Yesodei HaTorah*, or "Laws of the Foundations of the Torah." Here Maimonides sets out the foundation upon which all the other foundations rest.

For many, faith is distinct from knowledge. Belief begins where knowledge ends. But for Maimonides, faith *is* knowledge. It is only forged through rationally apprehending the existence of God. The first commandment of the Torah is to be acquainted with the proof— the foundation of all foundations.

The rational demonstration of God that appears in the first chapter of the *Hilkhot Yesodei HaTorah* is the indispensable foundation, without which the whole edifice of Torah would collapse. This proof also appears in the *Guide* (2:1) as part of the series of demonstrations that Maimonides presents for God's existence.[4] In addition to God's existence, he also proves God's unity and incorporeality.

First, Maimonides sets out to define the unity of God:

> This God is one; He is neither two nor more than two; He is simply one. His unity is not like any other oneness that exists in the world. His is not the unity of a kind that encompasses many other single particulars; and it is not like the unity of a body that is divided into parts and extremities; rather it is a unity that is entirely unlike any other sort of oneness in the universe. (*MT, Hilkhot Yesodei HaTorah,* 1:7)

The word "one" here does not correspond to any object in the world. There is no material thing that answers to Maimonides's description of the "one." Any physical object can be divided into secondary parts. My writing table is made up of four legs, the wooden surface that rests upon them, paint, and so forth. It is a cluster of different characteristics. In the material world, there is no oneness; there is only the *designation* of singularity. When we attribute the word "one" to certain objects, we are using a linguistic device.

It is impossible to attach the word "one" in its full meaning to anything in the physical world. Matter itself is divisible into parts, and form contains multiple elements. The only referent that may truly be called "one" is God. God alone is not "a kind that encompasses many other single particulars," nor "a body that is divided into many parts and extremities." God has exclusive rights to the category of oneness. Later we will see how, in the *Guide,* Maimonides created the "Doctrine of Negative Attributes" through which he made God compatible with the world by showing that God is not subject to any kind of verbal description. While, according to the *Guide,* there is no word that can be used to characterize God, in the opening chapter of the *Mishneh Torah,* Maimonides does just that. As opposed to any thing that exists in the world, only God can truly be described as one. It is not just that the word corresponds to God; it corresponds *only* to God.

The proof consists of several steps. Let us outline them and then follow them carefully:

1. The first step in the proof demonstrates that God's unity depends on God's immateriality.
2. The second step demonstrates that God's immateriality depends in turn upon God's infinitude.
3. The final step is the proof of God's unity that depends upon God's immateriality.

Now let us trace this three-part movement in more detail:

> If God were many, He would have a body and physicality, because items that are co-extensive with each other cannot be counted as distinct from one another except through occurrences that happen to their bodies. (MT, *Hilkhot Yesodei HaTorah*, 1:7)

Difference is a necessary condition of multiplicity. Objects that are not distinct from one another are not things; they are *a thing*. My writing desk is absolutely identical only to itself, because there is no difference between it and itself. It is a logical condition for the existence of multiple things that they are different from one another. However, there is no difference between two objects that are absolutely and essentially identical, and therefore it is not logically possible for there to be a multiplicity of identical objects. The distinction between objects that are the same in essence can only be meaningfully applied by virtue of differences in their physical characteristics.[5] It follows that if there are objects that are identical in essence, yet they are multiple, then they must also be immaterial. The concept of a triangle, for example, is single. There is no multiplicity of concepts of triangles. But there are many actual triangles. We have triangular roofs, triangular rulers, triangular slices of pizza. There are many physical triangles, but only one concept of a triangle.

If God were multiple, then God would have to be material, for the only way to create a distinction between the different parts of God would be through physical characteristics. The conclusion of the first step of the proof, then, is that if God is not physical, then God must be one.

Now it remains to prove the immateriality of God.

> If the Creator had a body, He would have a defined form for it is impossible that there should be a body that is not defined. And anything that is defined is limited in its power. (*MT*, *Hilkhot Yesodei HaTorah*, 1:7)

Finitude is an essential quality of any physical body.[6] The conclusion of the second step of our proof follows, namely, that the proof of God's immateriality depends on God's infinitude. The third step, then, is the proof of God's infinitude. Maimonides demonstrates this by reflection on the "motions of the spheres":

> This Existence is the God of the Universe, the Lord of the world. He moves the spheres through His infinite, unceasing power, for the spheres rotate constantly, and it is impossible that they should move without anything moving them; and He, may He be blessed, moves them, without a hand and without a body. (*Guide*, 2:1)

The astronomical fact that the "the spheres rotate constantly" is at the heart of Aristotelian proofs for the existence of God. From the perpetual motion of the spheres, Aristotelians infer God's existence. A "sphere" in the parlance of medieval astronomy is a ball made of transparent material that supports the stars or planets. The sphere of Mars, for example, is the sphere on which the planet Mars stands. The observed motion of Mars is in fact the movement of the sphere upon which it rests.

Matter is finite, but the motion of the spheres is perpetual and endless. According to medieval astronomy, the momentum and the circularity of the movements produced by heavenly forces testify to their eternity. This is the astronomical background to the Aristotelian inference: if the motion of the spheres is infinite, then the source of the motion must itself be infinite, because something finite cannot create something infinite—that would be logically impossible. The infinite movement of the cosmos has a source, and that source must, by definition, be infinite.

The proof of God's unity depends on the proof of God's immateriality, which in turns depends upon the demonstration of God's infinitude. The conclusion, then, is that the source of cosmic motion is infinite, and therefore it is non-physical and therefore it must be one.

> And the power of our God, may His name be blessed is not the kind of power that bodies have, since His power is infinite and unceasing, for the spheres are in constant motion. And since He has no body, such physical occurrences as would be necessary to ascribe to God—separation and difference—do not pertain to Him; therefore, He must be one. Know that this thing is a positive commandment, as it says, *The Lord our God, the Lord is one* (Deut. 6:4). (MT, *Hilkhot Yesodei HaTorah*, 1:7)

Reflection on the motion of the stars reveals the existence of a source for that movement; that source is infinite, non-material, and unitary.

The Foundation of Foundations?

God is the source of all motion, but there is nothing moving God. The immateriality of God negates any possibility that God might change. A God that is above time is also above motion and alteration.[7]

> It is written, *I am God who does not change* (Mal. 3:6). And if He were sometimes angry and sometimes happy, He would be changing. And these occurrences only happen to beings with dark, earthy bodies, those who dwell in houses of clay, and their foundation is dust. But He, may He be blessed, is far above all that. (MT, *Hilkhot Yesodei HaTorah*, 1:12)

A static, unchanging God is a God that does not hear prayer, does not pay attention to individual human needs and does not redeem history, for all of these assume change in God. The God that human beings reveal does not reveal Himself.

How can the Jewish religious system be based on the static God of Aristotle? The first chapter of the *Mishneh Torah* seems to undermine the doctrinal foundations of the Torah. But Maimonides does not identify the immutable unity of God as a threat to the Torah; rather, he understands this unity to be the foundation of all foundations and the pillar of all wisdom.

Yet without a God who reveals Himself to people and tells them to fulfill the commandments, what value is there to any of the mitzvot that Maimonides details throughout the *Mishneh Torah*? The God whose existence is provable by reason must somehow be compatible with the world of providence, revelation, prayer, and spiritual reward. However, in the *Mishneh Torah* there is no systematic, comprehensive attempt to mediate between the foundation of the one and other foundational beliefs, that is, between the static God and the dynamic elements of faith. Maimonides devoted another book to this project: *The Guide for the Perplexed*.

THE HIDDEN GOD OF THE *GUIDE*

The fierce desire to behold God's face is articulated in the Bible[8] and reinforced by early mystical literature.[9] This is the impetus behind Kabbalah, as well as large parts of Jewish philosophy. In opposition to this ancient tradition that seeks to characterize and describe God stands Maimonides, who maintains that one can say nothing at all about God. The only possible way to refer to Him is with silence.

> The most apt phrase concerning this subject is the dictum occurring in the Psalms, *Silence is praise to Thee* (Ps. 65:2), which interpreted signifies: silence with regard to You is praise. This is a most perfectly put phrase regarding this matter. For whatever we say intending to magnify and exalt on the one hand we find that it can have some application to Him, may He be exalted, on the other we perceive in it some deficiency.[10] Accordingly silence and limiting oneself to the apprehensions of the intellects are more appropriate—just as the perfect ones have enjoined

when they said, *Commune with your own heart upon your bed and be still* (Ps. 4:5). (*Guide*, 1:59)

Godliness, according to Maimonides, cannot be represented in language. One may not attribute any description to God, nor speak a single word about Him. All that one may say about God is what He is not:

> Know that description of God, may He be cherished and exalted, by means of negation is the correct description—a description that is not affected by an indulgence in facile language and does not imply any deficiency with respect to God in general or in any particular mode. On the other hand, if one describes him by means of affirmations, one implies, as we have made clear, that he is associated with that which is not He and implies a deficiency in Him. (*Guide*, 1:58)

That is to say, any attempt to praise God in words only diminishes God's stature. God is bigger than language, not just because of the perfection of God but also owing to the limitations of speech. Describing God in words implies placing God in a category that includes other things. For example, if we were to say that God is good, then we would be putting God in the class of good people, like Mother Teresa and the Baal Shem Tov. It may well be that God is better, much better even, than the other members of the group, but the difference between them is merely quantitative. Language places God and the world in the same category.[11]

The idea that God is beyond language is profoundly important; it means that God is utterly different from the world. The doctrine of negative attributes is founded on God's absolute otherness.

The God of Maimonides and the God of the Bible

Maimonides's God, who resists all description, seems very different from the God of the Bible, who is merciful, gracious, and a great many other things besides. Actually, however, there is no inconsistency.

Monotheism, the biblical faith revolution, was not just a mathematical operation. Monotheism did not simply reduce the number of gods from many to one. There was a period in which ancient Egyptians also believed in one God, the Sun God, but that was still an idolatrous culture. The biblical revolution focused more on the uniqueness of God than on His oneness. As opposed to the pagan world, which understood nature to be the place where the gods lived and identified different divinities with particular natural forces, the Bible removes God from nature.[12] This is the true core of the biblical revolution: making a partition between God and the world. God is not a part of nature and is not subject to the laws of nature. He created heaven and earth and is therefore distinct from heaven and earth. But if the Bible takes God out of the world, language still leaves Him in it. Even though it is in opposition to the anthropomorphic, scriptural conception of God, Maimonides's move nevertheless is congruent with the Bible. It brings the biblical theological process to completion: removing God from the world begins with God's liberation from nature in the Book of Genesis and ends with liberation from language in the *Guide*.[13]

Justifying the Doctrine of Negative Attributes

One should read the *Guide* according to Maimonides's instructions and connect the chapters according to their subject matter. The doctrine of negative attributes is set out in chapters 56–59 of part 1, but the justification for the doctrine is based on part 2, chapter 2 of the *Guide*. We will read these chapters in conjunction with one another in order to show the rational basis for negating descriptions of God.

At the beginning of part 2 of the *Guide*, Maimonides presents a series of proofs for God's existence. The doctrine of negative attributes is founded on what is sometimes known in Maimonidean scholarship as the metaphysical proof. In contrast to classical proofs, the metaphysical proof does not flow from reflection on the world (e.g., the motions of the spheres) but rather from a profound conceptual investigation.[14] One of the fundamental questions in ontology—the philosophical study of the nature of existence—is, In what class of existent things should we place the world? Maimonides lays out the different possibilities. There are three types of existing things: impossible existents, possible existents, and necessary existents. Impossible existents are objects for which some logical requirement prevents them from existing—that is, an object whose existence would entail a contradiction. For example, a triangle with angles adding up to 190 degrees is an impossible existent. If it had 190 degrees, it would not be a triangle. On the other hand, a possible existent is an object where there no logical barrier to either its existence or its non-existence (e.g., my desk). Finally, a necessary existent is an object that cannot possibly not exist.

In which of these categories of existent should one place the world? By definition, the world cannot be an impossible existent; it exists. Our experience shows that the world is full of possible existents. But is there anything in the world that is a necessary existent? This is a critical question, and its solution is essential for clarifying the nature of God. To arrive at the answer we must look more deeply at the distinction between possible and necessary existents.

Possible (or in modern philosophical terms, contingent) existents may exist, or they may not exist, because they are dependent upon other objects. The existence of my desk depends on the existence of the carpenter who made it, the wood from which it was fashioned, and also upon the fact that no fire has yet destroyed it. The dependency of its existence is the reason why its existence is merely possible.

In light of this explanation, let us ask once again: In addition to the possible existents that populate the world, are there also any necessary existents? Maimonides addresses this question by asking if it is possible to have a world in which there are only possible existents. After he has shown that such a world would be absurd, it follows, then, that in addition to possible existents there must be at least one necessary existent.

This is his proof: If all objects depend on other objects, and these other objects are dependent on still further objects, there is a problem, because a world composed entirely of possible existents cannot be grasped. Such a world is impossible. One may therefore infer from the existence of possible existents (such as my desk) that there must be at least one necessary existent that underwrites the existence of all the possible ones. This succession of dependent objects eventually requires one metaphysical nail, so to speak, that will hold the whole chain of possible existents in place.

This discovery of the existence of necessary objects has a very important consequence: we can say absolutely nothing about those things of whose existence we are certain. Any characterization of the necessary existent makes it dependent upon some larger category. If we say that it is good, then it depends on the category of good- ness. The use of words to describe the necessary existent denies its necessity; the very fact of giving the object a linguistic description testifies to its merely possible, but not necessary, existence.

A necessary existent exists beyond the bounds of language. This is the rational foundation for the doctrine of negative attributes. All that may be known about God as a necessary existent is that God exists, but we can know nothing at all about the nature of God who exists.

> I shall say that it has already been demonstrated that God may He be hon-
> ored and magnified, is existent of necessity and that there is no composition
> in Him, as we shall demonstrate, and that we are only able to apprehend
> that fact that He is and cannot apprehend His quiddity. (*Guide*, 1:58)

The wonderful thing about the metaphysical proof is that it dem- onstrates rationally that there is an area of existence that is not rational. The proof challenges the limits of reason. The existence of a realm that is accessible to reason and serves as the object of its investigation is grounded in a realm that is beyond the bounds of reason. Like the metaphysical proof for the existence of God, the doctrine of negative attributes is a transition from knowledge to knowing that one cannot know.

The doctrine of negative attributes also implies an important nor- mative principle. Maimonides is not content with merely negating descriptions of God. He demands that his readers invest great intellectual effort in eradicating qualitative statements about God's nature:

> These are some of the useful teachings of natural science with regard to the knowledge of the deity. For he who was no knowledge of these sciences is not aware of the deficiency inherent in affections, and does not understand the meaning of what is potential and what is in actuality, and does not know what privation attaches necessarily to everything potential and that which is potential is more deficient than that which is in motion—because in the latter case potentiality is passing into actuality. . . . For this reason, he does not have at his disposal a demonstration of the existence of God, or one of the necessity of negating these kinds of attributions in reference to him. (*Guide*, 1:55)

Maimonides reverses the way people often consider the relationship between science and religion. Learning about science contributes nothing to our knowledge of God; it only rules out things that we might have thought we knew about God. The more deeply a person understands how nature works, the more he understands that it is not divine. Studying science shatters the mythological view of nature.[15]

If God cannot be represented in language, then it follows not just that we cannot speak *about* God but also that we cannot speak *to* God. The universe "needs" a God whose existence we can prove, but not a God that we can worship. The perfect, static God of the *Guide* must, it would appear, be entirely indifferent to things that happen in the world. Maimonides describes the unchanging nature of God faced with the absolute destruction of the world that took place at the time of the Flood:

> It also says, *The Lord sitteth at the flood* (Ps. 29:10). It means that when the state of the earth is changed and corrupted, there is no change in the relation of God, may He be exalted, to things; this relation remains the same—stable and permanent—whether the thing undergoes generation or corruption. (*Guide*, 1:11.)

Let us return, then, to the issue that will accompany us throughout part 1 of this book: the unavoidable tension between God and religion. If basic elements of religion, such as providence, reward, punishment, and prayer, are to be meaningful, then God must be intimately involved. The more perfect God is, the more the metaphysical function of religion is diminished; by contrast, if God is less exalted and transcendent, then the role of religion will be correspondingly greater. We see, then, that the foundational tension in the *Guide* is not the one between Athens and Jerusalem, but rather between Maimonides's religion and his God.

We will see how Maimonides reinterprets the fundamentals of religion in order to make room for absolute divine transcendence. Most of the *Guide for the Perplexed* is devoted to this end. The first seventy chapters are dedicated to liberating God from the limitations of language. Maimonides enumerates and reinterprets the main terms in the Bible that appear to attribute physical or emotional traits to God.[16] After freeing God from language (and so too from the world), he devotes the next hundred chapters or so to rethinking the intellectual foundations of Judaism, central among them the concepts of creation, prophecy, and providence and the reasons for the commandments. I will discuss the question of creation extensively in part 3 of this book. Now, let us take on the issue of prophecy.

2

PROPHECY

God's perfection is not only a problem in talking about God. It can also be an obstacle to the possibility of God's talking to us. How, then, could Maimonides determine that prophecy is one of the basic principles of faith? In the *Mishneh Torah*, the Rambam declares, "Among the foundations of religion, one must know that God speaks to people in prophecy" (*Hilkhot Yesodei HaTorah*, 7:1). The Rambam's understanding of prophecy bridges God's unchanging nature and the idea that certain people can receive prophecy.

THE CLASSICAL IDEA OF PROPHECY

The Rambam considered our preconceptions to be the greatest obstacle to intellectual development. We maintain our belief in the ideas that are familiar to us. In general, the longer we hold an opinion, the greater our sense of certainty about it. We reflexively suspect new ideas. The psychological price of abandoning an old opinion and adopting a new one is often too high. *The Guide for the Perplexed* challenges us and seeks to free us from familiar thoughts that imprison us.

Maimonides begins his discussion of prophecy by describing the traditional view or preconceived notion: most people believe that prophecy is an act of God in which God reveals Himself to a particular person and transmits an important message. Prophecy is commonly thought of as a miraculous break in the natural order of things. The person who has a prophetic experience is, in that moment, lifted above the laws of nature. He or she bursts the bounds of normal existence and attains a kind of superhuman consciousness.[1] According to the Rambam:

> The first opinion—that of the multitude of those among the Pagans . . . and also believed by some of the common people professing our Law—is that God, may He be exalted, chooses whom He wishes from among men, turns him into a prophet, and sends him with a mission. According to them, it makes no difference whether this individual is a man of knowledge or ignorant, aged or young. The view of the ignorant masses . . . and also of some of our simple co-religionists, is that God selects anyone He pleases, speaks to him through prophecy and entrusts him with a mission. It makes no difference, in their view, whether the person is learned or stupid, young or old. (*Guide*, 2:32)

As the antithesis of this view, Maimonides presents the Aristotelian position:

> The second opinion is that of the philosophers. It affirms that prophecy is a certain perfection in the nature of man. This perfection is not achieved in any individual from among men except after a training that makes that which exists in the potentiality in the species pass into actuality, provided an obstacle due to temperament or some external cause does not hinder this, as is the case with regard to every perfection whose existence is possible in a certain species. For the existence of that perfection in its extreme and ultimate form in every individual of that species is not possible. It must, however, necessarily exist in at least one particular individual; if, in order to be achieved this perfection requires something that actualizes it, then that something must necessarily exist. According to this opinion, it is not possible that an ignoramus should turn into a prophet; nor can a man not be a prophet on a certain evening and be a prophet on the following morning, as if he had made some sudden find. Things are rather as follows: When, in the case of a superior individual who is perfect with respect to his rational and moral faculties, his imaginative faculty is in the most perfect state, and when he has prepared in the way that

you will hear, he will necessarily become a prophet, because that is a perfection that belongs to us by nature. According to this opinion, it is impossible that a person should be fit for prophecy and prepared for it, but not become a prophet, except to the extent that an individual having a healthy temperament should be nourished with excellent food, without sound blood and similar things being generated from that food. (*Guide*, 2:32)

Prophecy, according to this Aristotelian view, is a product of fully realized human perfection. Just as someone who develops his body to the utmost will become a model of physical fitness, so too, one who does the same for his spirit will be a prophet. This is the opposite of the traditional notion. The Rambam is saying that prophecy is a human spiritual achievement rather than an act of God.

One of Aristotle's great contributions to human thought was to articulate a new kind of "lack." Apart from "absolute lack," there is also a "lack of potential." Saying that a kitten is not a pine tree is different from saying that a kitten is not a cat. A kitten will never become a pine tree. That is not part of the kitten's potential. But the kitten *is* growing toward becoming a cat. The goal of its life, so to speak, is to overcome the lack that is inherent in mere potentiality and to actualize the full "catness" of its existence.

All of nature tends to move from potentiality to actualization, or, to put it in another way, from absence to reality. The movement toward full actualization is not a matter of choice. That is how nature works, with one exception: man. Human beings, according to Maimonides, are the only creatures that can choose to remain less than they can be.[2] A person can elect not to realize his potential and not to actualize his full human capacities. Unlike all other beings, man may remain a mere man-in-potential. The prophet, however, chooses to become a full human being and succeeds in doing so. His life's journey brings the potential intellect and humanity within him to full realization.

According to Maimonides, a person who does not actualize his intellect may have the external form of a human being but cannot be described as fully human. Extraordinarily, Maimonides calls such a person an animal, or creature.

> You know that whoever is not endowed with this form, whose significa-
> tion we have explained, is not a man but an animal, having the shape
> and configuration of a man. (*Guide*, 1:7)

It would appear that the prophet is not only no "superman" but is also one of the few people who can properly be called human.

This view resolves our opening difficulty. There is no contradiction between the notion of a static God and the dynamic occurrence of prophecy. God neither changes in the course of prophecy nor initiates the prophetic encounter. The change occurs only within human consciousness. According to this understanding of proph-ecy, God does not reveal Himself to humanity. Rather, humanity reveals God.

In addition to preserving the static conception of God, this under-standing of prophecy is also compatible with a stable natural world. According to Aristotle, the natural system is eternal and constant; the laws that govern it are unchanging. The "ignorant" view of prophecy as a miracle that overturns the laws of nature threatens this harmonious picture. Seeing prophecy as a human achievement is congenial with the Aristotelian vision of nature. Prophecy is not some exceptional break with natural laws but an effect of powers that are inherent in nature itself.

After having outlined the Aristotelian view, Maimonides explains his own position.

> The third approach is the opinion of our law and the foundation of
> our doctrine. It is identical with the philosophic opinion except in
> one thing. For we believe that it may happen that one who is fit for
> prophecy and prepared for it should not become a prophet, namely on
> account of the divine will. To my mind, this is like all of the miracles,

and takes the same course as they. For it is a natural thing that everyone who according to his natural disposition is fit for prophecy and who has been trained in his education and study should become a prophet. He who is prevented from it is like him who has been prevented, like Jeroboam, from moving his hand, or like the King of Arram's army going to seek out Elisha, from seeing. (*Guide*, 2:32)

The Torah, according to Maimonides, is consistent with the Aristotelian features of prophecy, except for one difference: a person may prepare himself for prophecy yet not merit it. Not everyone who has the potential for prophecy will receive it from God. Prophecy remains miraculous.

At first glance, it might seem that this change undermines the naturalness of prophecy as presented in the Aristotelian approach. In the Aristotelian view, the natural aspect of prophecy also reflects its necessity. It is impossible for a person who is prepared for prophecy not to achieve it. According to Aristotle, prophecy, like all natural phenomena, is bound by laws of causality. Training for prophecy is the cause, and the occurrence of prophecy is the necessary effect. In "the Torah's opinion," God breaks into this closed causal system, negates the natural necessity of prophecy, and blocks someone who is properly prepared from attaining prophetic experience.

Maimonides agrees with Aristotle's view of prophecy as a non-miraculous, natural process. One who is appropriately prepared should, in the natural way of things, achieve prophecy. Rather, it is the *prevention* of prophecy that is the miraculous occurrence here. This is not, in principle, different from other miracles; it is "according to the way of all miracles" (*Guide*, 2:32). Just as God can take away a person's ability to see, so too He can remove the ability to prophesy. The prevention of prophecy belongs to the phenomenon of miracles and is not conceptually connected to the phenomenon of prophecy. As far as the definition of prophecy goes, there is actually no difference between the Torah's view and Aristotle's: prophecy is a natural event and a human achievement.

The Naturalization of Prophecy
("Contradiction of the Seventh Kind")

The space that Maimonides allows for divine involvement leaves God outside the *concept* of prophecy but within the prophetic *event*, since God can block it from taking place.[3] Maimonides enlists scriptural support:

> Similarly, it may be said, as we shall explain, that in the passage, *Yea her prophets find no vision from the Lord* (Lam. 2:9), this was the case because they were in exile. However, we shall find many texts, some of them scriptural and some of them dicta of the Sages, all of which maintain this fundamental principle that God turns whom He wills, whenever He wills it into a prophet—but only someone perfect and superior to the utmost degree. (*Guide*, 2:32)

This is a powerful scriptural argument. "Yea her prophets find no vision from the Lord" implies that even those people who were fit for prophecy (i.e., "prophets") "received no vision from God." The human effort that should have called forth prophecy was answered with divine refusal.

Maimonides deploys this verse in another place as well. The mainstream Jewish doctrine is that prophecy ceased at the close of the biblical period. The question then arises: if God does not initiate prophecy, as Maimonides claims, why were there no more prophets after that point? One reason he gives for the cessation of prophecy does not rely on the extent of God's involvement: the climate of exile hindered the full actualization of human reason. Maimonides relies on the very same verse that we have just seen:

> This is indubitably the essential and proximate cause of the fact that prophecy was taken away during the time of the exile. For what languor or sadness can befall a man in any state that would be stronger than that due to his being a thrall slave in bondage to the ignorant who commit great sins and in whom the privation of true reason is united to the perfection of the lust of the beasts . . . and so it says, *her kings and princes*

are among the nations; there is no Torah, and her prophets find no vision from the Lord. (Guide, 2:36)

Since the kings and princes were among the nations, the prophets could find no vision. From this reading of the verse it appears that there is a causal relationship between exile and the cessation of prophecy. In this case, "her prophets find no vision from the Lord" serves as a proof for God's non-involvement in the cessation of prophecy. However, Maimonides read the same passage as supporting the idea of God's involvement in blocking the prophetic process. The same verse that is a justification for God's miraculous role in prophecy in one place is also an argument for the absolute naturalness of prophecy somewhere else.

This is an example of an intentional contradiction in the *Guide*. In the introduction to the *Guide*, the Rambam lists seven contradictions that one may find in writings the world over. The seventh is the contradiction intended to conceal certain ideas. Maimonides did not want all of his readers to understand the most complex and mysterious of his teachings. He acknowledged that he sometimes made contradictory points in order to keep his true opinion from the general public. Most Rambam scholars agree that when there is a contradiction between a conventional and a radical view, the latter is the Rambam's true opinion. This type of intentional contradiction for the sake of the concealment of esoteric ideas is known by Maimonidean scholars as a "contradiction of the seventh kind."

Some interpreters offer the following resolution: when he lays out the different possibilities about prophecy, Maimonides, by leaving room for God's involvement in the prophetic event, presents his own position as differing somewhat from the Aristotelian view. Thus he reassures his common audience. However, a few chapters later, Maimonides "winks" at the sophisticated reader and communicates a more subtle message, namely, that his real opinion is identical to Aristotle's, not just on the nature of prophecy, but also regarding its absence even where the preconditions have been met.

Who Is a Prophet?

Let us now try and understand the specific characteristics that a would-be prophet must have.

> This is emphatically not something that every person can attain. No one can reach it without arriving at perfection in the theoretical sciences and improving his moral qualities until they are as refined as they can possibly be; in addition, he must be naturally endowed with the most perfect imaginative faculty possible. (*Guide*, 2:36)

The personality of a prophet must combine three very different kinds of perfection: moral, intellectual and imaginative.

Moral Perfection: A moral person is not just someone who does good things, but also, and primarily, someone who has good qualities. Maimonides locates morality in the personality, which is the source of deeds, and not just in the actions themselves. He follows the Aristotelian conception that measures the moral quality of personal characteristics according to their degree of balance: "Good qualities are attributes of the soul that attain to a mean in between two bad characteristics, one of them being an excess and the other being a lack. One should aim for actions that are in the middle between these extremes."[4]

The "middle way" of Maimonides and Aristotle is frequently misunderstood. Balanced personal qualities do not always result in balanced actions. Well-balanced attributes lead to actions that are appropriate to one's objectives.[5] For example, responding to a minor irritant such as a fly in a manner that is halfway between anger and apathy is not following the middle path, because generally the proper way to react to a fly is with relative indifference. Similarly, the appropriate response to a grave injustice is not at the mean between anger and apathy; one should respond with righteous indignation. Balance means correct emotional calibration.

Through extensive training, people can reshape their personalities. Someone who attains moral perfection will have brought his personality into proper balance, meaning that one is able to maintain harmonious interactions with one's surroundings. This may be the greatest achievement of a person's life.

Imaginative Perfection: The imaginative faculty has two functions. First, it represents to us sensory impressions even when they are absent. "The imaginative faculty is a power that recalls our sense impressions after they have faded from the sensory organs that perceived them."[6] Second, it enables us to make new, complex images out of those impressions: "He may combine a bit of this with a bit of that, or separate one thing from another, and so the imaginative faculty can make compounds out of different perceptions, and create things that were never perceived by the senses."[7] A person may imagine an iron boat because he once saw one. He can imagine a bird because he has often seen such a creature. The imagination can render both of these images and connect them in order to create in one's mind the image of something that he never saw: "for example, a person may imagine an iron boat that flies in the air."[8]

The limit of the imaginative faculty depends on the hardwiring of the brain.[9] One has little ability to improve his imaginative capacity if it is innately limited. Some may achieve intellectual and moral perfection yet fail to attain prophecy because they do not possess a perfected imagination. Such people face a natural impediment to prophecy.[10]

The quality of the imaginative faculty varies from person to person. These differences consist in two features:

1. Imaginative Power: For most people, the objects of sense perception that are reconstructed in imagination seem faded in comparison with the sense perceptions themselves. When I imagine my desk, its colors and sense of presence are relatively weak compared to when I see it directly. However, there are some people who imagine objects in a way that is no less vivid and immediate than their sensory perception of the things themselves. For them, it can sometimes be difficult to distinguish between reality and imagination.

2. The capacity to create new constellations of images out of sense impressions differs from person to person. There are people who are unable to imagine anything very different from what they know. Others can burst through the bounds of experience and create worlds that don't exist. Imaginative perfection consists in the ability to re-create sense impressions that are as powerful as the original perceptions and to form them into new and extraordinary imaginary creations.

Intellectual Perfection: Reason is the ability to think about reality and to explain it in terms of its component parts. We seek the truth and desire deep knowledge of reality. Intellectual perfection means knowing truth for the sake of truth: "The point of truth is simply to know it as the truth."[11] Maimonides calls the person who attains intellectual perfection a philosopher.

A prophet has balanced moral qualities, a powerful imagination, and intellectual perfection. The prophet is a blend of saint, artist, and philosopher. A person who brings all of the rich resources of his humanity to full realization may become a prophet.

WHAT IS PROPHETIC EXPERIENCE?

How does the prophetic personality give birth to prophecy? How does this synthesis of moral, intellectual, and imaginative perfection produce revelation?

> Know that the true reality of prophecy consists in its overflowing[12] from God, may He be cherished and honored, through the intermediation of the Active Intellect toward the rational faculty in the first place and thereafter toward the imaginative faculty. This is the highest degree for man, and the ultimate term of perfection that can exist for his species; and this state is the ultimate term of perfection for the imaginative faculty. (*Guide*, 2:36)

Prophecy is an event that changes the normal relationship between imagination and intellect. Imagination, according to Maimonides, ordinarily is a threat to reason. It causes intellect to deviate from its course and to blur its goals. Reason, therefore, usually tries to free itself from the influence of imagination. In prophecy, however, instead of overcoming the imagination, reason must engage it in order to reach a spiritual breakthrough.

When intellectual attainments flood the imagination, a person is able to express intellectual concepts in imaginative language. When this happens, one can reflect visually upon his knowledge. The imagination represents theoretical knowledge as a powerful spectacle. The prophet is a philosopher who can visualize his philosophy as if it were a movie. This is also connected to Maimonides's psychology of dreams:

> *If there be a prophet among you, I the Lord do make myself known unto him in a vision, I speak with him in a dream* (Num. 12:6). Thus He, may He be exalted, has informed us of the true reality and essence of prophecy and has let us know that it is a perfection that comes in a dream or a vision. The word *mareh*, vision, derives from the word *ra'oh*, to see, This signifies that the imaginative faculty achieves so great a perfection of action, that it sees the thing as if it were outside, and that the thing whose origin is due to it appears to have come to it by way of external sensation. In these two groups, I mean vision and dream, all the degrees of prophecy are included, as shall be explained. It is known that a matter that occupies a man greatly—he being bent on it and desirous of it—while he is awake and while his senses function, is the one with regard to which the imaginative faculty acts when he is asleep, when receiving an overflow of the intellect corresponding to its disposition. It would be superfluous to quote examples of this and to expatiate on it, as this is a manifest matter that everyone knows. It is similar to the apprehension of the senses with regard to which no one whose natural disposition is healthy disagrees. (*Guide*, 2:36)

Dreams reflect our emotional autobiographies. We do not dream about the events of the day but about what caused an emotional reaction during that day. Someone who was angry will symbolically manifest anger in his dream. When a person is focused on his desires during the day, the desires will find expression in what he sees during sleep. This is why a philosopher who is intellectually perfect but ethically flawed does not achieve prophecy:

> For most of the thoughts of those who are outstanding among the men of knowledge are preoccupied with pleasures of this sense (the sense of touch) and are desirous of it. And then they wonder how it is that they do not become prophets if prophecy is something natural. (*Guide*, 2:36)

This phenomenon is not confined to dreaming. When a person is morally refined, his emotional energy is not dissipated in trivialities but rather is focused on unraveling the secrets of creation. A well-balanced character is not drawn to anger, envy, or lust; when he thinks about metaphysics, all of his emotional energy is devoted to the subject. The person whose emotions are riveted by "The Works of Creation"[13] and "The Works of the Chariot"[14] will see in his imagination (which represents the objects of desire) the secrets of physics and metaphysics.

> Now there is no doubt that whenever, in an individual of this description, his imaginative faculty, which is as perfect as possible, acts and receives from the intellect an overflow corresponding to his speculative perfection, this individual will only apprehend divine and most extraordinary matters, will see only God and his angels, and will be aware and achieve knowledge of matters that constitute true opinions and general rules for the welfare of human beings in their relations to one another. (*Guide*, 2:36)

The prophetic scene unfolds in the prophet's inner world. When Isaiah saw God seated on a throne, and when Ezekiel beheld the divine chariot, these visions were not external. Maimonides was not the first to make this assertion. There is a tradition in Judaism that locates such visions in the soul of the seer. The mystical world that coexists with the Rabbinic-talmudic universe is replete with accounts of ascents by mystics to the upper worlds. In these visions, they visit exalted, heavenly chambers, and their desire is to see the face of God. The descriptions of these celestial journeys are highly detailed and were collected in the *hechalot* literature—a genre of esoteric texts related to visions of ascents into heavenly palaces. Several hundred years later, Rabbi Hai Gaon was asked about the secret of these visions:

> When one wishes to behold the chariot, or to glimpse the chambers of the heavenly angels, there are ways to do so: he should fast for a number of days, place his head between his knees, and whisper many songs and praises. Thus he will gaze upon the seven chambers as if he is entering them one by one and look at what is in each. There are two tractates that the teachers of the *Mishnah* taught about this matter, *Hechalot Rabbati* and *Hechalot Zutri*, and this is public and well known.[15]

These sages would curl up into the mystical, fetal position, repeat names of God, enter into a deep trance, and embark on a journey to the heavenly chambers. According to Rabbi Hai Gaon, this flight to the upper worlds was a journey within the soul. That is where revelation happened. While Maimonides did not invent this idea, he did give it a psychological explanation. Visions take place in the consciousness of the prophet because the imagination of the morally perfect is liberated from the snares of lust and therefore free to represent metaphysical truths in a powerful, symbolic form.

In this light, one may discern a fourth ingredient in Maimonides's revolutionary account of prophecy. We have already seen that the Rambam understood prophecy as natural, not miraculous; it is a human achievement, not a divine initiative; and the prophet is a superlative human being, but not more than that. In addition, prophecy takes place within the prophet and not outside. Since prophecy is a symbolic representation of an intellectual phenomenon, once it has happened, a person reverts to the rational mode to decode the prophetic symbols. The intellect is garbed in imaginative form and then must itself interpret the prophecy. Prophecy enables reason to be self-reflective. The prophet activates his intellect through the mediation of imagination in order to understand his own thoughts anew.

This idea of prophecy as an internal phenomenon may seem to undermine the objective nature of the prophetic experience. If it is a human achievement that takes place within the individual, in what sense is prophecy divine revelation? Doesn't giving psychological explanations of prophetic process also imply its secularization?

The truth that reveals itself to the prophet is, according to Maimonides, absolutely objective and represents an external reality. The symbols that imagination creates for the prophet are conceived deep within him, but when he reflects upon and deciphers them he grasps a signified world that touches on the foundations of existence. Maimonides's prophetic conception of dreams stands in contrast to Freudian dream theory.

Freud viewed dreams as a secret, symbolic script that we must decode and interpret. In *The Interpretation of Dreams*, Freud wrote that, while the ancient world saw a dream as a letter received from the gods, he believed that a dream *was* a kind of letter, not from the gods but from a no less mysterious place: the unconscious. The dream is a symbolic communication from the unconscious to the conscious mind, a precious gateway to self-knowledge. The central role of dreams, according to Freud, is wish fulfillment. If we are able to interpret our dreams, we will thereby come to understand our deepest desires.

For both Maimonides and Freud, dreams are in a language of images that requires rational interpretation. In the Freudian dream, however, the knowledge that interpretation affords is limited to that of the dreamer's mind. The Maimonidean prophetic dream, on the other hand, bestows knowledge whose significance is far more profound. Prophecy is a moment when a person breaks through the boundaries of self.

The experience of prophecy is a symbolic representation of an objective truth. In general, however, scriptural accounts of prophecy set forth the truth without describing the accompanying drama. Many prophetic passages are monologues in which a prophet conveys ideas that are derived from an intellectual interpretation given by the prophet to images that he saw in his mind. Generally, the Bible does not disclose the whole creative process with readers—just the results. But sometimes the interpretation of the vision and also the vision itself are described: "and so too with other prophets; there are those who tell us the parable and its meaning, while others just tell us the meaning" (*MT*, *Hilkhot Yesodei HaTorah*, 3:7).

In some instances the Bible conveys the symbolic vision of the prophecy but not its interpretation: "And sometimes they speak just the parable, but not its solution, as in, for example, some of the words of Ezekiel and Zechariah—and in all of them they prophesy in riddles" (*MT*, *Hilkhot Yesodei HaTorah*, 3:7).

In Ezekiel's vision of the chariot, the reader is exposed to the prophet's inner world. We glimpse the products of Ezekiel's powerful imagination and contemplate their tumultuous symbols, but without explanation. The reader is expected to figure out what the vision means. In this sense, prophetic passages of the third kind make the reader a participant in the prophetic process. The final step, in which the prophet returns to rational consciousness and interprets the vision, is left to the reader. Here, the Bible is not merely presenting prophecy but also inviting us to take part in it.

THE POWER OF DIVINATION

Prophecy may also involve the capacity to discern the future:

> So too, the faculty of divination exists in all people . . . but in virtue of the strength of this divination the mind goes over all the premises and draws from them conclusions in the shortest time, so that it is thought to happen in no time at all. In virtue of this faculty, certain people give warnings concerning great future events. (*Guide*, 2:38)

The power of divination seems a paranormal intuition. The prophet is able to predict future events in a way that is so quick that the rational mind does not appear to be involved in the process at all. But this is an illusion.[16] According to Maimonides, the prophet's power of divination allows him to reflect very rapidly on the continuum of past and present events and thereby draw conclusions about what will happen in the future. This is actually an ordinary intellectual operation.[17] The faculty of divination simply accelerates the work of processing data and drawing inferences.[18]

THE PROPHETIC VISION

Maimonides's explanation of prophecy offers a new understanding of a number of scriptural passages. The Torah tells us that Abraham, who was sitting at the entrance to his tent, ran toward three men who were approaching and, without knowing that they were angels, extended extraordinary hospitality. According to Maimonides, the story never actually happened but rather was all a prophetic vision that took place in Abraham's mind.

> *And the Lord appeared to him by the tents of Mamre . . . and he raised his eyes and saw and behold three men were standing facing him"* (Gen. 18:1–2). For after he had first propounded the proposition that God appeared to him, he began to explain what the form of this proposition was; and he said that at first he saw three men and ran; whereupon they spoke and were spoken to. He who propounded this allegorical explanation says of Abraham's utterance: *And he said: My Lord, if I have now found favor in your sight, pass not away, I pray you from your servant* (Gen. 18:3) that it too is a description of what he said to one of them in a vision of prophecy, he says in fact *He said it to the greatest among them.* Understand this story, for it is one of the secrets." (*Guide,* 2:42)

These biblical descriptions enable us to behold, as it were, Abraham's inner visions. Maimonides claims that Jacob's struggle with an angel and the talking donkey in the story of Bilaam (Num. 22:22–35) also happened only in visions. The category of prophetic vision may be widened to include many other biblical episodes. The scholar Avraham Nouriel maintains, that according to Maimonides, even the binding of Isaac only took place in a prophetic vision.[19] Abraham did not rise early in the morning, or physically saddle his ass, or journey for three days, or actually offer his son on an altar. It all happened in a vision. This approach empties biblical narratives of historical significance. The prophetic vision is a continuous, symbolic, multivalent phenomenon that transforms biblical narrative from history into literature, from something that really happened into a parable.

Maimonides determines that although many of the biblical stories did not actually take place in reality, they are still true—because the lessons that emerge from their parables are true. If an event is historical, then it is something that happened in the past; if it is a parable, then it is a story that also "happens" in the present and the future. Turning story into allegory by placing it in the category of prophetic vision strengthens its meaning and transforms it from an isolated event into a universal truth.

On Mount Sinai

God's revelation to the Jewish people on Mount Sinai significantly challenges Maimonides's theory of prophecy. If prophecy requires preparation and training, how could a slave-people suddenly achieve prophecy in the middle of the desert? If prophecy is attainable only by a few extraordinary individuals, how could it be reached by the entirety of the Jewish people, so many of whom belonged to the "ignorant masses"?

Maimonides relies on the Rabbinic midrashim (narrative forms of Rabbinic commentary on the Bible) that distinguish between the first two commandments, which were heard by the whole people, and those that followed, which Moses alone received. The difference, according to Maimonides, is that anyone can fully grasp the first two commandments, which express God's existence and unity, by means of an entirely rational proof. Not so, however, with the latter commandments:

> The sages have a dictum formulated in several passages of the midrashim and also in the Talmud. This is their dictum: they heard *I* and *thou shalt not* from the mouth of the Mighty One. They mean that these words reached them just as they reached Moses our Master and that it was

not Moses who communicated them to them. For these two principles, I mean the existence of the deity and His being one are knowable by human speculation alone. Now with regard to anything that can be known by demonstration, the status of the prophet and anyone else who knows it are equal; there is no superiority of one over the other. Thus these two principles are not known through prophecy alone. The text of the Torah says: *unto you it was shown* (Deut. 4:35). As for the other commandments, they belong to the class of generally accepted opinions and those adopted in virtue of tradition, not to the class of intellecta. (*Guide*, 2:33)

The Jewish people, according to Maimonides, experienced a moment of philosophical illumination, but not prophecy. The revelation at Sinai proved God's existence, incorporeality, and unity. Maimonides believed that such proofs, although complex, were accessible to the masses. He even presented one such proof, as we saw above, in the first chapter of the *Mishneh Torah*, when he determined that knowledge of God was incumbent on the whole Jewish people. Maimonides's understanding of the Sinai moment reflects his trust in the potential for democratizing philosophy, even as he rules out the possibility of democratizing prophecy.

MOSES'S PROPHECY

Our description of prophecy applies to all Jewish prophets except Moses. His prophecy was qualitatively different:

> The proof from the Torah as to his prophecy being qualitatively different from that of all who came before him is constituted by his saying: *And I appeared to Abraham . . . but my name, the Lord, I made not known to them* (Ex. 6:3). Thus it informs us that his apprehension was not like that of the patriarchs, but greater—nor, all the more, like those who came before. As for the difference between his prophecy and that of all those who came after, it is stated by way of communicating information in the dictum: And there has not arisen a prophet since in Israel like Moses, whom the Lord knew *face to face* (Deut. 34:10). Thus it has been made

clear that his apprehension is different from all those who came before him in Israel, which is a kingdom of priests and a holy nation, and in whose midst is the Lord—and all the more so from the apprehension of all those who came in other religions communities. (*Guide*, 2:35)

Moses was unique, says the Rambam. In part 2, chapter 35 of the *Guide*, Maimonides declares that the term "prophecy," applied both to Moses and to other prophets, is "amphibolous," that is, equivocal. An amphibolous word is one "in which two or more essential meanings have, for whatever reason, been joined together and neither predominates" (*Milot Ha-higayon*, 13:57).

With amphibolous words, the similarity between the different meanings is coincidental rather than essential. The prophecy of Moses is of a different order than that of other prophets. His prophecy, and only his, had legislative force. Even the prophetical levels of Abraham, Isaac, and Jacob did not confer upon them this power. People followed them because of the power of their personalities, not because the people were commanded to do so. Maimonides distinguishes Moses from the other prophets and thereby reinforces Moses's authority. Maimonides's conception allows anyone—at least anyone whose imaginative faculty is not congenitally limited—to train, to prepare, and to reach the level of prophecy. However, if Moses's prophecy could be replicated in anyone, then a subsequent prophet claiming to have attained the same level could abrogate, amend, or supplement Torah law. Therefore, it was important for Maimonides to characterize Moses's prophecy as unique and not reproducible.

Some contemporary scholars claim that the Rambam's view is a necessary opinion, meaning that, in order to preserve the authority of *halakhah*, it is important that people accept the uniqueness of Moses's prophecy. But, they argue, Maimonides's real opinion was that the terms he ascribed to other prophets apply equally to Moses. Maybe Moses's prophecy was of a higher order than that of other prophets, but it was still the same sort of prophetic experience.

In chapter 2 of the *Guide*, Maimonides differentiates between divine law and human law. One of the ways to distinguish between the two is to look at who gave them:

> It also remains for you to know if he who lays claim to such guidance is a perfect man to whom a prophetic vision of that guidance has been vouchsafed, or whether he is an individual who lays claim to these dicta, having plagiarized them. The way of putting this to the test is to consider the perfection of that individual, carefully to examine his actions, and to study his way of life. The strongest of the indications that you should pay attention to this guidance is constituted by his renunciation of and contempt for the bodily pleasures, for this is the first of the degrees of people of science and, all the more so, of the prophets. (*Guide*, 2:40)

Since prophecy is an expression of human perfection, one may determine the authenticity of a particular prophetic message by examining the personality of the prophet. If he is indeed perfect, then it is possible that he has attained genuine prophetic experience. However, the paragraph quoted above is not describing ordinary prophecy; it refers to prophecy that creates law. Now, we saw earlier that Maimonides attributes this kind of prophecy to Moses alone. Since he previously stated that anyone who is not Moses and claims to have received a law-giving prophecy is a false prophet, it would appear that this passage undermines the idea of the uniqueness of Moses, because it grants that any prophet may be a source of legislation. Is this a contradiction of the seventh kind, that is, an intentional contradiction for the sake of the concealment of esoteric ideas?

That would not be the only contradiction. In part 2, chapter 35 of the *Guide*, part of the introduction to his teaching on prophecy, Maimonides writes that since his doctrine of prophecy does not apply to Moses, he will not mention him in the ensuing chapters: "And I will not relate to Moses's prophecy with a single word in these chapters, neither explicitly, nor in hints." Notwithstanding this emphatic declaration, Maimonides does mention Moses again—many times. He even illustrates parts of his theory using the example of Moses's prophecy. For example, he asserts that a sad person cannot have a prophetic experience, citing Moses as proof. Moses was so aggrieved by the sin of the spies that he did not prophesy for another forty years:

> Prophetic revelation did not come to Moses, peace be on him, after the disastrous incident of the spies, until the whole generation of the desert perished, in the way that revelation used to come before, because, seeing the enormity of their crime, he suffered greatly because of the matter. (*Guide*, 2:36)

The dissonance between Maimonides's professed intention not to mention Moses and what he actually writes reflects essential tensions in his teaching. Maimonides's theory of prophecy is based on the idea that the imagination of the morally perfect person represents what is in his intellect. This theory does not apply to Moses, because his prophecy is supposed not to involve imagination at all (*Guide*, 2:45). Nevertheless, Maimonides illustrates the imaginative variety of prophecy precisely through the example of Moses. These contradictions may be added to others that Rambam commentators have found in his treatment of Moses's prophecy.[20] Closing the gap between Moses's prophecy and that of others has far-reaching implications.

RELIGION AND REASON

Even if we emphasize Maimonides's straightforward writing and leave aside radical commentaries and contradictions of the seventh kind, we are left with a highly unusual approach to Moses's prophecy. According to Maimonides, the uniqueness of Moses's prophecy was that he connected directly to the cosmic intellect, without the intermediation of imagination. This was the greatest cognitive achievement in human history.[21] No one will ever reach such heights again.

Whether we stress the radical or traditional interpretation of his teaching, Maimonides's approach to this issue is a revolutionary departure in the history of Jewish thought. The Torah, in his view, is an intellectual achievement. Jewish rationalists prior to Maimonides, such as Saadia Gaon and Bachya Ibn Pakuda, labored to demonstrate the alignment of reason and Torah. Saadia, for example, gave rational proofs for the existence of God, the creation of the world, the existence of divine providence, a system of reward and punishment, and even for the revival of the dead. He sought to rationally prove the content of Jewish faith out of a deep conviction that the truth as conceived by reason must be the same truth that is revealed by the Torah. In his view, reason and Torah are two authentic ways of accessing truth and therefore cannot contradict one another. The task of the religious philosopher, then, is to harmonize them.

Maimonides, by contrast, does not try to make reason and Torah compatible. For him, there is no need to harmonize revelation and reason, because revelation reveals reason. One does not have to reconcile the two intermediaries between us and truth, because they are really one. According to Saadia Gaon, Torah exists in harmony with reason; according to Maimonides, Torah is the revelation of reason.

Maimonides recasts our conceptions of prophecy, the prophetic event, and the image of the prophet. He bridges the gap between a perfect, unchanging God and the ideas of revelation and prophecy. Maimonides opens up new perspectives on the Bible and on the Law, and in the process he creates a new image of a hero.

The Bible: Many of the biblical stories could be considered prophetic visions. Maimonides and those who continued his approach erode the image of the Bible as a historical book and treat its stories as parables that express Jewish prophecy. This has important implications for modern readers who are troubled by questions about the historical truth of Scripture.

The Law: The prophecy that expressed biblical legislation was not a disruption of reason; rather, it was reason's perfect expression: the Law is the product of intellect. One implication of this view is that all of the commandments may be explained rationally.

The Hero: Maimonides's God is perfect, pure, and unchanging, beyond space and time. In the prophetic process, the only thing that changes is the prophet's consciousness. The prophet is elevated above his physical needs and desires, connects himself to the cosmic intellect, and reveals metaphysical truths. Because of God's unchanging nature, alteration and initiative are transferred into the human realm. A new kind of religious hero appears: the perfect man, whose discoveries constitute revelation. An even more extraordinary expression of how divine perfection expands the human role may be found in Maimonides's teachings about providence, to which we now turn.

3

PROVIDENCE

In 1171, Maimonides's younger brother David, a trader in precious stones, was drowned on a voyage in the Indian Ocean. Maimonides, who was particularly close to his brother, was crushed by the loss and developed a serious heart disorder, fever, and melancholy. "I was at death's door," he wrote, adding that he did not rise from his sickbed for a year. He described his plight in a letter:

> Years have waned, but I still mourn and find no solace. And what could bring me solace anyway? He grew up in my lap. He was my brother and pupil. . . . My only joy was to see him. All my joy is gone. He has passed on to eternal life, leaving me shattered in a strange land. Whenever I see his handwriting or one of his books, my heart turns over within me and my grief comes awake again. *For, I will go down into the grave to my son mourning* (Gen. 37:35).[1]

David's death was not only a shattering personal tragedy for Maimonides; it was also a great financial blow. David's business success had enabled Maimonides to devote himself to study, research, and writing, free of material concerns. After his brother's death, how would Maimonides support himself? He could have earned a living as a rabbi and Torah teacher, but he rejected this option on the grounds that it was degrading and compromising for scholars to turn the Torah into a tool for making money. Instead, he went to work as a doctor, soon becoming the personal physician of the sultan.

His days were long and exhausting. From morning to night he was at the beck and call of the sultan's court and harem. Later, when his schedule became more arduous still, he wrote of the demands on him in a famous letter to his friend and translator Shmuel Ibn Tibbon:

> The sultan lives in Cairo and I live in Fustat; the two towns are two Sabbath leagues apart. I have a difficult time with the sultan; I must visit him every morning. If he himself or one of his children or harem members is sick, then I may not leave Cairo. I spend most of the day in the sultan's palace. Usually, I also have to treat some dignitary. In a word, I go to Cairo every morning at the crack of dawn, and if nothing keeps me there and nothing unforeseen occurs, I can come home only in the afternoon. Starving as I am, I find the antechamber full of people: Jews, non-Jews, nobles and lowly people, judges and officials, friends and foes, a motley company awaiting me with impatience. I dismount from my horse, wash, and entering the waiting room with the plea that they may not feel offended if they have to wait a bit longer while I partake of a hasty light meal, which normally happens only once every twenty four hours.[2]

Under such conditions, Maimonides wrote *The Guide for the Perplexed*. The greatest work of Jewish philosophy emerged not from a life of calm and equanimity but after years of profound grief and painful toil. When Maimonides writes in the *Guide* about suffering and evil, these were things that he knew firsthand.

We might be able to hear echoes of Maimonides's own life experience in the *Guide*'s teachings on these eternal problems of religious life. The issue of providence, God's involvement in our lives, is directly linked to the question of why tragedies befall us and may be the Rambam's way of making sense of his own loss.

DOES GOD CARE WHAT HAPPENS TO US?

One of the deepest human needs is to be noticed. People want attention. Parents satisfy this requirement when we are young, but the need does not go away when we grow up. The more important the person we are standing before, the greater the yearning we feel for that person's interest. God is the most important being in the cosmos. So the idea that God pays attention to us—providential concern—is one of the most profound religious needs.

The trust that God cares about the details of our lives gives us a sense of meaning and significance. It spares us from anonymity. Paradoxically, the people who most crave a sense that God is interested in their lives often are the furthest from being able to believe it. The conflict between emotional need and intellectual honesty is sharpest when we consider the question of divine providence.

At first glance, Maimonides's concept of God leaves no room for providence. A perfect, static God is not a God who shows interest in our lives. An intimately involved God would be a God who changes in response to us. Providence implies will, and will implies change. Attributing will to God implies that He lacks something. But a perfect God does not lack anything. The Rambam reinterprets providence in a way that is consistent with his idea of God.

The central issue in a discussion of providence is the problem of evil. For the Rambam too, one of the strongest arguments against providence is that bad things happen to good people and good things happen to bad people.[3]

THE PROBLEM OF EVIL

We experience a collision between our expectations of the world and what seems to be the reality. Reading the Bible makes us think that there should be a correspondence, or even a symmetry, between how we live and what happens to us. Good deeds ought to be rewarded, and bad actions should provoke punishment. The prophets promise that if we do what God wants, we will be saved from war, sickness, and hunger and that we will merit economic success and a safe and stable environment. The prophets also warn that if we do not obey God's commands, terrible things will befall us, both individually and collectively.

Theodicy, which means justifying God's allowing evil to exist, is the Christian tradition's way of grappling with this problem. The aim of theodicy is to break the connection between our experience of evil and the conclusion than we should therefore judge God to be evil. Some theologians have defended God's goodness by denying the *reality* of evil. The Hebrew Bible offers a different model of theodicy.

The rabbis of the Talmud read the Bible in a way that opens up the possibility that we might actually challenge God. In the face of the potential destruction of Sodom, Abraham courageously stands up to God and rebukes Him: "Should not the Judge of the whole world do justice?" (Gen. 18:25). Abraham argues, in effect, that God violates ethical laws when He kills the righteous: "Far be it for You to kill the righteous with the wicked" (Gen. 18:25). Moses echoes this idea before God vents His anger on Korach and his fellow rebels: "O God, source of the breath of all flesh! If one man sins, will you be angry at the whole community?" (Num. 16:22).

Prophets also confront God. Jeremiah poses to God the eternal riddle: "Why does the path of the wicked prosper?" (Jer. 12:1). This question resounds through Job and Psalms. The Talmud (*Menachot*, 29b) tells the story of Rabbi Akiva's torturous death at the hands of the Romans. It describes Moses looking down from heaven at Akiva's suffering. Moses turns to God and asks, "This is Torah and this is its reward?" Even from his celestial perspective, Moses cannot reconcile Rabbi Akiva's saintliness with the brutality of his death.

Biblical heroes do not justify God; instead, they voice their protest. Holding God to account is not a sign of religious weakness—it is a strength. However, this tradition virtually ceased by the Middle Ages. Thinkers of this period, in order to justify God, began to deny the existence of evil, and Maimonides struggled with the concept of evil against others' efforts to defend God against angry or skeptical protests.

Maimonides and Evil: Mythology and Therapy

At the beginning of chapter 12 in part 3 of the *Guide*, Maimonides poses a question about God's justice.[4] He does not, however, ask why there is undeserved suffering in the world. The question is phrased a little differently:

> Often it occurs to the imagination of the multitude that there are more evils in the world than there are good things. As a consequence, this thought is contained in many sermons and poems of all the religious communities, which say that it is surprising if good exists in the temporal, whereas the evils in the temporal are numerous and constant. This error is not found only among the multitude, but also among those who deem that they know something. (*Guide*, 3:12)

Maimonides addresses the melancholy argument that there is more evil in the world than good. He thinks that this is another example of a popular idea that is founded on an intellectual error. He believes that he can correct this mistake through the power of reason. The task is to persuade people to assess reality in a different way.

The Rambam does not concentrate on the extent of evil in the world. Rather, he argues for a shift in our point of view. The individual tends to project his personal distress onto the whole of existence. If a rainstorm ruins one's long-planned outdoor event, he might, in disappointment and pique, look at the world as a terrible place. It is hard for him to step back from his dismay or sadness and ask whether, from the point of view of the farmer who is desperate for rain, the world is also terrible at that moment. People paint the whole of reality in the hues of their own experience. The unstated premise underlying the claim that the world is bad is a certain self-centeredness, that is, the world is supposed to satisfy personal needs and that when it does not do so it is failing in its purpose. Liberating oneself from this egocentric point of view saves one from turning one's own pain into a theological problem.

It is important to note that Maimonides uses one word, "evil" (*ra'ah* in the usual Hebrew translations of the *Guide*), to encompass a range of undesirable eventualities spanning natural disasters, famines, war and other forms of human strife, addictive behavior, and harmful ways of living. But in contemporary English the word "evil" usually connotes deliberate and malicious human action.

It is counterintuitive for us to use the same word to cover the broad array of negative outcomes that the Rambam aggregates under one heading. However, his choice of terminology is closely aligned with his philosophical goals in his treatment of "evil." As we shall see, his point is precisely that these different sorts of harm have a lot more in common than most people think. The common factor, in the Rambam's view, is that most of them ultimately result from human agency. So, even though this may be jarring for readers, we will follow the Rambam's use of the same word, "evil," to refer to all of these diverse, negative phenomena. This dissonance is meant to help us question our assumptions about why bad things happen, and to seek their common denominator.

Maimonides describes three types of evil that lead people to claim that the world is bad. The first kind is the injury that nature causes to people; the second is the harm that people do to one another; and the third is the evil that we do to ourselves.

Human physicality makes us vulnerable to injury from nature, including sickness and natural disasters such as earthquakes and storms:

> The first species of evil is that which befalls a man because of the nature of coming-to-be and passing-away, I mean to say, because of his being endowed with matter. Because of this, infirmities and paralytic afflictions befall some individuals, either in consequence of their original, natural disposition, or they supervene because of changes occurring in the elements, such as corruption in the air or a fire from heaven and a landslide. We have already explained that divine wisdom has made it obligatory that there should be no coming-to-be except through passing-away. . . . Thus, this species of evils must necessarily exist. Withal you will find that the evils of this kind that befall men are very few and occur

only seldom. For you will find cities, existing for thousands of years, that have never been flooded or burned. Also, thousands of people are born in perfect health, whereas the birth of an infirm human being is an anomaly . . . they do not form a hundredth or even a thousandth part of those born in good health. (*Guide*, 3:12)

We cannot avoid the losses, disruptions, and traumas that occur in nature, but we can make our peace with them. They are an integral part of our being in the world. Likewise, to have a body is, as Hamlet puts it, to be subject to the "the thousand natural shocks that flesh is heir to."

The second type of evil is the harm that people cause one another, through crime or war, for example. Maimonides makes a distinction between crime that happens within a state and that is relatively limited, on the one hand, and war that is waged between states:

The evils of the second kind are those that human beings inflict upon one another, such as tyrannical domination of some over others. These evils are more numerous than those belonging to the first kind, and the reasons for that are numerous and well-known. The evils in question also come from us. However, the wronged man has no device against them. At the same time, there is no city existing anywhere in the whole world in which evil of this kind is in any way widespread or predominant among inhabitants of that city; but its existence is also rare—in the cases, for instance where, when one individual surprises another individual and kills him or robs him by night. This kind of evil becomes common, reaching many people, only in the course of great wars; and such events too do not form the majority of occurrences upon the earth taken as a whole. (*Guide*, 3:12)

Maimonides believes that the political framework can substantially limit the evil of war. In his view, war is more widespread than crime because there is no effective international authority that can limit this type of violence. This was certainly the case in his time, and it is arguably still true today. Maimonides lived in an age of violent political strife. In his childhood he was forced to flee Spain because of the Almohad invasion, which destroyed the highly developed Jewish community in Andalusia. As an adult he lived in Egypt, which still bore the wounds inflicted by Saladin's conquest.

The third kind of evil, that which a person does to himself, is caused mainly by bad habits. Chasing after sensual satisfaction, especially food and sexual licentiousness, is damaging to the body. As a physician, Maimonides stressed the importance of prevention and restraint.[5] He cautioned against the dangers of overeating, overindulgence in sex, and any excessive and repeated behavior that upsets biological equilibrium. "Most of the sicknesses that befall people are caused by eating bad foods, or by gluttonously filling their stomachs, even with good foods" (*MT, Hilkhot Deot*, 4:15). People who surrender to their unfettered physical desires will inevitably suffer as a result:

> This kind is consequent on all vices, I mean concupiscence for eating, drinking and copulation, and doing these things with excess in regard to quantity, or irregularly, or when the quality of the foodstuffs is bad, for this is the cause of all corporeal or psychical diseases and ailments. With regard to the diseases of the body, this is manifest. (*Guide*, 3:12)

What has Maimonides achieved philosophically through his division of evils into these three groups?

A basic principle emerges from this categorization. The closer a particular type of evil is to us, the more common it is. Damage caused by a natural event, which does not depend on human action, occurs least frequently. The harm that people do to one another is more common, and the evil we do to ourselves is the most widespread of all. Maimonides is not trying to ignore the presence of evil but to change our perception of its source. Many people feel themselves to be passive victims of cosmic evil. However, Maimonides transforms man from a hapless victim of evil to its primary cause.

Even with respect to harm from natural occurrences, Maimonides also implicates human responsibility. He describes the dangers to which people driven by uncontrollable lusts subject themselves:

In most cases such a man exposes himself to great dangers, such as arise in sea voyages and the service of kings; his aim therein being to attain these unnecessary luxuries. When, however he is stricken by misfortunes in these courses he has pursued, he complains about God's decree and predestination and begins to put the blame on the temporal world and to be astonished at the latter's injustice. (*Guide*, 3:12)

A merchant who makes dangerous sea voyages for business because he is driven to become rich is more likely to drown than a person who chooses a less potentially remunerative but also less risky way to earn his livelihood. He is not responsible for the storm, but he is responsible for his decision to go to sea. So the first stage in the *Guide*'s treatment of suffering is to challenge our sense of victimhood and to give us a far greater sense of responsibility for the consequences of our choices.

If one is the cause of his own pain, then he is also its cure, and herein lies the Maimonidean "therapeutic" approach. By changing our habits and aspirations, we can reduce or eliminate our suffering. We need to rid ourselves of the expectation of external redemption and accept responsibility for our condition. Theodicy—justifying God—does not help us to reduce suffering; on the contrary, it can hinder us. Maimonides shifts the source of troubles from God to man. He moves the discussion from theology to therapy.

THE SUFFERING OF THE SOUL

Maimonides's therapeutic approach to human suffering requires a clearer understanding of the source of psychological pain:

With regard to sicknesses of the soul due to this evil regimen, they arise in two ways: in the first place, through the alteration necessarily affecting the soul in consequence of the alteration of the body, the soul being a corporeal faculty—it having been said that the moral qualities of the soul are consequent upon the temperament of the body. And in the second place, because of the factor that the soul becomes familiarized with, and accustomed to, unnecessary things and consequently acquires the habit of desiring things that are unnecessary . . . and this desire is something infinite. For whereas all necessary things are restricted and limited, that which is superfluous is unlimited. If, for instance, your desire is directed to having silver plate, it would be better if it were of gold; some have crystal plate; and perhaps plate is procured that is made of emeralds and rubies, whenever these stones are to be found. Thus every ignoramus who thinks worthless thoughts is always sad and despondent because he is not able to achieve the luxury attained by someone else. (*Guide*, 3:12)

Someone who believes that his happiness depends on the extent to which he satisfies his desires is destined to suffer. A Buddhist commentator gave this elegant and simple definition of happiness: "Happiness is a consequence of attunement between what man wants and what he has. The greater the gap between those two things, the greater will be that person's suffering."[6]

Maimonides was neither the first nor the last to observe that, paradoxically, the pursuit of happiness is the cause of suffering.[7] The lust for sensory pleasure or wealth is insatiable. If a person craves honor and power, he will never be satisfied with what honor and power he attains. His desire for more will remain.

In the Buddhist tradition, one works through this problem by recognizing and renouncing desire. We can reach an alignment between what we want and what we have by extinguishing craving, or "thirst."[8] Consumerism, on the other hand, is driven by the quest for happiness. The basic illusion of consumerism is that more stuff will quench the thirst. The next purchase will bring one to the elusive goal of satisfaction.

The Rambam locates the source of suffering not in the *existence* of desire but in the way that desire tends to grow. Harmony is not achieved by utterly negating desire, but rather by cultivating desires that are in tune with reality. It is like a person who is trying to read a book while sitting in the middle of a playground full of noisy children. His inability to read the book makes him angry: "What kind of lousy playground is this where a person can't even read a book in peace?" Such dissonance expresses a mismatch between a person's expectations and the place where he actually is. The way to avoid frustration is to reassess one's expectations.

Underlying the sense of dissonance between one's desires and reality is the impulse to understand the world. Sadly, over the course of our lives, this beautiful, natural thirst to know is trampled, and other yearnings flourish in its place, only worsening our psychic pain. The Rambam offers a kind of philosophical therapy that can revive our sense of wonder and natural curiosity about the world. He believes that the ideal approach is to want to *know* the world. Only then will one experience harmony and avoid suffering.

Maimonides sees Job as an archetype for the process that people generally undergo when they confront suffering. Job suffers sudden and multiple afflictions: his wealth is taken, his children die, and his body is afflicted with terrible sicknesses. At first, Job responds by blaming the world and its Creator for what has happened to him:

> Now all men, I mean the vulgar, glorify God with their tongues and attribute to him justice and beneficence when they are happy and prosperous or even when they are in a state of endurable suffering. However, when the misfortunes mentioned in Job befall them, some of them become unbelievers and believe that there is little order in all that exists at the time when they lose their fortune; others hold to the belief in justice and order in spite of their having been stricken with the loss of their fortune, but do not keep patient if tried by the loss of their children. Others again are patient and keep an untroubled belief even when they lose their children, but none of them supports patiently the pain of the body without complaining . . . either with the tongue or in the heart. (*Guide*, 3:22)

When things are going well, we often do not question good and evil in the world. But when circumstances seem to turn against us we tend to see the world as the cause of our suffering. This is Job's reaction to adversity. At first, he experiences himself as a helpless victim of the afflictions that assail him, but then Job undergoes a transformation in consciousness that profoundly alters his relationship to suffering.

> The sages, in order to find an excuse for it, say a man is not to be blamed for what he does when suffering, meaning that he was excused because of his great sufferings. (*Guide*, 3:22)

In Maimonides's view, Job's faith becomes deeper and more sophisticated. At the outset, his belief is based on tradition, not on independent thought. By the end of the story, Job has reached a more profound faith, the fruit of his intellectual search. He learns that material resources are of limited value and comes to appreciate the genuine worth of intellectual enlightenment and knowledge of God. Job grows to reject his earlier yearnings and substitutes a new set of desires. By exchanging his physical appetites for spiritual ones, Job relieves his own suffering. It is not that the evils of the world have ceased to exist; rather, Job stops seeing them as evil. Difficult events in themselves are neither good nor bad. It is the way in which we experience them that makes the difference—and that depends on us.

Maimonides sees an allusion to Job's transformation in the fact that the opening of the story praises him as pure-hearted, upright, and God-fearing. The Bible does not call him wise at this point. Job had much to learn before he could earn that description.

Maimonides's approach here is radical. By transferring the source of evil from God to man, he turns the fact of evil into an idea: a human, mental construct. Maimonides recommends that we refocus our desires from satisfying our worldly wants to attaining knowledge of God by means of understanding the world. The urge to consume the world causes suffering; the desire to understand the world brings happiness.

FROM EVIL TO PROVIDENCE

Maimonides opens his discussion of providence by setting out the different theological options:

The opinions of people about providence are five in all. And all of them are ancient; I mean that they are opinions that have been heard about at the time of the prophets, since the true Law has appeared that has illumined all this darkness. (*Guide*, 3:17)

Maimonides first presents the view of nonbelievers, who deny that there is any providence in the world:

The first opinion is the profession of those who consider that there is no providence at all with regard to anything whatever in all that exists; that everything in it, the heavens and the things other than they, has happened by chance . . . and that there is no one who orders, governs, or is concerned with anything. This is the opinion of Epicurus. He also professes that there are atoms and holds that they mingle according to chance. Those in Israel who were unbelievers also professed this opinion; they are those of who it is said: *they have belied the Lord and said: It is not He* (Jer. 5:12). (*Guide*, 3:17)

According to the nonbeliever or heretic, there is no order to the universe and no external being to provide order. The chaotic nature of the world precludes faith in providence.

The second approach is attributed to Aristotle. Maimonides presents it as the opposite of the heretic's view. According to Aristotle, there is abundant, natural order in the world testifying to the existence of providential concern:

Aristotle has already demonstrated that this opinion is inadmissible; that it cannot be true that all things should have been generated by chance; and that, on the contrary, there is someone who orders and governs them. . . . The second opinion is the opinion that providence watches over certain things and that these exist through the governance and the ordering of one who governs and orders, whereas other things are left to chance. This is the opinion of Aristotle. (*Guide*, 3:17)

The argument between Aristotle and the heretic is about how nature works. According to the nonbeliever, the world is chaos;

according to Aristotle, it is cosmos, an orderly system. The universe reveals an extraordinary degree of order to anyone who investigates it deeply. This argument has important implications for the question of providence. According to Aristotle, order is evidence of a being that organizes the world. The fingerprint of divine concern is revealed in cosmic order. This idea is the basis for one of the most important proofs for God's existence—the teleological argument.[9]

This proof has different versions, but its core is that the universe cannot explain its own existence. Imagine a man who goes to a desolate place and sees a bunch of scattered stones. On climbing a hill and looking down, he sees that the stones are organized in the shape of an arrow. This is not merely an observation about the geometrical form of the stones; it is also evidence that someone else was there before him.[10] It shows that he is not alone.

Since nature cannot be the cause of its own harmonious organization, deep order imprinted on the world is evidence of a transcendent intelligence at work. This is the meaning of providence, according to Aristotle—an external wisdom that set up the world.

What about miracles? In the Aristotelian view, miracles are a problem. An event that breaks the laws of nature seems to disrupt the predictable and harmonious working of the world. Miracles break the rules, and the rules are the main evidence for God's existence. Jewish biblical commentators with Aristotelian views are troubled by the descriptions of miracles. They interpret stories like the parting of the Red Sea and manna in the desert as events apparently extraordinary yet also scientifically explicable.

This version of God's involvement in the world implies that there is no divine providence with respect to particular individuals. The laws of nature are blind to human biography. If two people fall from a high place, one a murderer and the other a saint, both will perish when they hit the ground. Gravity does not distinguish between the righteous and the wicked.

Maimonides then presents a third option: an extreme concept of providence, according to which God is fully involved in the world. Nature as an independent entity disappears. This view is attributed to the Ash'ariyya, an important Islamic school of thought which held that God decrees in advance everything that will happen; it is all God's will. The tree that falls in the forest is not brought down by the force of gravity but by a divine decision to fell that particular tree at that exact moment. Like that of the heretic, this approach denies the existence of laws of nature. However, whereas the nonbeliever declares that there is no natural law because everything is chance, this position holds that there is no nature because everything is God.

Many Jewish thinkers have criticized this view. Their objections are usually based on the observable fact that there *are* laws of nature. Otherwise it would be impossible to understand the order and regularity that we see in natural phenomena. The classic response of the Ash'ariyya and others[11] involves the idea of "hidden miracles," in which all of nature is subsumed within the category of miracle. According to this view, although it seems to us that the tree falls because of the laws of gravity, actually it is a hidden miracle. There is no essential difference between a tree falling—a hidden miracle—and the parting of the Red Sea—an open miracle. The two phenomena are both expressions of God's will at that moment.

A fourth view[12] that Maimonides presents is described as "the opinion of the Torah and of most of our sages":

> It is a fundamental principle of the Law of Moses, our Master, peace be on him, and of all those who follow it, that man has an absolute ability to act; I mean to say, that in virtue of his nature, his choice and his will, he may do everything that it is within the capacity of man to do. . . . It is likewise one of the fundamental principles of the Law of Moses our Master that it is in no way possible that He should be unjust, and that all the calamities that befall men and the good things that come to men . . . are all of them determined according to the deserts of the men

concerned through equitable judgment in which there is no injustice whatever. . . . *For all his ways are judgment* (Deut. 32:4). But we are ignorant of the various modes of deserts. (*Guide*, 3:17)

The Torah and Aristotle both describe a world in which there are laws of nature. In the Torah, miracles do not take the place of nature, but sometimes they intrude upon it. In contrast to Aristotle, however, in the Torah nature is not static, and human actions have their effect. God demonstrates His involvement not only in the laws of nature but also by sometimes miraculously breaking them.

These views express the relationship between God and the world in strikingly different ways. For the Aristotelian philosopher, God is limited by the laws of nature. According to the Torah, God is constrained by moral considerations. We are entitled to expect that God will not utterly flout moral laws and that He will not systematically punish the righteous or reward the wicked. According to the extreme theology of providence, God is not limited by any framework of law or expectations—neither by physics nor by ethics. God acts solely according to His own will.

After explaining these alternatives, Maimonides offers his own view of providence:

As for my own belief with regard to this fundamental principle, I mean divine providence . . . I for one believe that in this lowly world . . . divine providence watches only over the individuals belonging to the human species and that in this species alone all the circumstances of the individuals and the good and evil that befall them are consequent upon deserts, just as it says, *For all his ways are judgment* (Deut. 32:4). But regarding all the other animals and, all the more, the plants and other things, my opinion is that of Aristotle. For I do not by any means believe that this particular leaf has fallen because of a providence watching over it; nor that this spider has devoured this fly because God has now decreed and willed something. . . . According to me, divine providence is consequent upon the divine overflow; and the species with which this overflow is united . . . so that it becomes endowed with intellect . . . is the one accompanied with divine providence, which appraises its actions from the point of view of reward and punishment. If, as he states, the foundering of a ship and the drowning of those who were in it and the falling-down of a roof upon those who were in the house, are due to pure chance, the fact that the people on the ship were on board and that the people in the house were sitting on it is, according to our opinion, not due to chance, but to divine will in accordance with the deserts of those people, as determined in His judgments, the rule of which cannot be attained by our intellects. . . . Providence is consequent upon the intellect and attached to it. For providence can only come from an intelligent being. . . . Accordingly, everyone with whom something of this overflow is united, will be reached by providence to the extent that he is reached by the intellect. (*Guide*, 3:17)

The basic difference between the Torah's and Maimonides's view is the way in which providential care works. In the Torah, religious and ethical behavior is the basis for God's involvement. For the Rambam, on the other hand, the criterion is human intellectual attainment. From Maimonides's perspective, God does not distinguish between the righteous and the wicked, but rather between the wise and the foolish. The closer someone has come to reaching rational perfection, the greater is God's providential concern for that person.

Furthermore, reason is not just the cause of God's involvement in a person's life; it is also the medium through which one receives God's providence. God saves the rational individual by penetrating his consciousness: "Providence is consequent upon the intellect and is attached to it" (*Guide*, 3:17).

How, then, is the work of providence accomplished? Not by preventing disasters from happening in the rational person's vicinity. If, according to circumstances and the laws of physics, a particular building is "supposed to" fall down, it will. If meteorological conditions are such that a certain ship is going to sink at sea, it will sink. But God's providence is manifested by preventing a person from deciding to enter the shaky building or board the doomed vessel.

God does not uproot the laws of nature. Rather, He protects the wise through their minds.

This concept of providence begs many questions. First, it does not stand up to the test of experience. We see in life that wise people are not immune from tragedies and disasters. In addition, the theory raises problems of consistency within the Rambam's writings. By implying that God restricts the free choice of the enlightened individual in order to protect him from harm, the Rambam seems to be contradicting what he writes in other places: that God never interferes in human decisions. Maimonides makes this claim when explaining Moses's educational role after the Exodus from Egypt. Four hundred years of immersion in Egyptian paganism had left their mark on the Jewish people. The forty years in the desert were a kind of therapy that served to erase the fingerprints of idolatry. Maimonides asks why God needed to lead the people on such a long and arduous journey in order to free them from the after-effects of idol worship. Couldn't He have simply performed a psychological miracle? Why didn't He simply enter the Israelites' souls and wipe out the remaining tendencies toward idolatry? Maimonides then lays down an important rule: God does not take away our free choice.

> God does not change at all the nature of human individuals by means of miracles. Because of this great principle, it says, *O that they had such a heart as this* . . . (Deut. 5:26). It is because of this that there are commandments and prohibitions, rewards and punishments. . . . We do not say this because we believe that the changing of the nature of any human being is difficult for Him, may He be exalted. Rather, it is possible and fully within His capacity. But according to the foundations of the Law, of the Torah, He has never willed to do it, nor shall He ever will it. For if it were His will that the nature of any human individual should be changed because of what He, may He be exalted, wills from that individual, sending of prophets and all giving of a Law would have been useless. (*Guide*, 3:32)

A person's consciousness is his autonomous realm. Within it, he alone is sovereign. Here is the textual problem: According to part 3, chapter 17 of the *Guide*, human consciousness *is* a domain in which God intervenes, whereas in part 3, chapter 32, it is not. We have here a "contradiction of the seventh kind," which, as we discussed earlier, aims to conceal from the reader profound and sometimes radical ideas.

Rabbi Moses Ibn Tibbon, a medieval commentator on the *Guide*, made one of the earliest attempts to resolve this contradiction. He understood part 3, chapter 17 not as saying that God interferes in our thought processes but rather that human thought processes themselves *are* our divine, providential protection.[13] The wise man is protected from harm because he knows how to avoid getting into dangerous situations like unstable buildings and ships during storms. Reason, the godly part in each of us, is what protects us from harm.[14] This naturalistic reading finds support in the next chapter of the *Guide*:

> The fact that some individuals are preserved from calamities, whereas those befall others, is due not to their bodily forces and their natural dispositions, this being the meaning of the dictum "For not by force shall man prevail"—but to their perfection and deficiency, I mean their nearness to and remoteness from God. For this reason, those who are near to him are exceedingly well-protected: *He will keep the feet of his holy ones*; whereas those who are far from Him are given over to whatever may happen to befall them. For there is nothing to protect them against whatever may occur; for they are like one walking in darkness whose destruction is assured. (*Guide*, 3:18)

Just as vision protects one from stumbling on obstacles along the way, so reason acts as an inner eye guarding against danger. Someone who orders his life rationally, maintains his emotional equilibrium, doesn't smoke, and eats in a healthy way is much less likely to be exposed to pain and suffering. The eyes of reason will protect him from many of life's traps.

Ibn Tibbon's point is that rather than God protecting us, we protect ourselves. Our intellect, the godly within us, saves us from danger. This approach resolves the contradiction with part 3, chapter 32 of the *Guide*. Providence does not limit human freedom. On the contrary, it is a consequence of our choice to develop intellectually.

However, Ibn Tibbon's reading turns out to cause other problems. While his answer resolves the tensions between the chapters that we have seen so far (part 3, chapters 17 and 32), it contradicts what Maimonides writes in part 3, chapter 51, where he returns to the question of how God watches over the enlightened:

> Consider the "song on mishaps" (Ps. 91). You will find that it describes this great providence and the safeguard and protection from all bodily ills . . . so that neither those that are consequent upon the nature of being nor those that are due to the plotting of man would occur. It says: *That he will deliver you from the snare of the fowler . . . His truth is a shield and a buckler. You shall not be afraid of the terror by night nor of the arrow that flies by day; of the pestilence that walks in darkness, nor of the destruction that wastes at noon day* (Ps. 91:3–6). He then goes on to describe the protection against the plotting of men, saying . . . : *A thousand may fall at your side and ten thousand at your right hand; it shall not come near you. Only with your eyes shall you behold, and see the recompense of the wicked* (Ps. 91:7–8) . . . then it gives the reason for this great protection being effective with regard to the individual . . . : *Because he has set his passionate love upon him, therefore I will deliver him; I will set him on high, because he hath known my Name* (Ps. 91:14). We have already explained in preceding chapters that knowledge of the Name is apprehension of Him. (*Guide*, 3:51)

Providence confers protection upon the enlightened one. On a battlefield, thousands may fall, but the perfect man will walk away safe and sound. This is clearly different from part 3, chapter 17, where the Rambam says that a wise man should stay out of dangerous situations. Part 3, chapter 51 claims that even if wise people place themselves in peril, they will be protected. This is a big problem for

Ibn Tibbon's naturalistic understanding of providence. Can one really argue that wise people who walk on to a firing range will be saved because they have learned rational techniques for dodging artillery shells? Naturalistic approaches to providence simply do not cover graphic, miraculous descriptions such as "a thousand shall fall at your side and ten thousand at your right hand, but they shall not come close to you. With your eyes you shall behold and see the recompense of the wicked."

We seem to have reached an impasse. The idea of providence advanced in chapter 17, where God intervenes in human consciousness, contradicts the theory of freedom in chapter 34. The possible solution to this tension—full naturalization of providence—contradicts chapter 51, in which the enlightened are literally protected in extreme circumstances. What is the secret teaching about providence that these multiple contradictions conceal?

Resolving the Problem of Providence through the Problem of Evil

The key to resolving these contradictory ideas about providence lies in our earlier discussion of evil. It is not that the enlightened ones never encounter harmful events. Rather, they do not *experience* such incidents as being harmful. The thirst for knowledge of God frees them from dependence on this world; the spiritual life is their shield. People who love God with their whole being will enjoy total protection from the painful vicissitudes of this world. This is how we should understand the enigmatic words of the Rambam:

> Thus it has become clear to you that the true reason for a human individual's being abandoned to chance so that he is permitted to be devoured by the beasts is his being separated from God. If, however, his God is within him, no evil at all will befall him. For He, may He be exalted, says, *Fear not, for I am with thee; be not dismayed, for I am your God* (Isa. 41:10). He says: *When you pass through the waters, and I will be*

with you, the rivers shall not overflow you (Isa. 43:10). This is accounted for by the fact that everyone who has rendered himself so worthy that the intellect in question overflows toward him, has Providence attached to him, while all evils are prevented from befalling him. It says, *The Lord is for me, I will not fear; what can man do unto me?* (Ps. 118:6). And it says, *Acquaint now yourself with Him, and be at peace* (Job 21:21), meaning to say: turn toward Him and you will be safe from all ill . . . it is as if . . . this individual is protected because he has known Me and then passionately loved Me. You know the difference between the terms one who loves (*oheb*) and one who loves passionately (*hosheq*); an excess of love (*mahabbah*), so that no thought remains that is directed toward a thing other than the Beloved, is passionate love. (*Guide*, 3:51)

Absolute love of God saves a person from emotional dependence on anything else in the world. As we saw from Maimonides's explanation of Job, much of our suffering is subjective. Job's suffering ends when he stops experiencing the disasters of his life as disasters. Personal redemption comes from love of God. The more we love God, the more we will be freed from the pain and distress of this world. Providential protection, then, is a human cognitive achievement.

But did the author of the *Guide* manage to free himself in the way that he exhorts his students to do? As we saw at the start of this chapter, Maimonides wrote the *Guide* under almost unbearable circumstances.

Let us recall the Rambam's discussion of how running after wealth and sensory pleasures causes suffering. In his description of this kind of life, Maimonides cites two examples:

> Thus every ignoramus who thinks worthless thoughts is always sad and despondent because he is not able to achieve the luxury attained by someone else. In most cases such a man exposes himself to great dangers, such as arise in sea voyages and the service of kings; his aim therein being to attain these unnecessary luxuries. (*Guide*, 3:12)

Maimonides knew all about these experiences. His brother's business involved "sea voyages," and his own profession, chosen after his brother's death, was in "the service of kings." This is a wink from the master to his students throughout the generations. Maimonides himself was not fully free. He was not a guru, exhorting his students to strive for the peaks of enlightenment that he himself had reached. Maimonides did not believe that he had reached the summit. As a teacher, he did not merely show his students the way. He also admitted that he was walking the very same path beside them.

4

REDEMPTION

If God must be perfect and unchanging, how can we have a religion that relies on the idea that God listens to prayer, rewards the righteous, punishes evildoers, and wants our sacrifices?

The Kabbalists too felt this tension, and their solution was to reinterpret God. They understood the divine as having two aspects: one hidden and the other revealed. The revealed face of God is expressed in some of the *sefirot*,[1] which express the aspect of God that makes religion relevant: the God who rewards, punishes, answers prayer, and brings redemption. The concealed face of God, in contrast, represents the perfect, unchanging side of God.[2]

Because the Rambam believed that one cannot say anything substantive about God, his answer was to reinterpret not God but religion. We have seen in previous chapters how he reconceived the ideas of prophecy and providence so that they would be consistent with an absolute, perfect, and unchanging God. This chapter focuses on how the Rambam understood redemption.

The idea of redemption has come to occupy a central place in the intellectual and emotional life of the Jewish people. It is the source of a fierce hope in the hearts of Jews, and its relatively marginal place in the *Guide for the Perplexed* is surprising. In addition, while Maimonides extensively discussed the Messianic Era in the *Mishneh Torah*, he addressed it only briefly in the *Guide*. His description of a utopian future did not include the Messiah as an individual. Instead, in the *Guide* the Rambam reflected on some of the verses from the book of Isaiah that depict the perfect future toward which humanity is moving:

> Just as a blind man, because of absence of sight, does not cease stumbling, being wounded, and also wounding others, because he has no one to guide him on his way . . . [so too] if there were knowledge, whose relation to the human form is like that of the faculty of sight to the eye, people would refrain from doing any harm to themselves and to others.[3] For through cognition of the truth, enmity and hatred are removed and the inflicting of harm by people on one another is abolished. It holds out this promise saying: *And the wolf shall dwell with the lamb, and the leopard shall lie down with the kid* . . . (Isa. 11:6). Then it gives the reason for this, saying that the cause of the abolition of these enmities, these discords and these tyrannies, will be the knowledge that men will then have concerning the true reality of the deity. (*Guide*, 3:11)

In the messianic future, human distress will disappear. There will be no more hatred or war; peace and well-being will prevail. In Maimonides's view, there will be a single reason for this eclipse of suffering and the spread of goodness: intellectual enlightenment. In his metaphor, all human failures stem from blindness.[4] A man who cannot see is condemned to stumble, to be hurt, and to hurt others. Knowledge is compared to light. Because ignorance is the primary source of evil, knowledge must be the catalyst for redemption. The Rambam believed that human intellect drives the course of history. With the fulfillment of Isaiah's prophecy, "And the earth will be full of the knowledge of God as the waters cover the sea" (Isa. 11:9), the world will be a place where "the wolf and the sheep dwell together and the leopard lies down with the goat" (Isa. 11:6). Knowledge is redemptive; truth brings peace.

Uncharacteristically, the Rambam did not give a particularly well-ordered explanation of his views about redemption. Some have suggested that his belief in a rationalist redemption was not itself rationally grounded.[5] However, although Maimonides's explanations were relatively scanty in part 3, chapter 11 of the *Guide*, which ostensibly dealt directly with that subject, they were more extensive in other places that touch on it more tangentially. In particular, the Rambam wrote elsewhere that the spread of enlightened understanding has two very important social consequences: the elimination of economic deprivation and the end of war.

REASON AND ECONOMIC WELL-BEING

There is no necessary connection between the spread of reason and economic improvement. Indeed, in the introduction to *Mishneh Torah*, the Rambam wrote that the common people's pursuit of their foolish desires is what turns the wheels of the economy: "Were it not for such delusions, the world would be a wasteland" (80). Without mass consumerism, people would not invest capital, construct buildings, or create factories, and the economy would suffer. On the other hand, Maimonides mocked those who spent their whole lives pursuing wealth and despising the precious free time that they could have used to develop spiritually. For the Rambam, the headlong pursuit of economic success was illogical.

Maybe the spread of wisdom would lead to economic disaster. If people were to become more rational and spend more of their time pursuing enlightenment, consumption would diminish, economic activity would contract, and global productivity and wealth would be reduced. One might therefore think that in the utopian era, there will be less material prosperity, not more. According to this view, redemption could herald something very different from an age in which "all delicacies will be as common as dust" (*MT*, *Hilkhot Melakhim*, 12:5).

The Rambam's resolution of this problem relies on a distinction between wants and needs. In part 3, chapter 12 of the *Guide*, Maimonides argues that need in the world does not reflect a scarcity of resources but rather a limited human consciousness that cannot recognize the presence of plenty:

> Consider the circumstances in which we are placed. For the more a thing is necessary for a living being, the more often it may be found and the

cheaper it is. On the other hand, the less necessary it is, the less often it is found and it is very expensive. Thus, for example, what is necessary for man is air, water and food. But air is the most necessary, for nobody can live without it for a moment without perishing. As for water, one can remain without it for a day or two. Accordingly, air is indubitably easier to find and cheaper than water. Water is more necessary than food, for certain people may remain, if they drink and do not eat, for four or five days without food. Accordingly in every city you find water more frequently and at a cheaper price than food. Things are similar with regard to foodstuffs; those that are most necessary are easier to find at a given place and cheaper than the unnecessary. Regarding musk, amber, rubies and emeralds, I do not think than anyone of sound intellect can believe than man has strong need for them unless it be for medical treatment; and even in such cases, they and other similar things can be replaced by numerous herbs and earths. (*Guide*, 3:12)

In contrast to this amazing fit between needs and reality, there is no such alignment between human desires and their objects. People have fierce urges to gain honor, power, gold, or diamonds, but these things tend to be very rare. This is why there is subjective perception of scarcity. In a perfected world, people would desire only what they need, there would be no perceived scarcity, and people would feel satisfied:[6] "for the more people hope for luxuries, the harder they are to attain and so much energy is expended on superfluities that eventually necessities are not available either" (*Guide*, 3:12).

People in a fully rational society would know neither need nor perceived need. There might not be more objective riches, but there would be a general sense of wealth. The utopia of the *Guide* invites a transformation in human consciousness so that our subjective feeling of wealth does not depend on economic fluctuations in the world.

REASON AND PEACE

The Rambam claims that by virtue of the spread of reason, war will also disappear:

For when only the desires are followed, as is done by the ignorant, the longing for speculation is abolished . . . cares and sorrows multiply, mutual envy, hatred and strife, aimed at taking away what the other has, multiply. (*Guide*, 3:33)

Competition over scarce natural resources inevitably spills over into conflict. The rational perspective, on the other hand, is focused on the one, genuinely unlimited resource—the truth. The rules of zero-sum games do not apply to this commodity. One person understanding truth does not leave less truth available for others. The knowledge of God is accessible to all. A well-ordered society centered on the aspiration for enlightenment will refocus human desires away from scarce resources toward those that are limitless. Conflicts between people and nations will cease; wisdom will lead to peace.

This perspective on how wisdom can restrain man's violent urges gives rise to certain textual difficulties, for it appears to contradict other elements of the political theory that the Rambam presents in the *Guide*.

In a number of other places, Maimonides argues that political order is a condition for the successful pursuit of intellectual perfection. Where there is political instability with unpredictable outbursts of violence, the yearning for philosophy is weaker. The Rambam believed that the highest intellectual achievements were unattainable for one who lived under such a flawed political system. But the utopian model that we have just presented reverses this causality: intellectual perfection is a condition for political order, not the opposite.[7] It seems that in one place the Rambam implies that enlightenment will enable us to solve our political problems, while in another he states that perfecting our political system is a condition for reaching enlightenment. Which is it?

Moreover, we have seen that the Rambam viewed the dissemination of truth as a potential threat to the political order and that society needed to conceal the ultimate truths in order to preserve social stability. Here, however, the Rambam claims that the spread of truth facilitates peaceful political relations rather than threatening them. It appears, then, that the utopianism of the *Guide* does not sit easily with its politics.

THE UTOPIAN ANARCHISM OF THE *GUIDE*

Political systems mediate between two fundamental human characteristics: the need to be part of some collective and the need to express our immense differences from one another:

> There are many differences between the individuals belonging to it (the human species), so that you can hardly find two individuals who are in accord with respect to one of the . . . moral habits. The cause of this is the difference of temperaments . . . nothing like this great difference between individuals is found among the other species of animals, in which the difference between individuals belonging to the same species is small, man being in this respect an exception. For you may find among us two individuals who seem, with regard to every moral habit, to belong to two different species. Thus you may find in an individual cruelty that reaches the point at which he kills the youngest of his sons in his great anger, whereas another individual is full of pity at the killing of a bug or any other insect, his soul being too tender for this. The same holds true for other instances. (*Guide*, 2:40)

People have a profound need to live in societies. However, our multiple differences from one another make it difficult for us to come together in social frameworks that are non-coercive. Only though leadership that imposes law and order can we overcome our diversity sufficiently to enable the smooth running of society:

> Now, as the nature of the human species requires that there be those differences among the individuals belonging to it and as, in addition, society is a necessity for this nature, it is by no means possible that society should be perfected except—and this is necessarily so—through a ruler who gauges the actions of individuals, perfecting that which is deficient and reducing that which is excessive, and who prescribes actions and moral habits that all of them may always practice in the

same way, so that the natural diversity is hidden through the multiple points of conventional accord and so that the community becomes well ordered. (*Guide*, 2:40)

The function of law is to create norms that all are obliged to keep. Laws, including the Torah's laws, create a certain uniformity of human behavior, making it less likely that our differences will erupt in ways that threaten the social fabric. By blunting the full heterogeneity of its citizenry, the state enables social peace and political order.

The laws of the Torah have an additional purpose. Repairing the body politic is just one station on the road toward intellectual perfection. Peaceful political conditions create a climate in which intellectual pursuits can flourish.[8] So now we can discern a tension between these two functions of Torah—fostering greater uniformity of behavior on the one hand, and creating the conditions that enable the full spiritual and intellectual self-realization on the other.

According to Aristotle, the differences between people flow from their physical characteristics; things sharing the same essential nature can only exhibit differences if there are differences in their material substance. Maimonides mentions this idea in a different context: "individuals that are the same in their essence can only be differentiated from one another by accidents that pertain to their physical forms" (*MT, Hilkhot Yesodei HaTorah*, 1:7).

The basic form of man is the same for all individuals. In Aristotle's view, all the differences between people stem from differences in their material composition. This implies that the body and not the intellect is the basic cause of human diversity; this diversity in turn requires regulation by means of law and politics.

If our bodies are the cause of our differences, then it follows that focusing on the realization of our physical desires will magnify our differences and increase heterogeneity. On the other hand, a society that emphasizes intellectual activities will deemphasize the differences between people (because these are rooted in the physical). Philosophy is a pure, cerebral pursuit. Therefore a society that aspires to knowledge of God is one that will strengthen those parts of human nature that we have in common.

Maimonides writes explicitly, "the goal of the Torah is that human beings will become more alike" (*Guide*, 2:39). The Torah is meant to make us all converge toward a certain image of the perfect human being. In this sense, it is inimical to individuality. In a society that had fully realized the Torah's goals, all its members would become similar in respect of our spiritual and intellectual nature—the most essential part of us. If all would reach intellectual perfection, human heterogeneity would disappear.

It appears, then, that although one reason for the Torah's laws is to manage and moderate human difference, at the same time they also work to erase those differences. Is the goal of the Law to make the Law itself superfluous? At the same time, the Rambam staunchly defends the eternality of the Torah. Throughout his writings he rejects any interpretation of the Torah which suggests that the commandments might be "canceled" at some future time. However, by entertaining the notion that the *halakhah* is not an end in itself but rather a means to greater goal, the Rambam introduced a potentially anarchic element into his thought. Turning the Torah into a means can endanger its eternality, because when its goal is achieved, the Torah may then be seen as superfluous. Like Wittgenstein's example of the ladder which, once climbed, may be discarded, the utopian dimension of the *Guide* presents a society in which the Law has become a victim of its own success.

The redemptive vision described in the *Guide* appears to undermine the generally conservative cast of Maimonides's political thinking by suggesting the anarchic possibility of a utopia in which there will be no need for the Law. To gain a richer and more nuanced understanding of the Rambam's messianism, let us turn to his treatment of the subject in the *Mishneh Torah*.

The Messianic Era in the *Mishneh Torah*

The utopia of the *Guide* lacks most of the traditional messianic motifs we find in Jewish tradition. There is no description of the Messiah himself, no reference to the ingathering of exiles, or even any specific reference to the "Messianic Era." The *Mishneh Torah*, on the other hand, combines all these elements, and more, into a clear and systematic view of Jewish messianism.

Messianic expectation has been part of Judaism since the destruction of the First Temple. Many sources speculate about when the Messiah will arrive and what will happen when he does. Suggestions of portents and signs indicating the arrival of the redeemer have awakened messianic anticipation throughout history. There was an outburst of messianic hope in the Rambam's day. In his "Epistle to Yemen," Maimonides addressed a Jewish community that had been enthralled by the charisma of a would-be messiah. In his letter, Maimonides warned the community against vain speculations and expectations; he expressed similar warnings more pithily in the *Mishneh Torah*:

> A person should not busy himself with speculative legends, nor spend much time studying *midrashim* that deal with these [messianic] matters, nor make them central to his beliefs, because they do not bring a person either to fear or love of God. Furthermore, he should not try to calculate when the final redemption will come. The sages say "let the spirit of one who calculates the end rot." Rather, a person should wait and have faith. (*MT*, *Hilkhot Melakhim*, 12:5)

In the *Mishneh Torah*, the Rambam sought to challenge the widespread belief that the Messianic Era would bring about a drastic alteration in reality. Within Jewish tradition, there are elements that anticipate radical change in the Messianic Era in two large and important areas: alteration of the laws of nature and cancellation of some of the Torah's laws.

Changing the Laws of Nature

"And the light of the moon shall be like the light of the sun, while the light of the sun shall be seven times stronger than the light of the seven days of creation" (Isa. 30:26). There are biblical verses that describe drastic, cosmic changes in the future. Night will become day, the crooked will become straight, and hills will be flattened into plains. The Bible planted the memory of a wondrous past in the collective consciousness of the people: the exodus from Egypt, the appearance of manna in the desert, and the conquest of the Land of Israel. The miraculous, formative experiences of the Jewish people engender an expectation of a future in which the natural order of the world will be upended.

In the *Mishneh Torah*, the Rambam attacks this expectation. In the *Guide*, many miracles from the past are explained as parables; in the *Mishneh Torah*, too, future miracles are interpreted metaphorically:

> What is written in the Book of Isaiah about the wolf and the sheep, the leopard and goat lying down together is a parable . . . and all other such statements about the Messiah are likewise not to be taken literally, and in the days of the Messiah, the meaning of these parables and what exactly they were hinting at will become known to all. (*MT, Hilkhot Melakhim*, 12:2)

The order of nature, in Maimonides's view, is eternal and unchanging:

> Do not imagine that in the days of the Messiah any aspect of the laws of nature will be cancelled, or that there will be any innovation in the works of creation; rather, the world will continue to follow its natural course. (*MT, Hilkhot Melakhim*, 12:1)

The laws of physics are eternal; the macropolitical situation of the Jewish people will change. The future Messianic Era will manifest itself solely through a transformation in the Jewish political condition, from one of exile to a state of full Jewish sovereignty, and not through any change in the laws of nature. "The only difference between our world and the messianic world is our subjugation to the nations" (*MT, Hilkhot Melakhim*, 12:1).

ANNULLING LAWS OF THE TORAH

The messianic idea has the potential for anarchy. Many have believed that in the time of the Messiah, the mitzvot of the Torah would become irrelevant, or even be canceled: in the language of the Talmud, "mitzvot will be superfluous in the Messianic Era."[9] A central support for the connection between messianism and the negation of mitzvot was the notion that the Torah was limited to a certain period of time. Nachmanides, also known as the Ramban, one of the great medieval kabbalists, called the period during which mitzvot would be operative "the time of Torah."[10] The implication was that a certain stretch of history was allotted as the era of Torah. The Messiah's arrival would mark the end of this period and the start of a new era[11]—an era without laws.

These ideas were systematically elaborated in certain streams of kabbalistic thought.[12] Maimonides, however, disagreed. He declared that the *halakhah* was eternal. The messiah would not, in his view, make a "new covenant" or propound a new Torah emptied of legal content. "The essential point is this: the Torah and its laws will endure forever" (*MT, Hilkhot Melachim*, 11:7). Indeed, the Rambam believed that whereas in our time *halakhah* is only partially implemented, the Messianic Era will remove the obstacles to the full expression and observance of *halakhah*:

> The King Messiah who will be anointed in the future will restore the Kingdom as David to its former preeminence; he will rebuild the Temple and gather in the exiles of Israel. All the statutes that existed previously will return. We will offer sacrifices and observe the Sabbatical year and the Jubilee as they are described in the Torah. (*MT, Hilkhot Melakhim*, 11:1)

The Messiah will also identify the correct lineage of priests, Levites and of the tribes who had been scattered. He will enable *halakhah* to be fully actualized. In contrast to the more anarchistic view, according to the Rambam redemption will not end the era of Torah; rather, it will be the era of Torah *par excellence*.

A preoccupation with the future coming of the Messiah is an expression of discontent with the here and now. The idealized future will redeem what is lacking in the flawed present. The Rambam realized that in remolding the Jewish people's hopes for the future, he was also reconceptualizing their view of present reality. A messianic belief that the laws of nature will be nullified in the messianic future might reflect a contemporary withdrawal from the natural world into a realm of supernatural fantasy. Thus, Maimonides sought to base religious consciousness on awe of nature: the natural world bears the fingerprints of the Creator, and therefore studying its laws is a fulfillment of the positive commandment, "You shall love the Lord your God."

Maimonides understood that belief in a non-natural future was symptomatic of a distorted religious consciousness in the present. Similarly, the hope for a world without *halakhah* reflects a current recoiling from the *halakhah*. In the final chapters of the *Mishneh Torah*, the Rambam endeavors to reconcile his readers with *halakhah* by negating the expectation that law will one day be annulled.

Maimonides lowers our expectations of the Messianic Era. The main historical change that will occur in the messianic future is political: the restoration of full national independence to the Jewish people. The exile will end, and the people will be gathered to their land and will no longer be subject to foreign sovereignty. This naturalistic, historical process will be led by an exceptionally charismatic figure, the King Messiah. According to the "Epistle to Yemen," this leader will be greater than all of the biblical prophets apart from Moses.

The Rambam believed in the power of extraordinary individuals to alter the course of history. His view is echoed in the writings of the nineteenth-century political thinker Thomas Carlyle. Carlyle argued, contrary to determinist thinkers, that great leaders make history, rather than vice versa.[13] So, for example, whereas historians of a determinist bent might argue that if Theodore Herzl hadn't existed, then history would have produced another leader instead of him, Carlyle would have argued that, without Herzl, the State of Israel might never have been founded. Thinkers like Hegel and Marx believed that great people are formed by historical forces that are much bigger than any individuals.[14] Maimonides believed, like Carlyle, that extraordinary people steer the course of history, rather than the reverse. Abraham and Moses changed history in the past, the Rambam himself did so in his own era, and the Messiah will transform history in the future.

NON-UTOPIAN REDEMPTION

The messianic project is an enormous one. However, it is not an end in itself. Rather, messianism is a means; the end is to create sufficient free time and optimal political conditions for philosophical reflection. "The prophets and sages did not yearn for the Messianic Era in order to rule over or to dominate the nations, or to be honored by them and not to eat, drink and be merry; rather they wanted to be free to pursue Torah and wisdom, without any tyrant or task master who would make them desist" (*MT, Hilkhot Melachim*, 12:7). Sociopolitical peace allows peace of mind. A climate of perpetual insecurity and struggling for survival does not enable spiritual growth or intellectual development. The greatest benefit that the good society confers on its members is the freedom to think without distractions.

The ultimate goal of the Messianic Era is to provide the conditions under which people can pursue and reach truth and so become worthy of attaining the world to come. For the meaning of the world to come is bliss that comes from having reached intellectual perfection. The Rambam's messianism is a fulfillment of the political theory of the *Guide*: perfection of the body precedes perfection of the mind. The Messianic Era will perfect the physical world, paving the way for the ultimate spiritual perfection—the world to come.

The Rambam also discusses the status of *halakhah* in the Messianic Era at the end of his *Hilkhot Teshuvah* ("Laws of Repentance"). There, he attempts to revise what it is that the religious hope for in the future. The Torah promises that if we serve God, then we will flourish economically and succeed militarily. If, on the other hand, we rebel against God, we will suffer economic disaster and defeat in war. These promises are likely to influence our motivation for observing the mitzvot. Material success may become the central reason for keeping the Torah.

In *Hilkhot Teshuvah*, the Rambam reframes the future that religious Jews should hope for and thereby establishes a deeper motivational basis for observing *halakhah*. Maimonides neither negates the biblical promise of material flourishing nor treats it as a mere metaphor. Rather, he interprets it as a means to a greater end. Economic prosperity and victory on the battlefield are not the ultimate goals of religious life; they simply provide the conditions under which people can pursue intellectual and spiritual fulfillment. As the Rambam writes, "This is why the prophets and sages of Israel yearned for the Messianic Era: in order that they should have respite from the nations that don't allow us to pursue Torah and mitzvot fully and so that they should find some rest and peace of mind in order to increase wisdom and attain the world to come (*MT, Hilkhot Teshuvah*, 9:2). This description is not of a society that has attained wisdom, but of one where all have the opportunity to do so.

The Rambam's halakhic writings do not paint a picture of the spiritually perfected society. Such a description is found only in *The Guide for the Perplexed*. One might characterize the relationship between the messianic visions of the two books as follows: the utopia of the *Guide* is the ultimate goal of the Messianic Era as it is described in the *Mishneh Torah*.

Halakhah is eternal because physicality is part of our inexorable nature. The utopia of the *Guide* is therefore destined to remain an unrealized dream.

A hypothetical society that reached intellectual perfection would, like the Garden of Eden, have no need for law. Eden was a place without law, because its inhabitants knew God directly. The utopia of the *Guide* is a place where all have reached intellectual perfection, and therefore the physically rooted differences between people become insignificant. Maimonides treats the Garden of Eden story as a parable, removed from history. So too, he removes his future utopia from history. The one never happened in the past, and the other will not happen in the future. Universal intellectual perfection that renders law unnecessary may be an inspiring idea, but it is incapable of full realization.[15]

For Maimonides, redemption and utopia are not the same.[16] The redeemed society is one that is free to strive for utopia. It is a society that successfully reorients human desire from material plenty to intellectual and spiritual flourishing. The prophet Amos described the Messianic Era as a time of yearning: "Behold, days are coming, says the Lord, God when I will send a hunger in the land, not a hunger for bread, nor a thirst for water, but to hear the word of God" (Amos 8:11). Redemption will be characterized not by the satiation of desire but rather by its conversion from a hunger for bread to a hunger for the word of God.

The Rambam believed that the perfect society is ultimately unattainable. The philosopher Karl Popper convincingly showed how utopian systems (such as fascism and communism) that consider themselves to be perfect tend to become violent dictatorships.[17] The inner logic of utopian societies tends to make them hate difference. If you believe that the system is perfect, then dissent is by definition destructive and must be suppressed. Maimonides's messianic society does not fall into this trap. Its greatest achievement is to enable the pursuit of utopia rather than its realization.

The Rambam hoped for the establishment of an ideal society in the Messianic Era, in which all would be free to pursue knowledge and wisdom. This messianic time, however is not the final culmination of divine service; similarly, national redemption is not the ultimate goal—there is a higher purpose to history than both of these, and that is the spiritual redemption of every human being.

5

FROM NEGATIVE THEOLOGY TO EMPOWERING HUMANITY

The last decade has seen the rise of strident atheism as a cultural and literary phenomenon. Books such as Richard Dawkins's *The God Delusion* and Christopher Hitchens's *God Is Not Great* mounted all-out assaults on religion.[1] Hitchens and Dawkins argue that the beliefs of the world's religions are irrational, their God is vicious, and their followers have been responsible for most of the horrors and atrocities in world history. They maintain that religious belief has no redeeming features.

Militant atheists are strikingly confident that they know what religion is, what religious adherents think, and the specific nature of the God in whom people believe. In *The God Delusion*, for example, Dawkins characterizes God as "a vindictive bloodthirsty ethnic cleanser, a misogynistic, homophobic racist, an infanticidal, genocidal, filicidal, pestilential, megalomaniacal, sadomasochistic, capriciously malevolent bully."[2]

Numerous writers have noted Dawkins's fundamental ignorance of religious thought. In a review, the literary critic Terry Eagleton remarks about *The God Delusion*: "Imagine someone holding forth on biology whose only knowledge of the subject is the *Book of British*

Birds, and you have a rough idea of what it feels like to read Richard Dawkins on theology."[3] It is not hard to pillory Dawkins's description as a gross parody of what any major religion says about God.

A more sophisticated line of criticism, however, was advanced by Karen Armstrong in her 2009 book *The Case for God*.[4] Armstrong argues that the real problem lies in the attempt to say anything at all about God. She is witheringly critical both of religious traditions that make dogmatic claims about the nature of God and of polemical atheists who aim to deconstruct such claims. Both groups, in Armstrong's view, have missed the point of religion.

Armstrong advocates returning to the apophatic approach to religion. This was a stream found in all of the great traditions that "understood faith not as something people thought, but as something they did." Religious leaders in this tradition practiced, according to Armstrong, "a deliberate and principled reticence about God and/ or the sacred."[5] They were more concerned about what we are not able to know about the divine.

One need not subscribe to Armstrong's sweeping history and taxonomy of religious belief to agree with her that a little more "deliberate and principled reticence about God" would improve the tone and raise the level of contemporary public discussion of religion. In the history of religious thought, probably no one has been more careful to respect the limits of what can meaningfully be said about God than Maimonides. His "negative theology," which I outlined in the preceding chapters, was the cornerstone of *The Guide for the Perplexed*. It may also be the basis for a more productive contemporary discourse about God and religion. We began this part by talking about God and have moved, via discussion of three fundamental religious ideas—prophecy, providence, and redemption—to some conclusions about the Rambam's conception of human beings. A pattern emerges from our analysis of these three ideas. In each case, the Rambam radically recasts traditional beliefs.

Prophecy: The prophet is someone who is perfectly endowed with intellect and imagination, who attains prophecy after a lengthy process of education and moral training, and who, while not desiring political power, achieves a position of societal leadership by virtue of his prophetic status.

Providence: Providential protection is achieved through a process of study and spiritual refinement that leads a person to refocus his desires from the material to the spiritual so he is no longer emotionally dependent on the physical world and thus less likely to be disappointed by it.

Redemption: Human beings are active participants rather than passive objects of the redemptive process. The yearning for wisdom is redemptive, in that it displaces the desire for limited resources such as money, honor, and power, thereby reducing conflict and war.

The common denominator in the Rambam's treatment of these subjects is an ambitious attempt at refocusing *desire*. By directing human yearnings away from the physical and toward intellectual and spiritual goals, Maimonides sought to mold a new type of person who would be a more active religious agent.

THE LAW OF CONSERVATION OF *EROS*

People are born, according, to the Rambam, with an immense desire to learn. He adopted Aristotle's dictum, which opens the *Metaphysics*, that "all men by nature desire to know." Over a person's lifetime one's desire for knowledge tends to diminish. This does not happen automatically. The yearning for knowledge is crowded out as more physical desires are awakened. The Rambam describes how this happens:

> Even a perfect man, if he were to occupy himself much with these necessary things and all the more if he were to occupy himself with unnecessary things, and if his desire for them should grow strong, he would find that his theoretical desires had grown weak and had been submerged. And his demand for them would slacken and become intermittent and inattentive. (*Guide*, 1:34)

According to Maimonides, human *eros*, which we may define, following Plato, as passionate love that is not necessarily focused on a physical object, is essentially a single force. When *eros* is captured by the senses, intellectual desire is decreased. This dynamic can also work in reverse: strengthening our intellectual yearnings weakens sexual desire. This is implicit in the Rambam's discussion of male circumcision. He believed that one of the purposes of circumcision was to lessen the sexual urge so as to strengthen the desire for knowledge. As the Rambam expressed it in the *Mishneh Torah*, "A person should direct his thoughts to words of Torah and increase knowledge and wisdom, because thoughts of sexual sin are only overwhelming to a heart that is devoid of wisdom" (*MT, Hilkhot Issurei Bi'ah*, 22:21).

Maimonides believed that sexuality was a necessary evil for the continuation of human life, but for him there was no more potent force distracting human beings from their true purpose:

> As we have said, there are among men individuals to whose mind all the impulses of matter are shameful and ugly things, deficiencies imposed by necessity; particularly so the sense of touch, which, as Aristotle has stated, is a shame for us, and because of which we wish to eat, to drink and to copulate. Consequently, one's recourse to these things should be reduced to the extent that is possible; one should do them in secret, feel sorrowful because one does them, and not have them spoken and discoursed about; no gathering should be held with a view to these things. A man should be in control of all these impulses, restrict his efforts in relation to them, and admit only that which is indispensable. He should take as his end that which is the end of man *qua* man, solely the mental representation of the intelligibles. (*Guide*, 3:8)

However, the Rambam's opposition to uncontrolled sexuality did not stem from opposition to *eros*. On the contrary, he describes love of God in terms of fierce, erotic desire.[6] It was precisely his interest in channeling this desire toward wisdom that led to his suspicion of untrammeled sexuality. In one of his dialogues, Plato compares the human being to a charioteer with two horses. One horse is well behaved, representing our desire for knowledge, and the other is wild and rebellious, representing our physical desires. The rider's job is to subdue the horse of our earthly desires and let the horse of reason and intellect lead. For the Rambam there was only one horse. The drives for sexuality and for knowledge are at root the same. Our challenge is to make the yearning for knowledge rather than for sex the channel and outlet of our passions.

One might call this "the law of conservation of *eros*." We cannot crush our erotic desires, according to the Rambam, but we can redirect them. I would argue that this is the Rambam's view in his treatment of other urges too, for food, resources, and political power. In his discussions of prophecy, providence, and redemption we have seen how he advocates sublimating our material desires to higher ends and in the process molding a new kind of human personality.

INTERPRETING THE TORAH AND
THE AUTHORITY OF REASON

The Rambam challenged anthropomorphic understandings of the divine and argued instead for an incorporeal God to whom human language and human characteristics could not be attributed. To fortify his conception, Maimonides invested considerable effort in reinterpreting biblical verses that seemed to imply that God has physical characteristics. When the Bible applies words like "sit" and "stand" to God, it suggests to the reader a physical, embodied God. This was, for the Rambam, intensely problematic. Throughout part I of the *Guide*, the Rambam reinterpreted biblical verses that might be taken to provide a license for anthropomorphic beliefs and rendered problematic words and phrases metaphorically in order to free God of any physical attributes or associations with human linguistic descriptions.

As we have seen, the Rambam also recast key religious concepts such as prophecy, providence, and redemption so that they aligned more closely with his understanding of God. This too involved extensive reinterpretation of biblical verses and passages. The reader of the *Guide* cannot but be struck by the gap between the Rambam's understanding of core religious concepts and those of the Bible. The philosopher-prophet of the *Guide* seems very different from the prophets of the Bible; it is hard to imagine Isaiah, Jeremiah, or Ezekiel devoting his time to studying books of metaphysics. Similarly, the divine providence of the Bible does not much resemble the Rambam's concept. In the Bible, God interferes with the laws of nature and brings miracles to wreak vengeance on evildoers and redeem the righteous, apparently without any regard for the educational level of the people he is saving. In the *Guide*, by contrast, providential concern is primarily an intellectual and spiritual achievement of the perfected human being.

These far-reaching projects in biblical interpretation raise the important question of how Maimonides understood the degree of interpretative freedom that we have in reading the Bible. He addressed this issue in the context of the *Guide*'s discussion about whether the world was created, as the Bible teaches, or whether it had always existed, as Aristotle argued (a subject that I will address in part 3). After a lengthy analysis of the competing claims, the Rambam concludes that there is no decisive proof on either side. Nevertheless, he argues that the stronger argument lay in favor of the creation of the world. In the chapter where the Rambam explains his reasons for thinking this, he offers a rare glimpse into his approach to biblical interpretation:

> Know that our shunning the affirmation of the eternity of the world is not due to a text figuring in the Torah according to which the world has been produced in time. For the texts indicating that the world has been produced in time are not more numerous than those indicating that the deity is a body. Nor are the gates of figurative interpretation shut in our faces or impossible of access to us regarding the subject of the creation of the world in time. For we could interpret them as figurative, as we have done when denying His corporeality. Perhaps this would even be

much easier to do: we should be very able to give a figurative interpretation of those texts and to affirm as true the eternity of the world, just as we have given a figurative interpretation of those other texts and have denied that He, may He be exalted, is a body. (*Guide*, 2:25)

The Rambam avers that he does not decide in favor of creation because of the content of the biblical verses. If there were a decisive proof for the eternity of the world, then he would have no problem reinterpreting the Torah—whose opening words are, "In the beginning God created"—in line with the view that the world had always existed. Indeed, he writes that this would have been easier than his intensive effort to reinterpret the many biblical verses that could be taken give credence to anthropomorphism.

The idea that the commentator has considerable interpretative freedom was not new. The Rambam was continuing a tradition, in this respect, from the sages of the midrash and Talmud.[7] What *was* new, however, was how openly the Rambam declared what he was doing. Usually, interpreters of sacred scriptures take pains to emphasize their fidelity to the meaning of the authoritative text. The Rambam broke the rules of the game by stating explicitly that if he wished to, he could reinterpret the text to make it mean the opposite of what the plain sense suggests.

The Rambam does, however, place an important condition on when the reader may exercise such freedom. Only when there is a decisive proof in favor of a theological position is it legitimate to reinterpret the biblical verses to conform to that view. In the case of the incorporeality of God, which the Rambam believed to have been unequivocally demonstrated, he threw his whole weight behind the reinterpretation of biblical verses that seemed to suggest that God was physical. In the case of the creation of the world, on the other hand, where there was no decisive argument on either side, there was no mandate to reinterpret the verses in a way that contradicted their plain meaning.

The Rambam's approach to biblical interpretation was underpinned by a sophisticated conception of language. He understood that words often have many meanings and can be used metaphorically in multiple ways. How does one know when a word is being used metaphorically? One important condition is to understand the context. Knowledge about the cultural and intellectual context that was prevalent when the text was created can help identify when a literal interpretation of a given word or phrase would not have been entertained.[8] In such cases it is reasonable to think that the word or phrase is being used metaphorically.

If this is true, then we need contextual information that is external to the text we are trying to interpret in order to understand its elusive meanings and hidden aspects. According to the Rambam, any body of knowledge whose truth has been decisively demonstrated becomes part of the context that enables us to understand the text. So, for example, the Neo-Aristotelian theology of the Middle Ages, in particular the proof of the incorporeality of the divinity, became part of the contextual framework for texts about God. When we learn from external sources that God has no body, we realize that a verse that speaks, say, about the "hand of God" must be read metaphorically. Philosophical knowledge gives the reader the background that is necessary to interpret the Torah correctly. The Rambam did not think he was imposing philosophy on the Torah; rather, he believed that philosophy enables us to reveal the Torah's meaning.

In a certain sense, the Rambam believed that the biblical interpreter actually has little freedom. Once a truth has been unequivocally proved, the reader has no choice but to interpret the text in line with this truth. In this respect, philosophy may restrict our interpretative possibilities. The Rambam's openness to sources of knowledge outside the Torah does not necessarily result in openness in his interpretation of the Torah. Unlike the midrashic tradition, which promoted the plurality of possible meanings in the biblical text, for the Rambam, after a philosophical view was established as certain, only readings of the Torah that conformed with that view were possible.

This is what drove the Rambam to recast traditional understandings of prophecy, providence, and redemption. Once the existence of a God who was absolutely beyond human experience and language had been established beyond doubt, the Rambam was compelled to reinterpret the Torah's teachings on other basic religious concepts in accordance with this knowledge.

CONCLUSION

The New Religious Hero

In the process of reinterpreting fundamental Jewish concepts, the Rambam created a new model of religious greatness. Instead of the self-effacing saint, Maimonides offers as an ideal the thinker who creates his own life, world, and consciousness. Instead of the person who waits passively for God to save him from bad things, the Rambam holds up the image of one who works actively to prevent evil and molds his own consciousness so that he no longer experiences the difficulties of life as bad. Instead of the traditional prophet who waits for God to speak, the Rambam offers us a new religious hero who forms his own personality and educates himself to the point that he discovers God.

This new religious role model who emerges from the *Guide* bears some resemblance to the modern ideal that celebrated human autonomy as a supreme value. Many modern thinkers, most famously the German philosopher Frederick Nietzsche, believed that a precondition for the rise of free autonomous human beings was emancipation from tradition, God, and religion. Maimonides, on the other hand, did not see his ideal spiritual hero as a rebel against religion. He did not believe that God had to die for the new man to be born. On the contrary, he thought that a true appreciation for the exaltedness of God enabled the full spiritual flourishing of humanity. God's transcendence makes space for our creativity.

There is another aspect to the new religious ideal that Maimonides attempted to promote through his reinterpretation of traditional Jewish concepts. Against the view that God reveals Himself through great miracles, he argued that God's wisdom is revealed in the wondrous everyday workings of nature. The more deeply we understand the extraordinary complexity of the natural world, the more we will feel emotions of awe and wonder, which, according to the Rambam, are profound *religious* experiences.[1] The Rambam believed that amazement at the order of nature was a higher spiritual level than seeking evidence of miraculous departures from the order of nature. He viewed the need to constantly seek supernatural confirmation of religious beliefs as an expression of a kind of psychological disability:

> How great is the blindness of ignorance and how harmful! If you told a man who is one of those who deem themselves the sages of Israel that the deity sends an angel, who enters the womb of a woman and forms the fetus there, he would be pleased with this assertion and would accept it and would regard it as a manifestation of greatness and power on the part of the deity, and also of His wisdom, may He be exalted. . . . But if you tell him that God has placed in the sperm a formative force shaping the limbs and giving them their configuration . . . the man would shrink from this opinion. For he does not understand the notion of the true greatness and power in this. (*Guide*, 2:6)

The Rambam's goal was to form a new kind of sensibility that would be more excited and inspired by nature than by miraculous aberrations from nature.

We began this part of the book by asking whether distancing God from the world would empty religion of meaning by making God entirely inaccessible and unapproachable to human beings. We have found instead that the Rambam's conception of a transcendent God makes possible a new vision of religious life in which God's greatness does not belittle and infantilize but rather empowers and elevates.

PART 2
TORAH

In his 1784 essay "What Is Enlightenment?" Immanuel Kant argues that religious believers who obey traditional authorities are essentially infantile. They refuse to grow up. Like little children who are not responsible for their own thoughts or actions, Kant claims, believers hand over responsibility for their lives to others. "Enlightenment is man's emergence from his self-imposed immaturity," he declares. Enlightened people do not let rabbis or priests decide for them but rather decide to grow up and think for themselves.

The view of religion as infantilizing has become a staple of the contemporary polemic against religion.[1] Atheists look at believers and see overgrown children whose thinking was arrested in infancy. Maimonides, I believe, poses a serious challenge to Kant's perspective. According to Maimonides we do not need to outgrow religion; our religious beliefs can and should mature with us as we grow. *The Guide for the Perplexed* was a bold attempt to set out a grown-up religion.

In part 1 of this book we saw the immensity of the Rambam's view of God. We saw how this view required him to expand some of the key ideas of religion, such as prophecy, providence. and redemption, in order to match the extent of his thinking about the divine. In part 2 we move from God to Torah and address a similar question:

How does the Rambam ask us to expand our conception not just of God but also of the Torah? This part of the book will investigate the *Guide*'s profound understanding of Scripture, exploring the reasons for the commandments and also the nature of the revelation that produced them.

Before the Hebrew version of this book appeared in Israel, I worried about how the traditional religious community would react to the way I presented the Rambam's view of God. To my surprise, the response to that part of the book was very positive. However, some readers were angered by the section on the Torah. Many claimed that I had written that according to the Rambam, the Torah is not from God. In the light of that controversy, I should like to make clear that in the following section I do not argue against the divine nature of the Torah. I only attempt to explain how the Rambam understood the Torah's divinity.

6

IS THE TORAH DIVINE?

Toward the end of the *Guide*, the Rambam offers a well-known parable:

> The ruler is in his palace, and all of his subjects are partly within the
> city and partly outside the city. Of those who are within the city, some
> have turned their backs on the ruler's habitation, their faces being turned
> another way. Others seek to reach the ruler's habitation, turn toward it
> and desire to enter and stand before him, but up to now they have not
> yet seen the wall of the habitation. Some of those who seek to reach it
> have come up to the habitation and walk around it searching for the
> gate. Some of them have entered the gate, and walk around in the ante-
> chambers. Some of them have entered the inner court of the habitation
> and have come to be with the king, in one and the same place with him,
> namely in the ruler's habitation. But their having come into the inner
> part of the habitation does not mean that they see the ruler or speak to
> him. For after their coming into the inner part of the habitation, it is
> indispensable that they should make another effort; then they will be
> in the presence of the ruler, see him from afar or from nearby, or hear
> the ruler's speech or speak to him. (*Guide*, 3:51)

The meaning of the parable is that the true measure of a person's
greatness is closeness to God. And this closeness is measured by a
person's level of knowledge and understanding. The more one understands, the closer he is to God. The lowliest people in the parable are
those who are wandering around outside the city; they are likened
to people with no education. Next are those who are within the city

but outside the palace. These are like people who observe *halakhah* but do not have a systematic framework of religious thought; their faith is based on tradition, not on rational proof. Then there are those who wander around outside the place but cannot find the entrance. These, according to Maimonides, are sages of *halakhah* who do not know philosophy. Among those who have managed to enter the palace there are some who are closer to the king and others who are further away. Some walk about in the hallways, and a few succeed in reaching the chamber of the king. Within the chamber itself, a very small number arrive at the highest level of divine intimacy, which is knowing God through pure, philosophical thought.

This parable contains a surprising statement about the significance of *halakhah*. The Rambam attacks the traditional view that strict adherence to Jewish law brings a person close to God. Indeed, he maintains that those who devote their lives solely to *halakhah* had not even entered the palace:

> Those who seek to reach the ruler's habitation and to enter it, but never see the ruler's habitation, are the multitude of the adherents of the Law, I refer to the ignoramuses who observe the commandments.
>
> Those who have come up to the habitation and walk around it are the jurists, who believe true opinions on the basis of traditional authority and study the law concerning the practices of divine service, but do not engage in speculation concerning the fundamental principles of religion and make no inquiry whatever regarding the rectification of belief.
>
> Those who have plunged into speculation concerning the fundamental principles of religion have entered the antechambers. People there indubitably have different ranks. He, however, who has demonstrated to the extent that is possible of everything that may be demonstrated; and who has ascertained in divine matters, to the extent that is possible, everything that may be ascertained; and who has come close to certainty in those matters in which one can only come close to it—has come to be with the ruler in the inner part of the habitation. (*Guide*, 3:51)

And so, according to Maimonides, even the greatest halakhic authorities, who are considered to be among the giants of their generation, are not worthy to enter the king's chamber if they do not know philosophy. To reach the summit of religious life and to attain intimacy with God, one must study metaphysics. *Halakhah* regulates the norms of religious life, but philosophy determines spiritual development.

The Rambam's voice on this issue is barely heard today in traditional Jewish communities. Jews there believe that *halakhah* contains everything that is of real significance, and that *halakhah* is the only path to spiritual greatness. The stricter and more scrupulous the halakhic adherence, the closer one gets to God. A life of stringency becomes the only channel through which people can express their striving for religious greatness.

Maimonides, on the other hand, distinguishes between *halakhah* and the ultimate goals of spiritual life. He does not call for *halakhah* to be renounced or reformed. On the contrary, his halakhic teachings are generally conservative. But he places mastery of *halakhah* "outside the palace." Religious greatness comes not from preoccupation with halakhic severity but rather from grasping fundamental religious concepts.

In the first part of this book we discussed how the Rambam interpreted these big ideas. Now, let us consider how they are put into practice through the Torah and mitzvot.

Who Wrote the Torah?

The traditional religious description of revelation goes something like this: Thousands of years after God created the world and humankind, He revealed Himself and transmitted a body of knowledge that taught people how to live in the world He created. This body of knowledge was collected, organized, and redacted in texts that became known as holy books. These served as a sort of "recording" of revelation. They turned a onetime event into something that one could return to again and again. Whenever people wanted to know what God required of them, they could consult the holy books.

How far did the Rambam agree with this general view? Did he believe that God wrote a book? The Rambam does not address this question directly. However, based on certain comments scattered throughout the *Guide*, we may reconstruct how he grappled with the riddle of the Torah's origin.

The Rambam believed that he had demonstrated the fact of God's existence. But is it possible also to demonstrate that God wrote the Torah? Can one prove the Torah's divinity? Maimonides taught that nature bears witness to God's existence. But what sort of evidence within the Torah would count as evidence for the divine quality of the book? These are some of the questions that guide part 2.

As we saw in part 1, the subject of prophecy preoccupied Maimonides throughout the *Guide*. Prophecy happens when a person reaches the highest possible intellectual and spiritual levels and discovers exalted metaphysical knowledge. It is more than God revealing Himself to people; people also discover God. We saw that the Rambam treated Moses's revelation as unique in that it was the only revelation that led to the formulation of law.

In the *Guide*, Maimonides does not give a full and clear account of the nature of Moses's revelation.[2] There is only one chapter in which Maimonides directly addresses the unique, legislative character of Moses's prophecy.[3] This is the chapter in which Maimonides interprets the dialogue between God and Moses on Mount Sinai after the sin of worshipping the golden calf. This chapter appears in the section that deals with descriptions of God,[4] and thus it does not seem to be an integral part of the *Guide*'s discussion of prophecy. But the *Guide* reveals some of its secrets in places where you don't expect them, often mixed in with discussions of other subjects. Let us now study chapter 54 of part 1 of the *Guide* and try to understand, step by step, the Rambam's answer to the question of how the Torah was created.

From God's Wisdom to Natural Wisdom

The first ten chapters of Genesis describe the birth of humanity. They tell a string of stories about human sin that share a common theme. From the Garden of Eden, through the violence (*hamas* in Hebrew) that led to the Flood, to the Tower of Babel, we see a succession of stories in which people cannot reconcile themselves to their mortality. They try to become divine. Adam and Eve hoped that by eating the forbidden fruit they would cross the line that separated humanity from God. Finally, there is the story of the Tower of Babel, in which humans try to ascend to heaven to be like gods. Denying our human limits is a constant temptation.

However, when the Torah shifts its focus from the sins of individuals to the sins of the Jewish people as a whole, the nature of the temptation tends to reverse. Israel sins not by trying to come too close to God but by turning away from God.

The Torah presents Moses as a man who overcame this very human tendency to turn from God. He yearns for the utmost intimacy with the divine. In Maimonides's reading of the Torah, Moses on Mount Sinai reached the very summit of human consciousness. Yet just when he is at that peak of perfection, he wants even more. The Rambam identifies in Exodus 33 two specific requests that Moses makes of God:

> His request to know God's attributes is conveyed in his saying: *Show me now your ways, that I may know you*, and so on (Exod. 33:13). . . . Then he asked for the apprehension of His essence, may He be exalted. This is what he means when he says, *Show me I pray, your Glory* (Exod. 33:18). (*Guide*, 1:54)

Maimonides interprets the second of these requests as a prayer to "grasp God's glory, may He be exalted"—in other words, to know God. What does it mean to "know God"? It means to become God-like. The more deeply you understand God, the closer you come to God. The request to "know God," then, is Moses's wish to free himself from the limits of his humanity and to become God-like.

God refuses Moses's wish. He answers: "You cannot see My face, for no man may see My face and live" (Exod. 33:20). Moses is human and ultimately cannot escape the inherent limitations of his humanity.

Moses's other request, however, is granted. "Show me your ways," he begs of God. The Rambam understands this as a prayer to understand God's actions—how God works in the world. Moses wants to be able to understand the laws of nature. He is asking to grasp the secrets of physics, chemistry, and biology—and to know how the intricate systems of the natural world reflect God's wisdom. According to Maimonides, God grants this request. Moses attained a high level of understanding of the natural world:

> He received a favorable answer regarding what he had asked for at first, namely, "Show me your ways." For he was told, "I will make all my goodness to pass before you." In answer to his second demand, he was told, "You cannot see My face . . ." This dictum: "All my goodness"— alludes to the display to him of all existing things, of which it is said, "And God saw all that He had made and behold it was very good." By their "display" I mean that he will apprehend their nature and the way they are mutually connected so that He will know how He governs them in general and in detail. (*Guide*, 1:54)

The Rambam gives a deep, midrashic reading of God's answer. On the one hand, God says, "You cannot see My face." It is impossible to know God. On the other hand, God promises Moses, "I will cause all of my goodness to pass before you." The "goodness" that God shows Moses is identified with the "good" that God saw at the culmination of Creation, about which He says, "Behold, it was very good" (Gen. 1:31). Moses desires to understand how all the elements of nature fit together, perhaps like the modern search for a Theory of Everything, to explain the underlying unity of scientific laws.

The Rambam's reading of Moses's double request delineates the limits of human intellect. The cosmos is within the purview of our understanding. God, on the other hand, is beyond our mental grasp.

LEADERSHIP THAT IMITATES NATURE

However, Moses's curiosity about how the world works was not an end in itself. He wanted to understand nature in order to know better how to lead the people. If he understood how God ran the world, he would have a better idea of how to run society.

> This was Moses ultimate object in his demand, the conclusion of what he says being *That I may know you to the end that I may find grace in your sight and consider that this nation is Your people* (Exod. 33:13)—that is, a people for the government of which I need to perform actions that I must seek to make similar to Your actions in governing them. (*Guide*, 1:54)

From King David in the book of Psalms to Albert Einstein, people have meditated on nature in order to discern the ways of God. But according to Maimonides, Moses reflects on nature in order to gain political wisdom. We may recall that Moses's request to know God was denied but his prayer to understand nature was granted. He then translated what he had learned from nature into an understanding of leadership. Moses moves from theology to physics and then from physics to politics.

The Rambam's political thinking attempts to translate the wisdom of nature into wisdom for leadership. It is the politics of imitating nature. The seeds of this idea are scattered throughout the *Guide*'s discussions of Torah and mitzvot.

THE PRINCIPLE OF SPIRITUAL EQUANIMITY

One secret of good leadership that can be learned from the natural world is what the Rambam termed the principle of "spiritual equanimity"—a kind of profound indifference that a leader needs to cultivate about society's opinion of him. Leaders who are constantly concerned about their public image are bound to do a poor job, for it is impossible to lead well if one feels dependent on the approval of one's followers. Leaders who possess emotional self-sufficiency have a special resilience and inner strength. Therefore, one who aspires to be a real leader must, according to Maimonides, place knowledge of God above all else:

> It is likewise necessary that the thought of that individual should be detached from the spurious kinds of rulership and that his desire for them should be abolished—I mean the wish to dominate or to be held great by the common people and to obtain from them honor and obedience for their own sake. (*Guide*, 2:36)

To overcome the urge to gain honor and authority for their own sake, a person should meditate on the irrational foundations of the lust for power. If he thinks deeply about those whose admiration he craves, he will see their baseness and thus may free himself from the need for their approval.

> He should rather regard all people according to their various states with respect to which they are indubitably either like domestic animals or like beasts of prey. If the perfect man who lives in solitude thinks of them at all, he does so only with a view to saving himself from the harm that may be caused. (*Guide*, 2:36)

This release from the lust for honor and power frees the soul to receive prophecy. In Moses's case, his liberation from emotional dependence on the people was not just a condition for his prophecy; it was also a consequence of it. His deep understanding of nature refined his sense of independence from his followers.

Maimonides arrived at this conclusion in a somewhat roundabout manner. Moses described God by means of the Thirteen Divine Attributes that are specified in Exodus 34:6–8 ("God, the Lord, gracious and merciful . . ."). As Maimonides frequently emphasizes in the *Guide*, any attempt to understand in a literal fashion the relationship between human characteristics and God's attributes leads to theological confusion. Therefore, according to the Rambam's reading, the

Thirteen Attributes are not really describing God directly; rather, they are attributes of the world that God created. Nature, which bears the imprint of divine wisdom, is the manifestation of the Thirteen Attributes.

How is it possible, though, to attribute to nature characteristics such as "gracious," "merciful," and "long-suffering"? Maimonides's answer is that the Thirteen Attributes are a *projection* of human traits onto nature; of course, the natural world does not have feelings of its own. Sad people will talk about the gloomy heavens, and happy people may speak of white clouds chasing joyfully across the sky; an earthquake will make some people speak of the earth's rage, while others see the renewal of nature in the springtime as an outpouring of love.

Maimonides distances the Thirteen Attributes from the reality of God in two ways. First, he connects these attributes to God's wisdom, as expressed in the natural world, and not directly to God. Second, he acknowledges that ascribing these characteristics to nature is a human projection, not a description of nature as it really is. However, it is precisely this aspect of nature—that it readily lends itself to anthropomorphic projection of our emotions when in reality it has no feelings of its own—that the Rambam sought to emphasize in his approach to leadership. In Maimonides's view, a leader's acts should *appear* to be the result of feelings, but behind the mask they should be devoid of emotional considerations. Leadership imitates nature in the sense that policies and decisions are made according to rational principles, even though, in the eyes of those who are being led, the leader's actions may appear to be an expression of emotions like kindness or anger:

> It befits the governor of a city, if he is a prophet, to acquire similarity to those attributes, so that these actions may proceed from him according to a determined measure, and according to the deserts of the people who are affected by them and not merely because of his following a passion. He should not let loose the reins of anger, nor let passions gain mastery

over him, for all passions are evil; but on the contrary, he should guard against them, as far as this lies within the capacity of man. Sometimes, with regard to some people, he should be merciful and gracious, not out of mere compassion and pity, but in accordance with what is fitting. Sometimes, with regard to certain people, he should be "keeping anger and jealous and avenging," in accordance with their deserts, not out of mere anger; so he may order an individual to be burned without being angry and incensed with him and without hating him, because he perceives the deserts of that individual and considers the great benefit that many people will derive from the accomplishment of the action in question. (*Guide*, 1:54)

A capable leader might, for example, implement an economic policy that causes many people to lose their jobs. He may consequently be perceived as callous, whereas in fact he is acting wisely, out of sound economic considerations and for the benefit of the whole organization. Similarly, he might launch a surprise military attack and be seen as impulsive, while in reality he is operating from a well-thought-out geo-strategic plan. Good leadership emerges from wisdom but will often be perceived as flowing from emotion. A ruler who is motivated by anger or pity is actually reactive; some external event sways his emotions and causes him to do what he does. A skillful and effective leader, on the other hand, is an active one, molding reality in accordance with his intellect and will.

THE ETHICS OF IMITATING NATURE
What is a successful life, and how do I achieve one? These questions preoccupy many of us. The usual criteria for what counts as accomplishment—at least in the contemporary West—are a person's career and level of income.

The ancient Greek philosophers were also very much concerned with success,[5] but they measured it differently. For them, success was gauged not by which rung you reached on the ladder but by the quality of the character that you forged for yourself. According to Socrates,

Plato, and Aristotle, our character is our most important creation and the most significant measure of how well we have lived our life.

This Greek tradition merges with Jewish thought in the philosophy of the Rambam. Maimonides sees something essentially Jewish in the idea that we create our own character, and he argues that this notion is at the heart of biblical and talmudic culture. On this point, Athens and Jerusalem converge. Maimonides mines Aristotelian thought to broaden the variety of techniques that are available for building character. However, the Rambam draws on Aristotle for much more than that; he adopts Aristotle's basic position regarding the essential goal of building a human personality. Our investment in cultivating an ideal, balanced personality is central to our purpose in life.

One who wishes to cultivate such a personality will distance himself from extreme character traits and strive for a middle way. The Rambam took this Aristotelian goal and turned it into a religious obligation.[6] For him, creating a balanced personality and realizing the "Golden Mean" is the purpose of most of the mitzvot:

> If you examine most of the mitzvot from this perspective, you will find that they serve to train and educate the different forces within our souls. (Introduction to *Avot*, 238–39)

Why, though, did the Rambam assert that following the middle way is a *religious* obligation? Why is this the *divine* path? Maimonides was part of a medical tradition that emphasized the importance of *equilibrium*. He believed that health and illness are dependent on the proper balance between different elements in the body:

> For when a thing is as perfect as it is possible to be within a species, it is impossible that within that species there should be found another thing that does not fall short of that perfection either because of excess or deficiency. Thus, in comparison with a temperament whose composition is of the greatest equibalance possible in the species in question, all other temperaments are not composed in accordance with this balance because of either deficiency or excess. (*Guide*, 2:39)

Nature, then, represents balance, symmetry, and wholeness. The Rambam translates this characteristic from nature to the world of ethics. If equilibrium in nature is a mark of wholeness, and serious disequilibrium is a symptom of sickness, then so too is this the case in moral development: when our character traits are in balance with one another, it is a mark of excellence, and when they are unbalanced, that is problematic. Aristotle defined art as the imitation of nature; for the Rambam, the development of a balanced moral character, imitating the equilibrium of nature, is a person's greatest creative project.

Unlike other animals, which manifest their essential nature in the world whether they wish to or not, human beings have a choice. We can decide whether or not to fully become what we are meant to be. "It is quite clear that none of the elevated character traits grows within us naturally."[7] In the absence of any natural force impelling us toward moral perfection, we need an artificial mechanism to help us. That mechanism is education, which substitutes for nature. Yet although our moral qualities are not naturally produced, they can and, in the Rambam's view, should be an imitation of nature.[8]

Now we are in a position to understand why the Rambam identifies the middle way in ethics with the divine way. If, as Maimonides held, God's wisdom is imprinted upon the natural world, and if nature exhibits perfect balance and symmetry, then a path of moral development that strives for balance in our character traits will most closely imitate the divinely created natural order in our personalities.

Here the Rambam takes a further step. The perfect human being successfully imitates the perfection in nature. (This conclusion is consistent with the Rambam's theory of temperaments, which claims that the relative proportions of different elements in the body influence our general health; the healthy body is one where there is a balance between the different elements within it. For more on this see *Guide*, 1:34.) Since balance and symmetry are an expression of divine wisdom, Maimonides claims that one who succeeds in developing a balanced personality through observing the mitzvot imitates God.[9]

So far, then, we have seen two secrets that Moses learned from nature, one political and the other ethical: the ideal leader imitates nature by not letting emotions control his actions, and the ideal person imitates nature by creating a well-balanced character. I will now explain a third secret, one that enfolds within it the whole Torah.

THE TORAH AS IMITATION OF NATURE: TELEOLOGY

The key idea to understanding the Rambam's approach to Torah is that the Torah expresses the wisdom of nature, directed toward the social world. Let us look at some of the analogies between nature and Torah that are elaborated throughout the *Guide for the Perplexed*.

Teleology was a central principle of the natural science of the Rambam's time. Teleology assumes that everything in the world has a goal; nothing exists without a reason:

> A man endowed with intellect is incapable of saying that any action of God is vain, futile or frivolous. According to our opinion—that is, that of all of us who follow the Law of Moses our Master—all of His actions are good and excellent. He says *And God saw everything that He had made, and behold, it was very good* (Gen. 1:31). Consequently everything that He . . . has done for the sake of a thing, is necessary for the existence of the thing aimed at, or is very useful. (*Guide*, 3:25)

In contrast, however, to things that exist in nature, artificially created things do not necessarily have an inherent goal: "The philosophic opinion is similar, holding as it does that in all natural things there is nothing that may be described as futile; I mean to say everything that is not artificial" (*Guide*, 3:25). The Rambam makes the following analogy: Just as everything in nature has a purpose that science can investigate, so too, all of the mitzvot have a purpose that religious philosophy may uncover.

What everyone endowed with a sound intellect ought to believe on this subject is what I shall set forth to you: The generalities of the commandments necessarily have a cause and were set forth because of a certain usefulness. (*Guide*, 3:26)[10]

The analogy between Torah and nature is not confined to the fact that both have a purpose. Throughout the *Guide*, Maimonides discusses a succession of principles that, in his view, characterize nature and by analogy are also found in the world of Torah.

THE PRINCIPLE OF GRADUAL DEVELOPMENT

The Rambam opens part 3, chapter 32 of the *Guide* with a discussion about how change occurs in the natural world. He notes that there is a "principle of gradual development" that seems to be a law of nature. In the physical world, change appears to take place slowly and gradually. Maimonides gives the development of an infant as an example:

The deity made a wily and gracious arrangement with regard to all the individuals of the living beings that suck. For when born, such individuals are extremely soft, and cannot feed on dry food. Accordingly breasts were prepared for them so that they should produce milk with a view to their receiving humid food, which is similar to the composition of their bodies, until their limbs gradually and little by little become solid. (*Guide*, 3:32)

According to the Rambam, this principle of gradual development does not apply only in nature; we may also find it in the Torah:

Many things in our Law are due to something similar to this very governance on the part of Him who governs, may He be glorified and exalted. For a sudden transition from one opposite to another is impossible. And therefore man, according to his nature, is not capable of abandoning suddenly all to which he was accustomed. (*Guide*, 3:32)

Just as nature designs creatures that grow gradually and adapt to their developing needs, so too the Torah is attuned to the incremental pace of the Jewish people's spiritual development. This is the reason why the Torah, which aimed to effect a fundamental change in the people's relation to idolatry and primitive spiritual practices, does not proscribe the offering of sacrifices. Rather, as the Rambam explains in the same chapter, the Torah recognized that in the ancient world it would have been inconceivable for a religion *not* to require animal sacrifices. It would have been like, "The appearance of a prophet in these times who, calling upon the people to worship God, would say 'God has given you a Law forbidding you to pray to Him, to fast, to call upon Him for help in misfortune. Your worship should consist solely in meditation, without any works at all.'" (*Guide*, 3:32)

The Torah directed animal sacrifices as a concession to the religious reality of the ancient world in which it appeared, but not as an ideal form of worship. Human beings were expected to develop and grow beyond this mode of divine service.[11]

The Arbitrariness of Details

In part 3, chapter 26 of the *Guide*, the Rambam claims that we are limited in our ability to uncover the reasons behind all of the mitzvot. As we will see in our discussion of the reasons for the mitzvot, the human intellect can discover the overarching principles behind the commandments, but it will not always be able to penetrate beyond these general reasons to discover the reasons for all of the details. We might understand why the Torah commanded us to offer sacrifices, for example, but we will never understand why on a particular occasion we are supposed to offer a sheep rather than a ram: "No cause will ever be found for the fact that that one particular sacrifice consists in a lamb and another in a ram" (*Guide*, 3:26).[12] The reason why we cannot find reasons for all the details is that they are ultimately arbitrary. This arbitrariness is not just characteristic of the details of the commandments; it is found in all of existence:

This resembles the nature of the possible, for it is certain that one of the possibilities will come to pass. And no question should be put as to why one possibility and not another comes to pass, for a similar question would be necessary if another possibility instead of this particular one had come to pass. (*Guide*, 3:26)

The Rambam believed that there were strong parallels in the natural world for this combination of general principles that may be rationally comprehended, together with details that are arbitrary.[13] Maimonides thought, for example, that there are scientific principles that explain the paths of the heavenly spheres.[14] Nevertheless, he argued, *contra* Aristotle, that the speed and direction of their motions was arbitrary[15] and could not be explained by means of any teleological principle:

> For he [Aristotle] wished to give a cause for the fact that the sphere moves from the East, and not from the West; and he wished to give a cause for the fact that some of them are swift in motion, and others slow and that this is necessary because of the order of their position with regard to the highest sphere. . . . He wished to assign causes for all this so that these things would be ordered for us in a natural order that is due to necessity. However, he has not accomplished any of these undertakings. . . . [O]ne can say of all the matters that he has stated with regard to matters pertaining to the sphere, that he has assigned no clear cause with regard to this, and that the matter, as he sets it out, does not follow an order for which necessity can be claimed. (*Guide*, 2:19)

Just as, in nature, only the general principles are comprehensible, while many details cannot be fully explained, so too, our efforts to rationally explain the mitzvot can only be applied to the general underlying principles. As in the natural world, the small details are not subject to human understanding.

The Ineffectiveness of the Torah in Exceptional Cases

In part 3, chapter 34 of the *Guide*, the Rambam claims that we should not expect the Torah to have a direct, positive effect on everyone who fulfills its directives. The Torah is constructed in such a way that it will have a positive impact on most human beings, but not on all of them. There are exceptions,[16] those for whom the divine wisdom embedded in the Torah does not work.[17] "You must know that the Torah is not designed to suit exceptional individuals and its commandments are not appropriate for some small minorities of people" (*Guide*, 3:34).[18] As proof of this, the Rambam asks us to look at nature: "It is your business to reflect on the natural things, in which the general utility that is included within them nonetheless necessarily produces damages to individuals" (*Guide*, 3:34). This example serves to illustrate how the Rambam draws on his understanding of nature to deepen his understanding of the principles of the Torah.

Symmetry in the Torah

The Torah does not aim merely to mold the ideal person, who imitates the perfect balance of nature; the Torah itself imitates this balance:

> Things are similar with regard to this Law, as is clear from its equibalance. For it says, *Just statutes and judgments* (Deut. 4:8); now you know that the meaning of "just" is balanced. For these are manners of worship in which there is no burden or excess—such as monastic life and pilgrimage and similar things—nor a deficiency necessarily leading to greed and being engrossed in the indulgence of appetites, so that in consequence the perfection of man is diminished with regard to his moral habits. (*Guide*, 2:39)

Just as balance within a human being creates a perfectly healthy body, so too, balance between laws creates and constitutes the perfection of the Torah. The Torah mirrors the perfection of nature. This claim leads the Rambam to a conservative position on the issue of changing details in the Torah:

> And that is as it ought to be for when a thing is as perfect as it is possible to be within a species, it is impossible that within that species there should be found another thing that does not fall short of that perfection either because of excess or deficiency. Thus, in comparison with a temperament

whose composition is of the greatest equibalance possible in the species in question, all other temperaments are not composed in accordance with this balance because of either deficiency or excess. (*Guide*, 2:39)

The measuring stick for perfection in the Torah is taken from nature; perfection is balance.

Contemplation of nature is an important mitzvah, according to the Rambam.[19] The goal of such contemplation is to arouse an echo in the human heart—an inner feeling of love and fear of God. Maimonides extends his analogy between nature and Torah to a comparison between the awe that is aroused in us when we meditate on nature and what we may feel when we reflect on the wisdom behind the Torah's commandments. In his discussion of the reasons for the commandments, Maimonides writes: "Marvel exceedingly at the wisdom of His commandments, may He be exalted, just as you should marvel at the wisdom manifested in all the things He has made. It says: *The Rock, His work is perfect; for all His ways are judgment* (Deut. 32:4). It says that just as the things made by him are consummately perfect, so are His commandments consummately just" (*Guide*, 3:49).

The Rambam substitutes "imitate nature" for the traditional commandment to imitate God. The Torah's goal is to create people whose characters are modeled on the principles operating in nature, and a society whose laws are based on the observable laws of nature.

The analogy between Torah and nature is the hidden, organizing principle that underlies the Rambam's whole conception of Torah. Moses reflected on the world, understood the profound divine wisdom inherent in nature, and translated it into rules for creating an ideal society and perfect individuals. At the beginning of this chapter I posed the question of whether God wrote the Torah.[20] In *Bereshit Rabbah* the Midrash teaches that in the beginning God meditated on the Torah and created the world. We might paraphrase this and say that, according to Maimonides, Moses meditated on the world that God made and wrote the Torah. The Torah is indeed divine; the divine wisdom of nature is replicated in the Torah.[21]

7

REASONS FOR THE COMMANDMENTS

The Rambam's God is perfect, lacking nothing and needing nothing. The idea that such a God could require worship seems absurd. How then, should we understand the purpose of performing the mitzvot? Let us examine the guiding logic of the Torah's commandments.

The ancient, pagan world out of which the Torah emerged was replete with rituals that enabled people to control nature and events, or at least to feel as if they were. There were ceremonies to bring rain, rituals for ensuring fruitfulness, and religious rites intended to ensure victory in war. The texts prescribing the techniques of such ceremonies also specified their desired outcome. In the minds of their practitioners, one could no more separate the ritual from the result than one can today separate the act of dialing a phone number from making a connection. The meaning of the ceremony was defined by the hoped-for outcome.

The Bible is also full of rituals. The book of Leviticus, for example, is composed mostly of instructions for how to carry out ceremonies ranging from daily acts of eating to descriptions of the rites to be performed by the priests and Levites. One striking difference between the rituals of the Torah and those of other ancient religions is that the Torah almost always leaves out the desired outcome of a mitzvah. If other writings describe rituals as causes and the magical outcomes as effects, then the Torah is a book of causes without the effects. This was a radical change in the history of religion and a decisive break with the other religions of the time. Unlike modern deist philosophers who simply annulled ancient ceremonies, the Torah maintained ritual worship but paid little attention to its consequences. In the Torah, ritual is no longer a way of asserting control over the world. The worshipper approaches the religious act without expectations of the outcome. .

Ridding religious life of magical thinking about the results of our actions transformed the mitzvot from acts of power into expressions of weakness and humility. One's spiritual posture becomes like "the prayer of the lowly man when he is faint, and pours forth his plea before the Lord" (Ps. 102:1). The fulfillment of mitzvot is about obedience rather than dominance. The Torah thereby brought about a revolution not just in theology but also in religious psychology.

The Bible's relative indifference to the specific consequences of performing mitzvot left a vacuum that Jewish thought throughout the ages has attempted to fill. The project of interpreting the deeper meaning of the commandments was central to all the major streams of Jewish thought in the Middle Ages.

The kabbalistic contribution to this discussion was especially striking. According to kabbalistic theosophy, the higher spiritual worlds are in distress, so to speak, as a result of a rupture in the harmony between the *sefirot*[1]—the emanations from God through which the divine attributes are manifested. For example, there may be blockages in the flow of energy between the *sefirot* of *tiferet* and *malchut*, or perhaps an imbalance between the *sefirot* of *hesed* and *din*, indicating a disharmony in the divine world.

From a kabbalistic perspective, the main purpose in the life of every Jew is to help restore harmony and balance to the divine. Perhaps more than God redeems humanity, humanity needs to redeem God.[2] According to Kabbalah, the Torah places the tools for this cosmic rectification firmly in human hands. These tools are the mitzvot. *Halakhah* is the means by which we help repair the upper worlds.

This places an enormous responsibility on the shoulders of those who are keeping the commandments. This sense of the immense power of ritual to affect the world, which had been eclipsed by the biblical revolution, returned to Judaism via Kabbalah. Not only do religious ceremonies profoundly influence the world, but, according to central streams of Kabbalah, they also affect God. The question of whether Kabbalah thereby rehabilitated something like a pagan religious consciousness is a matter of dispute, but it is clear that by restoring a consciousness of the consequences of ritual acts, Kabbalah returned religious psychology to a central place in Jewish life.

Even without considering Kabbalah, however, the Bible does attribute a certain kind of causality to observance of the mitzvot. It is not a direct causal relationship between keeping particular commandments and specific consequences, but rather a connection between keeping the totality of the commandments and general societal well-being:

> And it shall happen, that if you will surely keep the commandments that I command you today, to the love the Lord, your God, and to worship Him with all your heart and soul, that I will give rain in your land at the proper time: the early rains and the later rains; and you will gather in your grain, wine and oil. I will give grass in your fields for your animals, and you shall eat and be satisfied. (Deut. 11:13–15)

Material sufficiency is a result of our obedience. This is not a mechanistic view of the relationship between particular rituals and reward. The Torah wishes to instill a more subtle expectation of reward, resulting from observance of the mitzvot as a whole.

In the *Guide*, Maimonides disputes the existence of even this indirect form of causation.[3] According to the *Guide*, Jewish religious rituals do not bring rain or heal the sick. Human ceremonies do not change nature, as the pagans believed. Observing the mitzvot of tefillin, tzitzit, or Shabbat does not restore the ruptured harmony within the *sefirot*, as the kabbalists claimed; no cosmic rectification is effected through the power of our acts. What, then, in the Rambam's view, is the point of keeping mitzvot?

The Rationality of the Mitzvot

Maimonides's answer is that, while the mitzvot do indeed affect the world, they do not directly influence God or nature. Instead, they work by transforming the person who fulfills them. We saw earlier that, for the Rambam, prophecy is not so much God's initiative as the individual's achievement. Similarly, in his view, providence is less about God's actions than about our achievement of a spiritual state in which we merit divine concern. So, too, we might say that the mitzvot were not given for God's sake but for man's—in order to shape a new kind of human being. If prophecy and providence are human spiritual achievements, then the mitzvot are methods through which we may attain these levels. Underlying all of the Rambam's writings about the reasons for the commandments is the notion that a person's character is his greatest achievement and that the mitzvot are, above all, tools to build a whole, balanced personality.

The Talmud distinguishes between *huqqim* (laws) and *mishpatim* (statutes). While the reasons for the *mishpatim*, such as "Do not murder," are perfectly clear, the reasons behind *huqqim*—for example, not mixing wool and linen, or sending out the scapegoat on Yom Kippur—are opaque. The Talmud says about them, "I, God, decreed it and you do not have permission to question them" (BT *Yoma*, 67b).

The Rambam suggests a novel way of understanding this talmudic distinction. He argues that, in fact, all of the mitzvot are capable of being fully understood. The difference between *huqqim* and *mishpatim* is not between some mitzvot that are rational and others that are not, but rather between those whose reasons are transparent and those for whom the reasons are hidden:

> Those commandments whose utility is clear to the multitude are called *mishpatim*, and those whose utility is not clear to the multitude are

called *huqqim*. The sages always say with regard to the verse: *For it is no vain thing . . .* (Deut. 32:47); *And if it is vain, it is because of you* (Jerusalem Talmud, *Peah*, I); meaning that this legislation is not a vain matter without a useful end and that if it seems to you that this is the case with regard to some of the commandments, the deficiency resides in your apprehension. (*Guide*, 3:26)

The *huqqim* also have reasons, but, unlike *mishpatim*, the reasons are not obvious; we have to dig deeper to find them. Revealing these hidden meanings was the goal of the Rambam's massive and ambitious discussion of the reasons for the commandments.[4]

UNDERSTANDING THE HUMAN WORLD

If the goal of the Torah is, according to the Rambam, to bring human beings to perfection, then a precondition for understanding the Torah is understanding the human world; anyone who wants to speak meaningfully about the reasons for the commandments needs to know something about psychology. Here, an understanding of the Rambam's psychology and anthropology is crucial for explicating how the mitzvot work to build character.

The Law as a whole aims for two things: the welfare of the soul and the welfare of the body. (*Guide*, 3:27)

There are two basic components—body and soul—that must be developed in order to build a whole human personality. The Torah works on both of them. When the Rambam speaks about the soul in this context, he refers primarily to the world of intellect. When he speaks about the body, he does not only mean our physical bodies, but also the whole political realm:

As for the welfare of the soul, it consists in the multitude's acquiring correct opinions corresponding to their respective capacity. . . . As for the welfare of the body, it comes about by the improvement of their ways of living with one another. This is achieved through two things. One is the abolition of their wronging of one another. This is tantamount to every individual among the people not being permitted to act according to his will and up to the limits of his power, but being forced to do that which is useful to the whole. The second thing consists in the acquisition by every human being of moral qualities that are useful for life in society so that the affairs of the city may be ordered. (*Guide*, 3:27)

The Torah leads humanity toward perfection: to political stability, emotional balance, intellectual wholeness, and the acquisition of correct views about the universe. The coming sections will focus on two particular aspects of how the mitzvot form human beings: first, the way they contribute to people's intellectual development, keeping us far from error and bringing us closer to the truth; and second, the way they mold human character traits and foster inner wholeness and balance.

Repairing the Soul: Toward Intellectual Perfection

Perfection of the soul, according to the Rambam, requires that we avoid common mistakes and misconceptions in our ways of thinking, and that we then embark on a philosophical journey that leads to the truth. This approach might seem surprising. The Torah does not actually teach its readers any systematic philosophy. It appears to lack all the usual ingredients of a philosophical work: it provides no statement of premises, or discussion of logical method, or any deduction of conclusions from first principles. The Torah presents no rigorously defined and examined body of knowledge. How, then, is the Torah supposed to keep us from error and aid us in our long, arduous climb toward truth?

Instead of intellectual investigations, the Torah demands commitment to action. The Rambam's educational approach was based on a deep belief in the power of deeds to subtly yet palpably affect our ideas. It is the practical actions mandated by the Torah that protect against intellectual error and bring us closer to metaphysical truths. The long-term persistence of well-grounded religious belief within any community depends less on the profundity of that community's philosophers than it does on the extent to which core beliefs are internalized in the souls of believers, through action.

The Rambam's analysis of the emergence of religion can help us to understand better the relationship between rituals and ideas. Let us reconstruct his understanding of four religions: the religion of the generation of Enosh, the philosophical religion of Abraham, Jesus's religion without commandments, and the normative Judaism of Moses.

THE RELIGION OF ENOSH

In the days of Enosh, mankind made a big mistake . . . The wise men of that generation were ignorant, and Enosh himself was one of those who erred. This was the mistake: they said, "since God created the stars and sphere in order to run the world, and set them in the heavens and gave them honor; and since they serve God, it is fitting that we praise and glorify them and give them honor also. For surely it is God's will, may He be blessed, to magnify and honor those who magnify and honor Him, just as a king desires that people give honor to the servants who stand before the king, thereby honoring the king himself." After this thought took root in their hearts, they began to build temples to the stars and to offer them sacrifices, and to sing their praises and to bow down to the stars, out of the false belief that they were thereby fulfilling the desire of the Creator. And this was how the worshippers, who understood the truth, would justify their practice: they would not say that there is no God apart from this star that we are worshipping. . . . Everyone knows that there is none besides God. Rather, their error and foolishness consisted in imagining that this emptiness was God's will.
(*MT, Hilkhot Avodat Kokhavim*, 1:1)

Some historians describe monotheism as a spiritual revolution that took place against the backdrop of a pagan world.[5] Maimonides, by contrast, describes a historical process that is exactly the reverse. In the beginning, humanity was monotheistic; polytheism sprouted out of monotheism. Paganism was born from a mistake that people made in the days of Enosh when they thought that the way to worship an abstract God was to bow down to the stars. This was not a philosophical error. The mistake was in their choice of method for worshipping God rather than in their understanding of the nature of God. It was a ceremonial error, not a theological one. But in the end it led to idolatry: not merely bowing down to stars, but also believing in them.

> As time passed, the glorious and awesome Name of God was forgotten from the mouths and minds of men and they no longer knew Him. Men, women and children knew only the images of wood and stone, and the temples which had, through human folly, been consecrated so that people could worship the images and swear by their names. Even the wise men and priests among them believed that there is no God, save for the stars and spheres whose images were depicted. But as for the Rock of all Worlds, no one knew Him, except for a handful of individuals such as Hanoch, Methusaleh, Noah, Shem and Ever. (*MT, Hilkhot Avodat Kokhavim*, 1:2)

This narrative illustrates the Rambam's guiding principle that belief follows where action leads.

ABRAHAM'S PHILOSOPHICAL RELIGION

This story of humanity's descent into idol worship serves as the background for the appearance of Abraham. Abraham was born into a world that had forgotten the truth. Through force of intellect he succeeded in revealing it anew. Maimonides portrays Abraham as a philosopher who meditated on the cosmos.[6] By reflecting on the eternal motion of the spheres, Abraham grasped the unbridgeable difference between God and the world. Here is the Rambam's description:

> From the time when that great man was weaned, he began to wonder, even from when he was a child, thinking to himself, "How is it possible that this sphere should be in continuous motion, without anyone moving or guiding it. Surely it is impossible that it should move itself!" He had nobody to teach or instruct him, for he was mired in a world of foolish

idolaters in Ur of the Chaldees. His father, mother and everyone around him worshipped idols, and he worshipped with them, but all the time, his heart was restless,[7] until he came to the true path as a result of correct reasoning; he knew that there is one God, and that He guides the spheres and created everything, and that there is no God besides Him. Abraham realized that the whole world was wrong and that what had caused them to err was their worshipping of stars and images, until the truth had become lost. (*MT, Hilkhot Avodat Kokhavim*, 1:3)

Abraham began to teach his discoveries and to gather followers who were convinced of the truth of these new-old ideas. This community wandered around the ancient Near East until it reached the Land of Canaan, where, led by Abraham and then by his offspring, it settled and continued to develop. The Rambam depicts Abraham's followers as a group united by loyalty to certain philosophical truths; there is no mention in the Rambam's account of laws, rituals, or commandments that bound them together.

At the height of the group's flourishing, a famine forced them to travel south into Egypt. A lengthy sojourn in Egypt engendered a spiritual crisis. The children of Israel were subjected to cruel and degrading slavery by their Egyptian hosts. Harsh external conditions brought about profound inner changes—the midrashim tell of a profound devastation of the people's spiritual identity—until Abraham's descendants had almost entirely lost their philosophical heritage. As the Rambam expresses it:

Time wore on, and Israel in Egypt learned from the ways of their neighbors and began to worship idols like them; all except for the Tribe of Levi, who held fast to the ways of their ancestors, and never worshipped idols. But they were an exception. The principle that Abraham had implanted was uprooted and the descendants of Jacob went back to making the same mistakes as everyone else. (*MT, Hilkhot Avodat Kokhavim*, 1:3)

Abraham's revolution did not survive dramatic changes in the community's political and economic circumstances. The trauma of the Egyptian exile caused Abraham's legacy to be all but forgotten.

According to Maimonides, by the time of Moses there were just a few isolated individuals who knew God: "In those days no one except a very few people knew of the existence of God" (*Guide*, 1:63).

There is a connection between the loss of monotheistic belief in the days of Enosh and the spiritual decline of Abraham's descendants in Egypt. Enosh's generation forgot God by choosing the wrong rituals. One may infer from a close reading of the Rambam's narrative here that Abraham's descendants lost their body of knowledge through not having any rituals. Maimonides finds a common meaning in both stories: the walls that defend knowledge from ignorance and worship of God from idolatry are not made out of philosophical arguments. The truly effective barriers are constructed not of ideas but from religious acts. Rituals that sustain group identity and reinforce its core principles are necessary for long-term survival and flourishing. Enosh buttressed his ideas with false rituals; Abraham did not support his ideas with any legal superstructure at all. This lack of appropriate commandments and rituals caused both communities to lose their knowledge of fundamental philosophical truths. Maimonides articulates this principle explicitly in the *Guide*:

> You know from what I have said that opinions do not last unless they are accompanied by actions that strengthen them, make them generally known, and perpetuate them among the multitude. (*Guide*, 2:31)

THE CHRISTIANITY OF JESUS:
RELIGION WITHOUT COMMANDMENTS

We may identify the same ideas that underlie Maimonides's descriptions of Enosh and Abraham in his analysis of the birth of Christianity. The Rambam's relationship to Christianity was complex and ambivalent. On the one hand, he believed that Christianity had an important role to play in the world by spreading knowledge of God and thereby paving the way for universal redemption. On the other hand, he viewed it as a false religion that is essentially idolatrous.[8] Notwithstanding this ambivalence about the existence of Christianity after the fact, however, the Rambam's opinion of the *emergence* of Christianity was unequivocal. He saw it as a dangerous development, pregnant with potential for disaster:

> Also Jesus of Nazareth, who imagined himself to be the Messiah and was killed by a bet din, had already been foreshadowed in one of Daniel's prophecies, as it said, *And the lawless sons of your people will assert themselves to confirm the vision, but they will fail* (Dan. 11:14). Could there possibly be any greater failure than this? All of the prophets predicted that the Messiah would save and redeem Israel and strengthen observance of the *mitzvot*; then this man came along and caused Israel to be put to the sword, and the remnant of the Jewish People to be scattered and humiliated, and he supplanted the Torah and deceived most of the world into worshipping a God who is not God. (*MT, Hilkhot Melakhim*, 11:4)

Jesus began a process that caused both physical and spiritual destruction: the exile of the Jewish people and the spread of idolatry. How did it happen that he caused most of the world to worship "a God who is not God"? How was he able to lead so many to idolatry? In his "Epistle to Yemen," the Rambam addresses the question:

> The inventor of this religion was Jesus of Nazareth . . . who was a Jew. He thought that he had been sent by God to clarify all of the doubtful points in the Torah and that he was the Messiah whose coming had been predicted by all the prophets. He reinterpreted the Torah in a way that led to the nullification of the Torah and its commandments. The sages, may their memories be for a blessing, understood his intentions and before his impact became very strong, did what was fitting to him.[9]

Here the Rambam distinguishes between Jesus and Christianity. Jesus did not found Christianity, but he began a process that led to its establishment.[10] Maimonides attributes to Jesus a new way of interpreting the Torah—an interpretation that rejected the binding nature of the mitzvot. In the "Epistle to Yemen," Maimonides writes about what Jesus initiated, that is, the abrogation of the commandments.

In the *Mishneh Torah*, the Rambam describes how, as a result, much of the world was swept up by an idolatrous religion.

According to the Rambam, Christianity developed in stages: the initial stage was a change in Judaism's legal structure, and thereafter a transformation of Jewish beliefs—from monotheism to a different religion that the Rambam regarded as being tainted with idolatry. Once again, as in the generation of Enosh, changes in practice lead to a sea change in faith.

There are also parallels between the unintended consequences of Abraham's revolution and the emergence of Christianity. Abraham erred, Maimonides implies, in not creating a system of ritual or mitzvot that would bind together his philosophical community. Christianity ultimately canceled the commandments. Both communities ended up in idolatry.

Two pervasive principles emerge from Maimonides's discussion of Enosh, Abraham, and Jesus:

1. Correct religious ideas will not endure in the long term unless they are supported by a system of rules and practices.[11]
2. Fundamental changes in laws lead to changes in fundamental beliefs.

MOSES'S COMMANDMENT-BASED RELIGION

Moses's mission was to succeed where these pioneers had failed (or, in the case of Christianity, would fail in the future). He needed to forge a community in which religious beliefs would be internalized by all members and would be transmitted to future generations. For Moses, mitzvot were the mechanism that would preserve and communicate the fundamental ideas of Judaism.

Pure philosophy may, perhaps, be a transformative force for a few exceptional individuals. But history shows that to make philosophy an active force in the world, it must be preserved and lived by a group of people over an extended period of time. Human instability and weakness mean that ideals are fragile in the crucible of experience if they are not rooted in clearly defined actions. Because of their practical nature, the mitzvot are able to protect and perpetuate the theoretical truths of Judaism.

Reasons for the Commandments

There are two kinds of commandments in the Torah. There are mitzvot that aim to distance people from false notions, and there are mitzvot that aim to draw people closer to true beliefs. Rambam believed that the Torah did not view people as blank slates. It was dealing with thousands of years of conditioning by pagan religions that had implanted false ideas deep in human consciousness. The Torah invested great efforts in uprooting idolatrous preconceptions. Abraham succeeded, at least for a time, in freeing his followers' minds from idolatry, using argument and persuasion. Moses employed a different approach: the mitzvot were designed to erase idolatrous beliefs from the consciousness of those who fulfilled them. The educational power of ritual is the Torah's weapon of choice for defeating paganism.

According to the *Guide*, there are two basic methods that the Torah uses in its struggle against idolatry: distancing and appropriation. There are mitzvot whose goal is to distance people from idolatry and all its symbols and ceremonies. And there are other mitzvot that aim to take away the magic of pagan religions by appropriating some of their main characteristics.

Distancing Commandments

Ancient, universal, pagan religion (which the Rambam calls the "religion of the Sabians")[12] believed in the divinity of the heavenly bodies. Maimonides tells his readers that he invested considerable intellectual energies in learning about the Sabian religion. Out of a belief that the Torah is trying to undermine the idolatrous mind-set, the Rambam put on his anthropologist's hat, so to speak, and set out to explore pagan culture. He hoped thereby to better understand the forgotten rationales for some of the Torah's commandments.

One of his conclusions was that Sabianism had been extremely successful through the judicious use of fear in its rituals. Ancient

Sabian ceremonies were full of threats against the safety of anyone who dared to miss the magical rites. The Rambam thought that a number of the Torah's commandments are responses to Sabian ceremonies. For example, the Sabians venerated cows as holy animals, and therefore prohibited their slaughter:

> As for the slaughter of oxen, the majority of idolaters abominated it, as all of them held this species in very great esteem. Hence you will find that up to our time, the Indians do not slaughter oxen, even in countries where other species of animals are slaughtered. (*Guide*, 3:46)

The Torah's choice to designate oxen as sacrificial animals was therefore a profound protest against paganism. When a Jew in the ancient world slaughtered a cow, he was also at the same time erasing pagan conditioning that had been etched on his consciousness.

Sabian priests used to cast spells on trees, believing that this would cause the trees to grow faster and produce more fruit. The average length of time for a new tree in Israel to bear fruit is three years. The Torah prohibits eating fruit from a tree until at least three years after it was planted.[13] According to the Rambam, the purpose of this prohibition is to remove the temptation to use magic in order to accelerate the tree's development. The Torah sets a clear limit. Even if the tree naturally grows more rapidly than the average, it is still forbidden to eat the fruit for three years.

Yet another example was the Sabian priests' custom of wearing ceremonial robes of wool and linen mixed together. Known as the prohibition of "*shatnez*," the Torah forbade such mixtures. According to the Rambam, one cannot understand this biblical law without the background information about the ritual dress of idolatrous priests.

The Torah was not content with mere declarations against idolatry; it also demanded action. There are many more examples throughout the *Guide* where the Rambam demonstrated that fulfilling mitzvot served an anti-pagan purpose. Obviously, as time has passed, the pagan rituals that underlie some of the Bible's prohibitions have been forgotten. Only the prohibitions remain. Stripped of their original context, they may appear pointless. However, Maimonides's anthropological investigations, through which he reconstructed rival religious cultures that were contemporaneous with the Torah, revealed the importance of those prohibitions in the battle to uproot idolatry.

The Rambam's views on this subject were formed by extensive study of ancient pagan and astrological texts. He read everything that he could possibly find in this field. Maimonides's profound investment in researching idolatrous culture is surprising. He was, after all, passionate about the need to devote one's leisure time to worthwhile intellectual pursuits. In one place, he attacks people who spend their time studying astrology, writing, "How many men who are great in years if not in wisdom have wasted their lives learning those books [of astrology]" (*Guide*, 3:37). Why, then, did the Rambam invest so much energy in mastering and interpreting pagan writings?

The answer apparently is that the Rambam did not believe that pagan writings should be studied for their inherent value. Rather, he dedicated himself to studying them so as to better understand a far more significant text, the Torah. For him, studying Sabian literature was an extension of learning Torah. Just as Aristotle's writing contained metaphysical knowledge that was necessary for unlocking secrets of the Torah, so too, researching pagan writings yielded anthropological knowledge that was critical for a proper understanding of the reasons for the commandments.[14]

Mitzvot of Appropriation

Abraham neither legislated rules nor commanded rituals. According to the Rambam he did, however, establish the Temple Mount as a center for worshipping God:

> It is known that idolaters sought to build their temples and to set up their idols in the highest places they could find there: *upon the highest mountains* (Deut. 12:2). Therefore, Abraham our Father singled out Mount Moriah, because of its being the highest mountain there, proclaiming upon it the unity of God and he determined and defined the

direction toward which one should turn in prayer, fixing it exactly in the west. For the Holy of Holies is in the west. This is the meaning of the dictum of the sages: "the indwelling is in the west." They, may their memory be blessed, have made clear in the gemara of the tractate *Yoma*, that Abraham our father fixed the direction toward which one should turn in prayer, I mean the Temple of the Holy of Holies; in my opinion, the reason for this is as follows: inasmuch as at that time the opinion generally accepted in the world was to the effect that the sun should be worshipped, and that it is the deity, there is no doubt that all men turned when praying toward the east. Therefore Abraham our father turned when praying on Mount Moriah—I mean in the sanctuary—toward the west, so as to turn his back upon the sun. (*Guide*, 3:45)

Abraham chose Mount Moriah as a ceremonial site because it was *already* a place of worship—to the god of the sun. In that very place, Abraham established a sanctuary to God. He appropriated the tradition and the popular belief that this was a holy mountain, but transformed it from a place where people worshipped nature to one where they served the God of nature. There is a strand in talmudic tradition that continues this tradition and asserts that "the *Shechinah* is on the west."[15] On the Temple Mount, people bowed down toward the Holy of Holies, which was located on the western side of the mountain. Thus the old customs were precisely reversed. At a place where people had bowed down to the sun, the followers of Abraham's religion turned their backs on the sun to worship God.

Mountain peaks are conceived in the human imagination as mystical places where heaven and earth meet. Primitive pagans tended to place their statues on mountaintops, trying to draw down the influence of heavenly bodies and channel it to people via the mediation of pagan priests. The Temple was also located on a mountain (or at least a hill), but at its summit was placed not a statue but, inside the ark, the tablets of the Ten Commandments, upon which were engraved, among other things, "You shall not make for yourselves any statue."

This interpretation of the Temple Mount shows that part of the Torah's approach to idolatry was to appropriate and transmute some of its critical ingredients. Another excellent example of this strategy is animal sacrifice. According to Maimonides, the sacrificial offering of animals was an ancient, idolatrous mode of worship. When the Jewish people lived as slaves in Egypt they were immersed in this practice. The only ways of worship that they knew were offering animals and burning incense. The Torah sought to align itself with people who were receiving it and therefore commanded that they continue offering animals and burning incense, except that now, instead of sacrificing to idols, they were to sacrifice to the God of Israel. Like the martial arts technique of defeating your opponent by turning his own strength against him, the Torah enlisted the power of idolatrous methods in order to overcome idolatry.

By means of these two approaches—anathematizing pagan rituals along with appropriating some of their essential elements and sublimating them into the system of mitzvot[16]—the Torah set out to defeat idolatry. In the Rambam's view, the strategy was a tremendous success. Idolatrous culture, which had been pervasive, virtually disappeared.

FORMATIVE MITZVOT

In addition, there are mitzvot whose goal is to help believers internalize certain essential truths. An outstanding example of this type is Shabbat. The idea that God created the world was a subject of intensive discussion throughout the Middle Ages, and especially in the *Guide*.[17] The Torah, however, does not give logical, philosophical proofs that the world was created of the sort advanced by medieval theologians. To implant the idea of creation in human consciousness, the Torah eschews intellectual argument, offering instead the commandment to keep Shabbat. As the Rambam explains:

> Perhaps it has already become clear to you what is the cause of the Law's establishing the Sabbath so firmly and ordaining death by stoning for breaking it. The Master of the prophets (Moses) has put people to death

because of it. It comes third after the existence of the deity and the denial of dualism. For the prohibition against the worship of anything except Him only aims at the affirmation of the belief in his unity. You know from what I have said, that opinions do not last unless they are accompanied by actions that strengthen them . . . therefore we have been commanded rest in order to bring together two things: the belief in a true opinion, namely the creation of the world in time . . . and the memory of the benefit that God bestowed on us by giving us rest from under the burdens of the Egyptians. (*Guide*, 2:31)[18]

For Maimonides, Shabbat is the living embodiment of the idea of creation. Keeping Shabbat instills the idea of creation deep in the soul of one who observes it, because Shabbat itself was an inseparable part of the work of creation. For the Rambam, though, Shabbat is more than just a theological declaration translated into the language of action.[19] Shabbat does not merely express faith in creation; it also molds and deepens that faith. As we saw above, Maimonides believed that the power and endurance of ideas depends not on the force of the intellectual arguments behind them but on the durability of the rituals, practices, and forms of life within which the ideas are embedded: "Ideas that are not rooted in actions will not last" (*Guide*, 3:31).

Judaism's ritual commandments have been a subject of controversy since time immemorial. Beginning with the prophets who attacked the hypocrisy of ritual observance that neglected morality—from Jesus's disciple Paul, who abrogated the practical commandments for Christians, to Rabbenu Bachya Ibn Pakuda—there have been many who have criticized halakhic Jews for excessive focus on detail at the expense of spiritual awareness.[20] Among the modern exponents of this view were Spinoza and Kant. Each of these figures shared the general critique of Jewish ritual, namely, that mechanical observance of commandments anesthetizes human consciousness and causes us to forget fundamental religious truths.

The Rambam made the opposite claim, namely, that ritual observance does not distract us from fundamental beliefs, and actually is necessary for us to internalize those beliefs. The laws are the defensive wall of ancient monotheism that have enabled it to survive and spread.

Another belief that the Torah attempted to entrench in human consciousness was faith in man. The Torah teaches that human beings have free choice. People do not merely chart their own course in life; they also mold their own personalities. We are not entrapped by our habits or by life's circumstances. Instead, we have the power to free ourselves from all of these and create ourselves anew. In Jewish tradition, this power is called *teshuvah*.

A condition for doing *teshuvah*, according to the Rambam, is belief in *teshuvah*. Someone who does not believe that he can change his basic patterns of behavior or the structure of his personality will never succeed in doing so:

> It is manifest that repentance also belongs in this class, I mean to the opinions without the belief in which the existence of individuals professing a Law cannot be well-ordered. For an individual cannot but sin and err, either through ignorance—by professing an opinion or a moral quality that is not preferable in truth—or else because he is overcome by desire and anger. If then the individual believed that the fracture can never be remedied, he would persist in his error, and perhaps disobey even more because of the fact that no stratagem remains at his disposal. If, however, he believes in repentance, he can correct himself and return to a better and more perfect state than the one he was in before he sinned. (*Guide*, 3:36)

The Rambam locates his discussion of the mitzvot of *teshuvah* in the *Guide* in a surprising place: next to those commandments that he describes in the "Laws of Foundations of the Torah" (the first section of *Mishneh Torah*). That is to say, besides all of the theological claims that we are meant to believe in relation to God, *teshuvah* is the vital belief that we need to have about the potential for improvement and repair in relation to man. Faith in *teshuvah* is also established not merely by words and declarations, but through ceremonies and deeds:

> For this reason, there are many actions that are meant to establish this correct and very useful opinion, I mean the confessions, the sacrifices in expiation of negligence and also of certain sins committed intentionally, the fasts, and the general commandment to repent from any sin. (*Guide*, 3:36)

According to the Rambam, the fast of Yom Kippur was also instituted to reinforce our belief in the reality of *teshuvah*:

> Similarly, the penalty of being cut off is entailed by partaking of unleavened bread during Passover, and of food during the day of fasting (Yom Kippur) because of the hardship imposed by this kind of abstention and because of the belief to which these actions lead. For these are actions that fortify opinions that are fundamentals of the Law, I mean the Exodus from Egypt and its miracles, and the belief in repentance. (*Guide*, 3:41)[21]

Maimonides further explained the power that the Day of Atonement has on our consciousness when he elucidated the importance of the ritual of sending away the scapegoat to Azazel, which took place on the Day of Atonement in the Temple:

> Since the goat that was sent forth into the wilderness served only to atone for great sins, so that there was no sin offering of the congregation that served as atonement in as great a measure as that goat, which was, as it were, the bearer of all the sins, it was not to receive at all such treatment as being slaughtered or burnt or sacrificed, but had to be removed to as great a distance as possible and sent forth unto *a land that is cut off* (Lev. 16:22), I mean one that was separated from habitation. No one has any doubt that sins are not bodies that may be transported from the back of one individual to that of another. But all these actions are parables, serving to bring forth a form in the soul, such that a passion for repentance should result: we have freed ourselves from our previous actions, cast them behind our backs, and removed them to an extreme distance. (*Guide*, 3:46)

The scapegoat ritual, according to the Rambam, is a parable acted out in dramatic form. The spectacle is meant to stir the souls of all who see it to do *teshuvah*. It dramatizes the idea that our sins have been taken far away and are no longer a part of our personalities. The psychological separation from our self-image as sinners is necessary for us truly to separate from sin. Belief in the possibility of change helps make change possible. The scapegoat ceremony is therefore not a substitute for *teshuvah*,[22] but a facilitator of the process. This is also the deeper purpose of confessions and sin offerings: all these rituals inspire a sense that we can free ourselves from past patterns of behavior.

BETWEEN COMMANDMENTS AND CHARACTERISTICS

The goal of the Torah is the perfection of humankind. That, of course, raises the following questions: What is the perfect human being? What does human excellence consist of? This is an issue that preoccupied the ancient Greek philosophers, and the Rambam's ideas about this were influenced by Athens.

According to Socrates, the "special excellence" of human beings is acquired through the intellect. Excellent moral characteristics are reached by applying thought and understanding. As a corollary, immoral behavior is caused primarily by ignorance. The identification of sin with intellectual error, which flows in turn from identifying moral excellence with correct understanding, goes against most people's ethical intuitions.

Aristotle led the common-sense revolt against Socrates. According to Aristotle's *Ethics*, it is possible for a man to know what is right and still do what is wrong. If Socrates were to see a doctor smoking, for example, he would immediately conclude that this is a bad doctor who obviously doesn't know that smoking is harmful. For Aristotle, on the other hand, the man could be an excellent doctor. He could have a profound and detailed understanding of the damaging effects of nicotine on the body and nevertheless still smoke. According to

Aristotle, learning does not necessarily affect a person's will, emotions, or actions. Human personality is complex and multilayered. Bridging the gap between knowledge and its internalization requires an additional process. Just as we get our bodies in shape through training, so too, our personalities and emotions are also formed and developed through training. This training takes place through habituation to ethical actions.

As we saw in the previous chapter, Aristotle defined the perfect personality as the perfectly balanced one, in which all character traits are midway between the extremes; generosity is a balance between stinginess and extravagance, while courage is the proper balance between cowardice and foolhardiness.

The Rambam followed most of Aristotle's views on this subject. Like Aristotle, he believed that our characters were our most important creations[23] and that building character is a lifelong task. In his book *Shmoneh Perakin (The Eight Chapters)*, Maimonides divided the human soul into five parts. Moral perfection is not located in the intellect but in the "appetitive part" of our personalities. Intellectual perfection does not necessarily give rise to moral behavior; these qualities reside in different parts of our souls.

Character traits are an inclination toward certain kinds of actions. A good indication of the presence of a certain quality in a person is how easy—or hard—it is for him to fulfill the kind of action that typically flows from that trait. For example, a generous person is not necessarily one who gives to charity each day, but rather one who, when called upon to give, can do so easily. A courageous man is not necessarily one who performs deeds of valor all the time, but one who can, without too much difficulty, act bravely when required.

The generous man is able to give and the courageous one to endanger himself not because these acts transcend natural inclinations, but rather because they are an expression of their characters. If a stingy man begins to train himself in giving, it will be hard for him at first, but after a few times something loosens up and it becomes a little easier and, after still more practice, giving will start to come naturally. When this happens, he knows that generosity has taken root in his soul. Character does not only generate action; action also forms character:[24]

> Know that these excellences and flaws in character only take root in the soul through frequent repetition of the actions that come from those characteristics. If the actions are good ones then the result will be excellent character traits, and if the actions are bad then the result will be character defects. (Introduction to *Avot*, 236)

Just as an athlete trains the body in order to come closer to physical perfection, so too, one who aspires to ethical perfection must be constantly training the personality.

These ideas give us a new perspective on the mitzvot. If deeds form character, then the mitzvot, as a system of habitual actions, will have a profound and far-reaching effect on the personality of one who fulfills them. The Rambam's conception of the soul is crucial to his understanding of the reasons for mitzvot. The purpose of most of the commandments is to form character, or in Rambam's words, "in order that the character of each individual should tend toward excellence. Most of the commandments are designed to achieve this kind of moral perfection" (*Guide*, 3:54). The mitzvot are a system of actions whose repetition has a therapeutic and edifying effect on the personality.

Aristotle's teachings in his *Ethics* turn out then to be key to interpreting the underlying reasons for many of the mitzvot.[25] Let us look at a few examples of how Aristotelian psychology helps the Rambam to discover the inner meaning of some of the commandments. Recall first of all that for Aristotle, intellectual excellence does not guarantee ethical excellence. A person can fail to do what he knows to be right. Aristotle attributes this failure to *ekrasia*, or weakness of the will. Remember our smoking example: someone can be fully cognizant of the damage he is doing to his health by smoking yet still not be able to kick the habit.

Aristotle's view suggests a different way of understanding human immorality. Most people who do bad things are not inherently cruel or evil; they lie, cheat, and commit adultery not because they are bad but because they are weak. Ethical failings signify weaknesses in the soul. If so, then the solution for people who know what is right but cannot do it is not to lecture them but to help them to strengthen their wills by training their characters. According to the Rambam, this is what large parts of the Torah are all about.

For example, practicing kashrut, the mitzvot commanding us to only eat certain types of food, has the effect, in the Rambam's words, of "cutting down the desire for sensory gratification that can turn eating, drinking and pursuit of what is most pleasurable into an end in itself" (*Guide*, 3:35). The role of kashrut is to restrain the excesses of human behavior in everything that has to do with food. Kashrut creates mindfulness around the act of eating, compels us to forgo opportunities to satisfy our desire for food (if is not kosher) or to delay gratification (e.g., by waiting between eating meat and milk). Kashrut is a daily training in disciplining our desires. As the Rambam puts it: "The commandments and prohibitions of the Torah come to restrain all of our basic physical impulses" (*Guide*, 3:8).

Another example is the Rambam's understanding of the mitzvot of first fruits and other offerings to the Temple. The Torah requires a person to give up some of his property, whether fruits or flocks or money, and give it over to God. Fulfilling these commands can have a profound effect. The act of giving some of what we have to God loosens attachment to property and cultivates generosity, making it easier to give, not just to God, but also to those around us.

The Torah's explicitly ethical commandments, such as "Do not steal" and "Do not commit adultery," are accompanied by another group of mitzvot that train human character. How should we categorize this latter group, whose purpose is to strengthen the will for good and restrain destructive desires? Are they mitzvot "between a person and his fellow man," or are they rather between man and God? In a remarkable passage, the Rambam seems to create a new category for these commandments:

> All the other groups deal with the relation between man and God. For every commandment, whether it be a prescription or a prohibition, whose purpose is to bring about the achievement of a certain moral quality, or of an opinion, or the rightness of actions, which only concerns the individual himself and his becoming more perfect, is called by them between man and God, even though in reality it may sometimes affect relations between man and his fellow man. (*Guide*, 3:35)

According to the Rambam, many mitzvot that are traditionally termed "between man and God" are better described as "between man and himself." More than serving God, they strengthen our characters. Mitzvot between a person and himself are indirectly connected to the mitzvot between man and his fellow man, because without the capacity for self-restraint, ethical laws are virtually meaningless. A person who has undergone the training of keeping kashrut should be better able to withstand the temptations of lying, stealing, and adultery.

The mitzvot thus have a dual effect: they cultivate correct beliefs and they build character, contributing thereby to the perfection both of the soul and the body. Over the course of twenty-five chapters of the *Guide*, Maimonides reveals the deeper reasons for the commandments. His interpretations make the pursuit of human perfection central to the meaning of the mitzvot. Because of this, *The Guide for the Perplexed* has stood for centuries as the major alternative to the streams in Jewish thought which argued that the primary purpose of the mitzvot is to please God.

8

MAN AND THE TORAH

The Rambam held that the primary purpose of the mitzvot is to perfect human beings, on the spiritual, physical, and societal levels. However, at a number of places in his writings Maimonides clearly implies that man is *not* the focus and goal of the mitzvot. The Jewish thinker who most strongly opposed the anthropocentric reading of the Rambam was the renowned Israeli scholar Yeshayahu Leibowitz.[1]

LEIBOWITZ'S QUESTION

Based on a close reading of the Rambam's introduction to the last chapter of the talmudic tractate *Sanhedrin*, Leibowitz infers that Maimonides places great religious significance on our motivations for learning Torah and fulfilling mitzvot. In that introduction, the Rambam describes the evolution of religious motivations by means of a classic example:

Understand the following parable, and afterwards pay attention to what I have to say about it. Imagine that a young boy is taken to a teacher to learn Torah. . . . The teacher finds it necessary to encourage the boy to learn by offering him things that small boys like as an incentive. He says, "If you learn well, I will give you nuts, or figs, or a piece of sugar." The boy applies himself to learning, not because of the learning itself—he does not understand its value—but in order to get the thing that he wants. This ulterior purpose is much more important to him than the learning; he will value the learning and work hard at it because it is a means to obtain his real desire—the nuts or the piece of sugar. (*Commentary to Mishnah*, *Introduction to Helek*)

The Torah itself does not offer sufficient enticements to the young boy who begins to study. In the Rambam's example, one must offer the beginner supplementary motivation, for example, through treats like nuts or figs. However, as the child matures, these incentives lose their effect, and there needs to be a different motivational strategy:

> When he grows up and becomes smarter, and the things that he used to value now seem trivial and his wants become a little more sophisticated, the teacher motivates him using these new desires. He may say to him, "learn well and I will buy you those nice shoes, or that impressive garment." The boy will persevere at his studies, not because of the learning itself, but because of the item of clothing, which is his real goal and motivation. (*Commentary to Mishnah*, *Introduction to Helek*)

Later on, the clothes and nice shoes don't do it for him anymore. Then the teacher may motivate him by offering money, which gives the boy freedom to buy whatever he wants. When he grows older still, he comes to value honor more than money, and the esteem and public recognition he receives for his learning become central motivations for his Torah study:

> Then the teacher motivates him with what has become most important to the student, by saying: "learn in order that you will become a rabbi and a judge and so that people will give you honor and stand before you and do your bidding, and your name will become great in your lifetime, and after your death, like so-and-so." Then he will learn in order to achieve honor and praise, but in truth all of these motivations are unworthy. (*Commentary to Mishnah*, *Introduction to Helek*)

In this story, learning represents fulfillment of the mitzvot. The story describes how motivation for religious observance develops. Initially, people's reasons for observance tend to be egocentric; some fulfill the commandments as an insurance policy against going to hell;

others see them as a guarantee of health and prosperity for them and their families. There are also more edifying reasons for observance, such as the belief that fulfilling the mitzvot is conducive to creating a more moral society or a stable family life. But those who fulfill the commandments for these reasons are not serving God; they are serving themselves or their own values. For them, the mitzvot are a powerful tool for advancing their personal interests and goals. However, the Rambam teaches that at a more advanced stage of religious growth this changes:

> Furthermore, the sages taught *His desire for His mitzvot is very great* (Ps. 112:1). "For His *mitzvot*," and not for the reward of the *mitzvot*. Thus the great sages used to teach the most enlightened of their students: "do not be like servants who serve their master in order to receive some good; be like servants who serve their master for no reason except that he is the master, and it is therefore fitting to serve him: in other words, serve out of love." (*Commentary to Mishnah; Introduction to Helek*)

> Anyone who is involved in Torah in order to receive a reward, or so as to avoid punishment is learning "not for its own sake." And anyone who is involved in Torah neither out of fear, nor to receive reward, but from love of the Master of the whole world who commanded him thus—he is learning for its own sake. The sages said "a person should always be involved in Torah, even not for its own sake, because out of that will come involvement for its own sake." (*MT, Hilkhot Teshuvah*, 10:5)

Love of God is a spiritual state in which a person transcends selfish motivations. One can infer from these passages that the commandments should not be understood as a tool for self-realization. Rather, one who follows the mitzvot should strive to take himself out of the picture, so to speak, and see service of God as the only worthy motivation for religious endeavor:

> This level is an exceedingly high one, and not every wise person is worthy of attaining it. It is the level of Abraham our forefather, who

the Holy One called his lover, because Abraham served God only out of love. This is the level of serving God that Moses commanded us saying, *You shall love the Lord your God with all your heart, all your soul and all your might* (Deut. 6:5). From the moment when one loves God as He should be loved, one will fulfill all of the *mitzvot* out of love. (*MT, Hilkhot Teshuvah*, 10:2.)

Leibowitz argued that it was no accident that the Rambam chose Abraham as the model for love of God. Abraham is the most striking example in the Bible of someone who freed himself from all selfish motivations in his devotion to God. The moment of the *Akedah*, when Abraham demonstrated his willingness to slaughter his only son, was also the point at which Abraham succeeded in killing the last of his selfish reasons for divine service. Abraham was ready to give up everything for God. The sacrifice of Isaac did not take place, but the sacrifice of Abraham's egocentric motivations did, and this is the real drama of the story.

Leibowitz (who was not known to be a great lover of Christianity) compared the binding of Isaac to the crucifixion of Jesus. He pointed out the similar yet contrasting central motifs of these foundational stories of Judaism and Christianity. In the crucifixion story, God sacrifices His son in order to redeem humanity, whereas in the binding of Isaac, a man is prepared to sacrifice his son in order to serve God.[2] This is the difference, argues Leibowitz, between an idolatrous creed that places man at the center and monotheistic religion, where God is at the center.

But does Leibowitz really speak for the Rambam, or at least for a certain strain in the Rambam's thought? Over the course of twenty-five chapters of the *Guide*, Maimonides developed a clear vision of how the mitzvot train and refine the soul of the one who lives them. Yet he also wrote that it is a mistake to understand the mitzvot as being focused on man, and that one should attempt to transcend this point of view. What is the real purpose of mitzvot according to the Rambam? Is the focus God, or man?

The Torah and Nature

Even more difficult challenges to any anthropocentric understanding of the Torah can be found in other areas of the Rambam's religious thought. In one of the later chapters of the *Guide*, Maimonides raises the question of the purpose of existence and examines the possibility that man could have been the purpose of creating the universe with its myriad stars, spheres, and constellations. After all, since human beings benefit from the light of the heavenly bodies, whether sunlight during the day or the glow of the stars at night, might one not conclude that these bodies were made in order to serve us? Maimonides rejects this option as absurd:

> However, this does not apply to the stars; I mean to say that they do not exist for our sake so that good should come to us through them . . . according to what I have made clear to you, concerning the nature of the constant overflow of the good from one thing toward another. (*Guide*, 3:13)

The Rambam is saying that the benefit that flows from the stars to us occurs in any event. It is not the purpose for which the stars were created but merely a necessary consequence of their nature. Man is indeed the summit of the created world, yet the earthly, material universe is ultimately a lowly thing compared to the spheres and heavenly bodies, which the Rambam considered to be above and distinct from the earthly, physical world. As the Rambam put it: "Man is the most perfect and noble thing that has been created from this inferior matter, but no more than that" (*Guide*, 3:13). When the enormous gulf separating man from the spheres and heavenly bodies is considered, it becomes clear how small and insignificant we are, and how absurd it is to think that man is at the center of the universe: "If his being is compared to that of the sphere . . . it is very, very lowly" (*Guide*, 3:13).

In the next chapter of the *Guide*, the Rambam advances another argument to reinforce his claim that it is absurd to think of man as the purpose of creation:

What man ought also to consider in order to know what his own soul is worth and to make no mistake regarding this point, is what has been made clear concerning the dimensions of the spheres and of the stars and the measures of the distances separating us from them. . . . It had been demonstrated that the distance between the center of the earth and the highest part of the sphere of Saturn is one that could be covered in approximately eight thousand seven hundred years of three hundred and sixty five days each, if each day a distance is covered of forty of our legal miles, of which each had two thousand of the cubits used for working purposes. Consider this great and terrifying distance. (*Guide*, 3:14)

The cosmos is, of course, immense. After giving his readers a sense of its enormous dimensions, the Rambam suggests a thought experiment: compare the size of the universe to the size of man. This comparison should lead not just to an appreciation of the insignificance of man but also to letting go of the whole anthropocentric conception of the world.

The Rambam's exhortation that we reflect on nature in order to understand our proper status in the world is reminiscent of an earlier Andalusian Jewish philosopher, Rabbenu Bachya Ibn Pakudah, who also tried to make meditation on the natural world a religious duty. His approach was different from the Rambam's, however. Bachya's reason for encouraging contemplation of nature was his belief that doing so would lead to an appreciation of the wondrous attunement of the world to all human needs:

The sky above is like a beam, and the earth below is like a comfortable bed and the stars are arranged around us like candles, and all beings are provided with whatever they need, and man, as master of the house uses everything around. Different types of plant are available for his benefit, and different species of animals serve his pleasure, as King David said. . . .
The order of the rising and setting sun, determining the times of day and night and the sun's movements creating cold and warmth, summer and winter, each season with its particular benefits.[3]

The cosmos is designed to enable human life to flourish. The wondrous feature in nature that so excites Bachya's religious passion is its anthropocentric order—the way it is all perfectly set up to meet man's every need. The Rambam, in contrast, believed that contemplation of nature would destroy any illusions of anthropocentrism. For Bachya, reflecting on the world awakens a consciousness that "for my sake the world was created," whereas for the Rambam it gives rise to a sense that "I am dust and ashes."

Maimonides is making a dual claim here. The first part is that it is hard to believe that the purpose of the cosmos in all of its vast enormity is really man. The second part is that it is impossible to assume that the spheres and the intelligences that guide them, which are on a higher, metaphysical plane than human beings, were created in order to serve man:

> Seeing the difference that there is between them [i.e., between man and the spheres] concerning the nobleness of substance, it would have been most disgraceful if what is nobler served as an instrument for the existence of what is most base and vile. (*Guide*, 3:14)

The Rambam makes a considerable effort to persuade his readers that even though they were, in a physical sense, at the center of the universe (or at least they believed themselves to be so in the medieval period, when the geocentric understanding of the universe was still dominant), they were not the center of the world from the perspective of its purpose. The world was not created to serve man.

THE VARIETIES OF RELIGIOUS EXPERIENCE
There are two problems with the Rambam's teaching about the mitzvot. First, there is an apparent contradiction between the twenty-five chapters of the *Guide*, which assume that the purpose of the mitzvot is the perfection of man, and other places in the Rambam's writings which imply that their purpose is not for man's sake at all. Second, the conception of the mitzvot in the *Guide* that places man at the center seems to be opposed to the

Rambam's idea that we should try to free ourselves from our self-important sense that we are the center of everything, by reflecting on the vastness of the universe and grasping how marginal and insignificant we truly are.

However, a careful reading of the *Guide* shows that there is not necessarily any contradiction between these different strands of thought. In fact, the chapters that deal with the reasons for the mitzvot do not discuss the *motivation* that should accompany fulfillment of the commandments. The purpose of these chapters is to show the *rationality* of the mitzvot rather than to discuss from a subjective point of view why someone might choose to fulfill them. If these chapters were meant to serve a motivational purpose, one might well conclude that they do a poor job. Understood as arguments for why one should keep the commandments, some of the claims do not seem convincing today, given that they refer to the struggle against Sabian idolatry thousands of years ago. We need to distinguish clearly between the reasons why the mitzvot were given and the proper motivations for fulfilling them. They should be fulfilled in order to serve God, but the rationale for giving them was to improve man.

This is a little like a mother trying to feed a child who is not interested in eating. She promises him prizes as a reward for eating, as a result of which the child yields to her entreaties. The child's motivation for eating is to get a prize, but the purpose of his eating is not the prize, but rather that he should be healthy. This distinction between the motivation of an action and the goal of an action is as important as it is common. Think about obeying the law, for example: the most common motivation for obeying the law is fear of punishment, but the goal is social order. Or take learning in university: the main motivation of students might be to receive a diploma, but the purpose of universities is to establish a well-educated society.

This was the response that my teacher, Professor Aviezer Ravitsky, gave to Leibowitz's critique.[4] According to the Rambam, we should strive to observe the mitzvot out of pure-hearted devotion to God, and at the same time we should know that they were given for the purpose of perfecting man.

Religious motivations that place man at the center and express an instrumental attitude toward the mitzvot are improper and are termed *she'lo lishmah*, not for their own sake. A more elevated kind of motivation for devotion to religious actions, one that places God at the center, frees a person from egotistical considerations. One who serves God *lishmah*, for the sake of Heaven, seeks no reward for fulfilling the mitzvot but does so in an act of self-negation before God. According to the Rambam, a theocentric orientation toward the mitzvot is not merely an attitude toward doing them but can also be an *effect* of fulfilling them. How can a certain kind of motivation for keeping the commandments be an outcome of their fulfillment? One who dedicates himself to the mitzvot undergoes a process of change, which gradually transforms his motivation:

> Anyone who is involved in Torah in order to receive a reward, or so as not to be punished is doing so "not for its own sake." But anyone who is involved in Torah neither out of fear, nor to receive a reward, but out of love for the Master of the whole world who commanded it—is doing so "for its own sake." The sages said that a person should always study Torah, even if not for its sake, because from doing so, he will come to learn for its own sake.
>
> Therefore, when one teaches children, women and ignorant people, one should initially teach them to serve God out of fear, in order to receive reward, until their understanding grows, they become wiser, and little by little one reveals to them the secret, until they gain true knowledge and are able to serve out of love. (*MT, Hilkhot Teshuvah*, 10:5)

The mitzvot themselves remake our attitude toward keeping them. A person can begin to observe the commandments because he views them as a helpful tool for self-realization, but the very act of following them frees him from this self-centered approach, and he becomes genuinely focused on serving God. But how exactly do the mitzvot work to effect this change? The key to understanding this process is to be found in one of the final chapters of the *Guide*. But let us approach this question by means of William James's classic work, *The Varieties of Religious Experience.*

James offers the following elegant definition of the religious phenomenon:

> Religion . . . shall mean for us the feelings, acts and experiences of individual men in their solitude, so far as they apprehend themselves in relation to whatever they consider the divine.[5]

According to James, a religious person is one who lives his life as a response to the sense that something exists that is above and beyond his earthly life. People's patterns of behavior are usually a collection of responses to events and stimuli that they encounter in their lives. Curiosity is a response to facing puzzles, and seeking food is a response to feeling hungry. Religious actions, on the other hand, are a response to an invisible reality.

Later in the book, James sharpens his definition of religion:

> It consists in the belief that there is an unseen order, and that our supreme good consists in harmoniously adjusting ourselves thereto.[6]

Based on his research of religious experiences across a range of cultures, James explains that one of the most fundamental religious phenomena is the sense that things exist in the world that cannot be apprehended by our intellect or through our senses. Human beings have the ability to sense very powerfully the presence of things that cannot be rationally understood. James terms this kind of experience "the presence of the hidden."

Maimonides in the *Guide* also discusses the nature of intense religious experience in the context of describing the profile of extraordinary individuals:[7]

> Man does not sit, move and occupy himself when he is alone in his house, as he sits, moves and occupies himself when he is in the presence

of a great king; nor does he speak and rejoice while he is with his family and relatives, as he speaks in the king's council. Therefore, he who chooses to achieve human perfection and to be in true reality a man of God must give heed and know that the great king who always accompanies him and cleaves to him is greater than any human individual. (*Guide*, 3:52)

The religious psychology that the Rambam discusses in this chapter is very reminiscent of James's evocations of religious experience. The Rambam describes people who feel "the presence of the hidden" very intensely. They live their lives as a response to the presence of God in their worlds. This kind of spiritual state guides the way a person acts:

Understand this well. Know that when the perfect men understand this, they achieve such humility, such awe and fear of God, such reverence and such shame before Him, may He be exalted—and this in ways that pertain to true reality, not to imagination, that their secret conduct with their wives, and in latrines is like their public conduct with other people. This, as you will find, was the way of our most renowned sages with their wives: *One uncovers a handbreadth and covers up a handbreadth* (BT *Nedarim* 20a–b). They also said, *Who is modest? Whoever behaves by night as he behaves by day* (BT *Berachot* 62a). You know already that they forbade walking around with an erect carriage because of the biblical dictum, *The whole world is full of his glory* (Isa. 6:3); all this being firmly intended to establish the notion that I have mentioned to you, that we are always before Him, may He be exalted, and walk about to and fro while his Indwelling is with us. And the greatest among the sages, may their memory be blessed, avoided uncovering their heads, because man is covered about by the indwelling. They also spoke little for this reason. We have already given in the Commentary on *Avot*, the explanation that was needed concerning the habit of speaking but little: *For God is in heaven and thou upon the earth; therefore let thy words be few* (Eccles. 5:1). (*Guide*, 3:52)

This strong sense of God's presence inspires religious acts, but it is also, according to the Rambam, the consequence of fulfilling the commandments.

This purpose, to which I have drawn your attention, is the purpose of all the actions prescribed by the Law. For it is by all the particulars of the actions and through their repetition that some excellent men obtain such training that they achieve human perfection, so that they fear, and are in dread and in awe of God, may he be exalted, and know who it is that is with them, and as a result act subsequently as they ought to . . . I refer to the fear of Him, may He be exalted, and the awe before His command. It says, *If you will not take care to observe all the words of this Law that are written in this book, that you may fear this great and glorious name, the Lord your God.* (Deut. 28:58). Consider how it is explicitly stated for your benefit that the intention of all the words of this law is one end, namely that you may fear His name, and so on. The fact that this end is achieved through actions, you can learn from its dictum in this verse: *if you will not take care to observe.* For it has already been made clear that this refers to actions prescribed by commandments and prohibitions. (*Guide*, 3:52)

In this chapter, the Rambam reverses the cause-and-effect relations about religious experience that James implies. Observing the commandments is not just a consequence of feeling the presence of God; fulfilling them also creates a sense of God's presence. Actions mold not merely ideas and personality characteristics, as we saw earlier; they can also form a powerful religious sensibility. Creating a sense of devotion to God is one of the main achievements of the mitzvot. Indeed, according to the Rambam, this is their main goal.

How should we reconcile part 3, chapter 52 of the *Guide* with the twenty-five chapters that give reasons for the mitzvot? If there are rational reasons for observing the commandments, then when a person follows them, isn't he then responding to a revealed logic rather than to a hidden presence? The distinction between the subjective motivations for keeping mitzvot, on the one hand, and their goals, on the other, is also helpful here. In part 3, chapter 52 the Rambam is talking about the consciousness of the one who is commanded rather than the psychological effect of the commandments. A person can fulfill the commandments for all kinds of subjective reasons, but the experience of fulfilling them and living the intensive religious life that they mandate deepens a person's sense of the presence of the hidden God who commands them. This sense of presence in turn gives rise to feelings of submission and self-abnegation.

There is a parallel between the psychological effects of meditating on nature and of practicing Torah. Contemplating nature creates a sense of humility in the face of the cosmic vastness of the universe; practicing the mitzvot of the Torah generates humility in the face of the presence of God. Both of these acts can dispel the illusions of anthropocentrism and confer on us a new, spiritual consciousness. According to the theosophic school of Kabbalah, the mitzvot influence God. According to the Rambam, they train and mold human beings—but they shape a kind of person who is constantly involved with God. The mitzvot refine and improve our character, while at the same time diminishing our sense of self-importance.

The mitzvot lead us along a path that is both intellectually and emotionally therapeutic. The intellectual path consists in first of all purifying from our notion of God all material attributes, and subsequently purifying it of all attributes whatsoever. The emotional path consists in purifying our motivations first from physical drives, and then in cleansing our motivations of all human-centered considerations. The further a person advances on this path, the less will his conception of God be influenced by physical images, and the less will his motivation be affected by material factors. Our understanding of God evolves together with the evolution of our motivation for serving Him. In the Rambam's writings, these motivations are usually described separately, but actually they are closely related. True spiritual achievement consists in removing one's conception of God from worldly factors and in liberating oneself from enslavement to the ego.

9

THE UNIVERSALITY
OF THE TORAH

The commandments were designed to help people become more natural, in the sense of being more balanced and whole. But if nature, which is universal, reflects the Torah, why isn't the Torah universal? Why was it given only to Jews?

THE UNIVERSAL GOD OF NATURE

When God revealed himself to Israel on Mount Sinai, He began with a personal introduction: "I am the Lord your God who took you out of the Land of Egypt" (Exod. 20:2). God introduces Himself, so to speak, with a fragment of autobiography, the part that is most relevant to His encounter with the Jewish people: their liberation from slavery. A moment before He asks for Israel's absolute allegiance, God states the historical drama that created that obligation. God saved Israel, and from this flows the exclusivity that He demands from Israel. The early national history of Israel was marked by the liberation from Egypt, the drama of wandering in the desert, and the miraculous military victories that Israel won upon entering the promised land. This history is the source of God's authority, but it is also a principal source of religious inspiration for the Jewish people.

The Rambam proposes an alternative source of authority. Instead of basing God's authority on history, he bases it on nature. The perfect order of the cosmos bears witness to God's perfection.

Substituting nature for history at the center of religious life has far-reaching consequences. One important implication is how we understand the uniqueness of the Jewish people. National history is necessarily particularistic. Every people has its own story. Basing religion on history emphasizes the distinctiveness of the religious group. Nature, on the other hand, is universal; it is blind to differences between religions and peoples. The sun shines on every nation. So when nature becomes the basis for religious authority, the boundaries between religions are inevitably blurred. Basing religion on nature weakens particularism and emphasizes common, universal themes. The God of nature is the God of all peoples.

Halevi, who grounded the Torah in history, emphasized not just the Jewish people's difference from other nations but also their superiority. God chose the people of Israel from all the nations on the face of the earth because He found in them certain qualities that were absent from all the rest. According to Halevi, Israel has a special connection to the divine. All people can achieve philosophical perfection, but only Israel can reach the level of prophecy. The summit of religious life is blocked for other peoples and is attainable only by one nation, the Chosen People.

Many religions believe that God communicates with human beings by way of intermediaries. This was the function of the priests in Mesopotamian cultures, of the king in Egypt, and it is the role of the pope in Catholicism. Halevi also thought that God conducts a conversation with human beings, but for Halevi, the mediator is not a chosen individual but rather the Chosen People. Israel is a kingdom of priests with an open channel to God.

Did Maimonides believe that God communicates directly with non-Jews? Whereas Halevi saw prophecy as a special faculty that is distinct from ordinary wisdom, the Rambam considered prophecy a natural extension of wisdom. As we saw, Maimonides viewed prophecy as something that happens in a man who has successfully combined three types of perfection: perfection in moral qualities, intellect, and imagination. In such a person, intellect and imagination join forces to create the prophetic experience. Intellect is a universal quality that all people share; imagination, according to the Rambam, is a faculty that not only people but also that animals have. He thought of prophecy as resulting not from a choice by God to confer it on a particular person but rather from a human initiative to cultivate the forms of perfection that will bring him or her to prophecy. If so, then surely any person from any religion could become worthy of prophecy. If there is no fundamental obstacle, either conceptual or genetic, to non-Jews receiving prophecy, then one cannot insist that the Jewish people function as God's exclusive channel for communication with humanity.

This would also imply that God's providential concern is not devoted exclusively to Israel. For Maimonides, such divine concern is a consequence of our level of understanding and thirst for knowledge. But intellect and the yearning to know are human traits that transcend ethnic limitations. It follows that the criterion for providence is whether or not you are enlightened, not whether you are Jewish.

The Chosen People have no monopoly, then, either on prophecy or on providence. But they do have one big advantage: the mitzvot. As we have seen, the commandments of the Torah serve as a kind of personal training program that is designed to bring us closer to moral and intellectual perfection. When non-Jews fall short of the level of prophecy, this is not due to any innate incapacity on their part. The limitation is cultural. Just as someone who aspires to become a great athlete will need to follow the best possible training regime, so too, prophecy and providence are more available to Jews than to other people because they have the most successful educational program. The Torah is uniquely suited to lead to prophecy. The Rambam did not think Jews were inherently better that other people, but he did believe that the Torah was superior to any other body of spiritual teaching.

One of the fundamental differences between the *Guide* and the *Mishneh Torah* is their attitude toward non-Jews. Whereas the *Guide* does not distinguish between Jews and gentiles, the *Mishneh Torah* records many such distinctions throughout its fourteen books.[1] Philosophy is blind to ethnic differences; *halakhah*, on the other hand, insists on them. Many of the laws of the Torah apply differently to Jews and non-Jews.

But the Rambam's philosophy does not contradict *halakhah*. Generations of scholars and interpreters of the *Guide* argued that the *Guide* and the *Mishneh Torah* represent two very different spiritual sensibilities. However, the consensus among modern scholars is that the distance between these two works is not so great.[2] (The bridge between the two books was built by the Rambam himself, who wove in philosophical ideas throughout his halakhic works.) Nevertheless, the place where the gap between *halakhah* and philosophy seems widest in Maimonides's thought is around this question of the relationship to non-Jews. Despite his philosophical universalism, the Rambam is committed to a separatist halakhic tradition that treats Jews and non-Jews differently in significant ways. Should we assume, then, that the universalism of the *Guide* is qualified by the particularist *halakhah* of the *Mishneh Torah*?

The Relationship to Non-Jews
in the *Mishneh Torah*

I would argue that the Rambam's commitment to the traditional halakhic system does not really undermine the egalitarianism of his philosophy. Maimonides created a unique space for universalism within his halakhic discourse. In a number of places in the *Mishneh Torah*, the Rambam concludes a halakhic discussion by summarizing the relevant legal obligations and then giving instructions to those who want to go beyond the strict halakhic requirements. *Halakhah* lays out the norms of religious behavior, but those who strive for spiritual excellence can choose to transcend the letter of the law. In these passages, Maimonides tended not to focus on voluntary stringencies that one might choose to adopt in halakhic observance. Instead, he often took a kind of meta-halakhic leap in the direction of universalism.

For example, the *halakhah* is replete with instructions about how an owner should treat his Jewish slave, namely, with kindness, concern, and sensitivity. There are so many rules institutionalizing this relationship that the sages said, "If you acquire a Jewish slave, it is as if you acquire a master for yourself." However, the *halakhah* does not codify one's obligations toward a non-Jewish slave. After detailing all of the rules that regulate the relationship with a Jewish slave, the Rambam had this to say about how to treat a slave who is not Jewish:

> It is permissible to give a Canaanite slave hard work to do. Even though this is the law, saintliness and the ways of wisdom require that a man be merciful and pursue justice. Therefore one should not place a heavy yoke on a non-Jewish slave, and one should give him food and drink from whatever the master eats and drinks. The early sages would give their slaves whatever they themselves used to eat and drink and would take care of the food for their slaves and animals before they sat down to eat. As it says, *Like the eyes of slaves toward their masters, and of maidservants toward their mistresses* . . . (Ps. 123:2). Therefore, they should not be despised, either in deed or word. The Torah permitted us to take them as slaves, but not to humiliate them; one should not scream and yell at them, but rather speak gently and listen to their complaints. This is explicit in the praiseworthy ways of Job, who said, *Did I ever brush aside the case of my servants, man or maid, when they made complaint against me? . . . Did not One form us both in the womb?* (Job 31:13–15). (*MT*, *Hilkhot Avadim*, 12:8)

Here, Maimonides is not satisfied with the particularist *halakhah* that only regulates how owners should behave toward slaves from their own community. He insists that "saintliness and the ways of wisdom" require us to go beyond the *halakhic* norms and to act with compassion toward all. The morally excellent individual is not the one who is extra strict about particularistic obligations to his own people, but rather one who seeks to go beyond them and embrace a universal commitment to all people. It is interesting to note that the Rambam bases this universalistic ethics on a biblical verse that stresses the shared nature of humanity: "Did not One form us both in the womb?" The God of nature, creator of the world, is the God of the non-Jewish Job just as He is the God of Israel. Nature is indifferent to nationality; treating nature as a source of authority implies a blindness to ethnic differences. A Jew who lives according to *halakhah* is required to love the whole halakhic community; however, a Jew who is guided by an understanding of nature is enjoined to love all human beings, since all were created in the image of God.

Maimonides did not change *halakhah* in order to make it more universal. Instead, he created a non-halakhic space of moral excellence where a universal ethic could flourish. This type of excellence builds on the normal feelings of solidarity that people have toward others from their ethnic group and channels these emotions toward the rest of humanity. By creating this special moral space, the universalist philosopher of the *Guide* inserted himself into the halakhic discussion of the *Mishneh Torah*.

HOLY OF HOLIES

At the beginning of this section I pointed out that one of the key differences between *halakhah* and philosophy is that *halakhah* expresses the religious norm, whereas philosophy articulates the aspiration to religious excellence. In the parable of the king in his palace, the Rambam places experts in *halakhah* outside the king's palace, whereas the philosophers are inside.

Separating spiritual excellence from *halakhah* has far-reaching implications. So long as it is inextricably connected to halakhic observance, religious excellence is only accessible to Jews. Freeing it from *halakhah* implies a democratization of the highest reaches of religious achievement.

In the *Mishneh Torah* the Rambam is explicit about the universal nature of spiritual excellence. At the end of the section about the laws of the sabbatical year and Jubilee, he writes about the special political and economic status of the tribe of Levi. The members of this tribe were not required to work for a living or to go to war. They were exempt them from these obligations so that they could devote themselves to philosophical study. They were free of the day-to-day struggle of life in order to inquire into the meaning of life. At the end of this passage, the Rambam comments:

> Not just the Tribe of Levi, but any person in the world whose spirit moves him and who wishes, on his own initiative, to stand before God and serve Him by striving to know Him, and who follows the straight path, and removes from his neck the yoke of the manifold calculations that most men are involved with—he becomes sanctified as holy of holies. God is his portion and his inheritance forever. He will merit to receive whatever he needs in this life, just as the priests and Levites did. As David said, *God, you are my inheritance and my cup; you support my way* (Ps. 16:5). (*MT, Hilkhot Shmitah v'Yovel*, 13:13)

The members of the tribe of Levi become a metaphor for all people who choose to devote themselves to a life of study and contemplation and the pursuit of truth. Levi is a symbol for all those who aspire to reach the summit of human existence. In this surprising passage, the Rambam affirms that his ideal of religious excellence is accessible to all people regardless of their ethnic group. Moreover, he adds a new metaphor, the idea of the "holy of holies," the most special and distinctive space in the Jewish universe. The Holy of Holies may never be entered, except by the High Priest on the Day of Atonement, the holiest day of the year. The Rambam takes a symbol for the most rarified religious reality and applies it to something that is universally accessible. The metaphor signals the democratization of his version of religious excellence and an access to high levels of spiritual achievement for anyone willing to strive for them.

The *Guide* implies that the peaks of religious experience are open to all people. In the *Mishneh Torah*, this is not just obliquely implied; it is stated explicitly. Still, our original question remains: although truth is universal, the path that leads to it—the Torah—is particular. Did the Rambam believe that there are roads to the truth that do not follow the way of *halakhah*? When he opened up the Holy of Holies of philosophical perfection to all-comers, was he conceding that Judaism has no monopoly on pathways to truth?

The *Mishneh Torah* hints at the radical answer to this question. One of the ways in which *halakhah* influences human personality is by training us to have refined personality traits. The Torah itself embodies perfect balance, and its intensive training program allows us to internalize this balance. The role model that the Rambam chose to exemplify this path is Abraham: "The one who follows this way brings goodness and blessing on himself, as it says, *in order that the Lord may bring about for Abraham what He has promised him* (Gen. 18:19)" (*Hilkhot Shmitah v'Yovel*, 13:11). This is a surprising choice, because Abraham, according to the Rambam, did not have the Torah. The Rambam did not go along with the talmudic rabbis' project of recasting Abraham as an observant Jew who kept all the commandments. The Rambam's Abraham had just eight mitzvot: the Seven Noachide Laws plus circumcision.

Abraham, then, is the archetype of one who was able to actualize the goal that the Torah and mitzvot direct us toward, but without the mitzvot themselves. How was Abraham able to develop a perfectly balanced personality without the mitzvot to guide him? Maimonides does not tell us. However, the choice of Abraham as a model for spiritual greatness without the Torah strongly hints at the Rambam's real view: that the path to religious excellence does not depend on keeping *halakhah*, as he writes at the end of the *Hilkhot Shmitah v'Yovel*, but rather that it is open to all.

The figure of Abraham recurs throughout the Rambam's writings. We saw earlier how the Rambam uses Abraham's story to reinforce the importance and prestige of *halakhah*. Abraham's attempt to preserve philosophical truth within a non-halakhic community ultimately failed. Nevertheless, the Rambam's depiction of Abraham also assumes that for certain people, at least some of the time, the truth can appear (and also disappear) even without the benefit of *halakhah*. The Rambam acknowledged that great spirits who are not Jewish can reach perfection and touch the truth.

Halakhah alone cannot bring a person into the king's palace. It can, however, take him up to the entrance, where he can decide whether or not to step over the threshold. The Rambam seems to have thought that the likelihood of non-Jews reaching perfection without *halakhah* is not high, and moreover, if they reached it they would be unlikely to maintain that level for long. Nevertheless, he believed that it was possible. In this sense, the universalist philosophy of the *Guide* triumphed over the halakhic particularism of the *Mishneh Torah*.

CONCLUSION

Rising to the Level of Understanding

A few years ago I carried out some unscientific research. I interviewed friends about their first-ever time in synagogue and asked them if they had experienced a particular moment of spiritual uplift during the prayer service. Most of them answered that, although they found most of the ritual tedious, there had been at least one moment that pushed their religious buttons, so to speak. Surprisingly, most said that the parts of the service that had been most inspiring were the sections in Aramaic. Being obscure to most native Hebrew speakers, these portions of the service aroused a sense of mystery. There is a certain kind of excitement and awe that people often feel in the face of what they cannot understand. The Rambam was aware of this very human tendency and wrote in the *Guide* that some people believe that identifying the reasons for the mitzvot would actually empty them of meaning:

> There is a group of human beings that consider it a grievous thing that causes should be given for any law; what would please them most is that the intellect would not find a meaning for the commandments and prohibitions. What compels them to feel thus is a sickness that they find in their souls, a sickness to which they are unable to give utterance. . . . [They believe that] if however there was a thing for which the intellect could not find any meaning at all and that does not derive from something useful, it indubitably derives from God. (*Guide*, 3:31)

Groucho Marx famously once said that he didn't want to belong to a club that would have him as a member. Likewise, we might say that there is a tendency for people to say, "Anything that I am capable of understanding cannot be worth understanding." Maimonides understood that this attraction to that which transcends understanding stems from a sense of insecurity about the powers of one's intellect; anything that falls within the purview of our understanding is automatically thought of as unimportant. Throughout the *Guide*, the Rambam argues against such feelings of inferiority about the human mind. Time and again he stresses that intellect is central for the full realization of religious life.

The Rambam interprets the concept "the image of God that is in man" as being the understanding. This threefold identification between God, the essence of the human being, and the intellect is at the heart of the Rambam's teaching. Identifying the godly in human beings as our minds does not diminish God; it exalts our intellects. The essential religious act is not one of transcending understanding, but of rising to the level of understanding.

In the first part of this book we saw how the foundational ideas of Judaism are consistent with rationality. In the second part I have sought to show how divine revelation is a revelation of reason. The gap between reason and revelation has been erased, and with it, apparently, human perplexity. In part 3, however, we will see that Rambam identified deeper sources of perplexity elsewhere in the human condition.

PART 3
PERPLEXITY

The Guide for the Perplexed is, as its title declares, directed toward those who are perplexed. As Maimonides writes about the book in his introduction,

> Its purpose is to give indications to a religious man, for whom the validity of our Law has become established in his soul, and has become actual in his belief—such a man being perfect in his religion and character, and having studied the sciences of the philosophers and come to know what they signify. The human intellect having drawn him on, and led him to dwell within its province, he must have felt distressed by the externals of the Law and by the meanings of the above-mentioned equivocal, derivative or amphibolous terms, as he continued to understand them himself, or was made to understand them by others, hence he would remain in a state of perplexity and confusion. (*Guide*, introduction, 5)

The *Guide* is aimed at those who grew up within Jewish tradition, were exposed to the achievements of science and philosophy, and felt that the contrast between Judaism and the surrounding culture required them to choose one or the other. Make no mistake, the person to whom the *Guide* is addressed is no ordinary man; the Rambam emphasizes that he is an exceptional individual:

To sum up, I am the man who when the concern pressed him and his way was straitened and he could find no other device by which to teach a demonstrated truth other than by giving satisfaction to a single virtuous man while displeasing ten thousand ignoramuses—I am he who prefers to address the single man by himself, and I do not heed the blame of those many creatures. For I claim to liberate that virtuous one from that into which he has sunk, and I shall guide him in his perplexity until he becomes perfect and finds rest. (*Guide*, introduction, 16–17)

10

CONTRADICTIONS

The perplexity in the *Guide* stems from confusion about the gaps, and sometimes contradictions, between two bodies of knowledge: Jewish tradition on the one hand and science and philosophy on the other. This is essentially a problem about reconciling two fundamentally different sources of knowledge: revelation and reason. Religious scriptures and traditions derive their authority from exceptional moments in which God revealed Himself to chosen individuals and communicated to them a body of doctrine and instruction. The knowledge that was thus conveyed was turned into a corpus of holy writings that was then accessible to people, including those of future generations, who had not experienced the revelation. Aristotelian philosophy, in contrast, sought to employ reason to answer the big questions about the world. Its insights were collected into books of thought, to which new insights were continually added over time, creating the body of knowledge that is philosophy. Someone who is seeking the ultimate source of authority must choose, in effect, between God and man.

On first impression, the goal of the *Guide* seems to be to resolve the tension between these two sources. Through innovative interpretations of biblical beliefs, the Rambam identified the core of philosophical truth that they contain. Moreover, throughout the book he elucidates the nature of revelation: it is not an alternative to reason as a source of knowledge about the world, he explains, but rather an achievement of reason itself. Turning revelation into the most elevated expression of reason collapses the barriers between two worlds of authority and overcomes the perplexity arising from the apparent tensions between them.

However, the deeper a reader swims in the *Guide*, the more he becomes aware of a new and more serious kind of perplexity—that which lies within reason itself. The writings of Aristotle, which some had thought to comprise the sum of all human wisdom, turned out not to contain exhaustive and reliable truth about reality after all. In particular, the field of astronomy, upon which metaphysics had been based, was shown to be seriously flawed. This undermined the whole intellectual structure that had been built on it.

In one of the pivotal sections of the *Guide*, the Rambam describes the intellectual quandary in which he found himself as a result of the collapse of the certainty of astronomy: "The extreme predilection that I have for investigating the truth is evidenced by the fact that I have explicitly stated and reported my perplexity regarding these matters" (*Guide*, 2:24). This puzzlement had an impact on many of the great questions of philosophy: What is the structure of the universe? Was the universe created, or has it existed forever? Is there a God? Is there life after death? All of these questions were subject to deep philosophical disagreements, arguments that demonstrated the inherent limits of reason. The perplexity of reason itself is the subject of this final section of the book.

The *Guide* is a masterpiece of careful and precise writing, and its goal is to lead the reader on a long and sometimes discomfiting journey. The reader is meant to arrive at the end of the book having acquired new understandings of human existence, including some that are likely to shake up his comfortable assumptions.

The Rambam laid out five approaches to providence, three possible positions with regard to prophecy, and three different ways of understanding creation. This diversity of opinions in the *Guide* has fostered lively disagreement over the centuries about what Maimonides *really* thought. There were some who understood him to be an Aristotelian philosopher, others who took him to be a mystic, and still others who thought he was a conservative traditionalist. The *Guide*, which presented so many arguments, itself became a focus of intense argument. Why did the Rambam obscure his real opinions? Surely not for the reason that the book of Job does. The Rambam claimed that there are fundamental theological questions inherent in the book of Job that had been obscured by the author, who did not wish the masses to know that basic issues of faith are subject to controversy:

> Together with that notion, he [Elihu] says all that they have said . . . namely Job and his three friends . . . as I have mentioned to you, the notion expressed by another among them. This is done in order to hide the notion that is peculiar to the opinion of each individual, so that at first it occurs to the multitude that all the interlocutors are agreed on the selfsame opinion; however, this is not so. (*Guide*, 3:23)

But in the *Guide*, Maimonides has no qualms about revealing the existence of such disagreements. We can gain an inkling of why he does this from the Rambam's halakhic work, the *Mishneh Torah*. Whereas the talmudic tradition is full of arguments about halakhic issues, the *Mishneh Torah* simply presented the final halakhic decisions shorn of the talmudic disputes that lay behind them. In a letter to Rabbi Pinchas the Judge, the Rambam explained that he omitted the underlying arguments because he wished to accord *halakhah* absolute authority. Arguments may awaken questions and doubts about the binding force of the halakhic norms and so weaken people's commitment to keeping them. *The Guide for the Perplexed*, on the other hand, which explicitly sets out a range of different opinions and arguments, was written with the goal of undermining the reader's absolute commitment to any one point of view.

Moreover, in a number of places the Rambam expresses conflicting views. He surely understood that these tensions would arouse doubts and questions as to the real doctrine of the *Guide*. It appears that this deliberate ambiguity was part of his purpose. But why?

Generations of interpreters of the *Guide* concluded that that when the Rambam planted two inconsistent opinions in the text he actually believed one of them to be incorrect and placed it there in order to camouflage his true view. However, there is another possibility—that Maimonides himself was genuinely undecided about which of the two positions was correct.

In an important article, Yair Lorberbaum develops a striking insight.[1] The conventional view is that this kind of contradiction appears in the *Guide* in order to conceal the Rambam's true position by presenting a contradictory view as a sort of a smoke screen. Loeberbaum shows that this is not always the case. There are some instances of contradiction in the *Guide* where the Rambam identified himself completely with one of the two views. However, there are many other instances where he appears to make two contradictory claims. The *Guide* is the canvas upon which Maimonides worked out his own greatest philosophical dilemmas. He did not choose one position or the other, but rather inhabited the tension between them.

The struggles of interpreting the *Guide* are the struggles of the *Guide* itself. In the following chapters we will examine the contradictions of the *Guide* and see how the Rambam used them as a tool for presenting his own central dilemmas about the world, about God, and about humanity.

11

THE CREATION
OF THE WORLD

The concept of creation has always been a philosophical battlefield, and particularly so in the Middle Ages. Was the world created from nothing at a certain moment in time? Has it always existed? Some of the most fundamental theological problems turn on the issue of creation. It, of course, implicates questions about the nature of God, the role of miracles, and the possibility of human free will. In the *Guide*, the Rambam took up the issue of creation in the last six chapters of part 1 and continued to address them at least through chapter 25 of part 2.

The effort to demonstrate rationally that the world had been created was associated primarily with a strain of Islamic thought known as the kalām. The proof of creation lay at the heart of kalām theology and served as a basis for other essential beliefs. From it was derived a proof of God's unity, and from God's unity flowed the principle of God's incorporeality.[1]

The threefold proof of creation, of God's unity, and of God's incorporeality is found in many medieval theological texts.[2] The Rambam gathered different versions of the proof and summarized them in three chapters of the *Guide* (1:74–76). First, though, he purged the arguments of the florid rhetoric in which they were usually garbed:

> Do not demand of me that I set them forth in their terminology and at such length as they do. However, I will inform you of what every one

of them intends and of the method he uses in order to adduce proof establishing the creation of the world in time or refuting its eternity. I shall draw your attention with brevity to the premises used by the author of each method. When you shall read their lengthy books and famous works, you shall not find in them in any respect, in the proofs they adduce with regard to the subject in question, a single notion in addition to what you will understand from my exposition here. However, you shall find a lengthier exposition and resplendent and fine diction. Sometimes they used rhymed prose and symmetrical words and choose eloquent language. Sometime also they make their diction obscure intending to astonish the listener and to strike terror into the student. (*Guide*, 1:74)

The Rambam enumerated seven different variations of the kalām's proof that the universe was created. I will sketch just one of them.

A glance at the world suffices to show that many objects renew themselves. A fertilized egg becomes a human being, a date pit grows into a date tree, and so forth. The inference is that if renewal is a characteristic of things in the world, then it also applies to the world as a whole:

Some of them think that any single happening occurring in time may be adduced as proof that the world has been created in time. . . . [T]he same inference, he says, applies to the world as a whole. Thus you say that he believes that whatever rule may be found with regard to one particular body must necessarily be applied to everybody. (*Guide*, 1:74)

The Rambam attacked this argument, just as he refuted the six other "proofs" that the world was created. Maimonides did not think that all of the arguments of the Mutakallimun (followers of the kalām) were completely invalid; he regarded some of them as being more convincing than others. However, none of them was a decisive demonstration. It was enough to be able to cast reasonable doubt on the arguments of the kalām in order to be refute their claim to be offering absolute, decisive proofs.

After claiming to prove that the world had been created, the Mutakallimun went on to try and derive from this the principle of God's unity. The Rambam gathered together five of their attempts to deduce God's unity from creation, but he found that these arguments too were not convincing. He also criticized their efforts to derive God's incorporeality from the principle of His unity. One can gauge the Rambam's impatience with these arguments from his praise of one of the sages of the kalām who claimed that ultimately we can only base our belief in the world's creation upon the authority of religious sources and scriptures:

> One of the Mutakallimun was so wearied by those tricks that he affirmed that the belief in unity was accepted by virtue of the Law. The Mutakallimun considered this statement as very disgraceful and despised him who made it. As for me, I am of the opinion that he among them who made this statement was a man of a most rightly directed mind, averse to the acceptance of sophistries. Accordingly, as he did not hear in their speech anything that was in truth a demonstration and found that his soul was not at peace with what they considered a demonstration, he said that the belief in unity was a thing accepted from the Law. (*Guide*, 1:75)

The greatness of this theologian, according to the Rambam, was that he had freed himself from the self-deception that led others to treat inadequate arguments for the creation of the world as convincing. This self-deception stems from a desire to believe in the creation of the world, and it manifests itself in an inability to distinguish between proofs that are truly rigorous and those which are not.

The Rambam's broader critique of the arguments of the kalām is that they undermine belief in the stability of scientific laws and thereby cripple our ability to derive any theological conclusions from nature. Only if the natural world is stable and regular can we make reliable inferences from our observations of its operation. According to the Rambam, the kalām's proofs are ultimately self-defeating. The conclusions undermine the premises:

Your soul should not be led into error by the circumstances of these men engaged in speculation, neither by what has happened to them, nor by what has come from them. For they are like one who flees from torrid heat into fire. For they have abolished the nature of being and have altered the original disposition of the heavens and earth by thinking that by means of these premises, it would be demonstrated that the world was created in time. In consequence whereof, they have not demonstrated the creation of the world in time and have destroyed for us the demonstrations of the existence and oneness of the deity and of the negation of His corporeality. For the demonstrations, by means of which all this can be made clear, can only be taken from the permanent nature of what exists, a nature that can be seen and apprehended by the senses and the intellect. (*Guide*, 1:76)

The implication here is that someone who seeks firm proofs regarding the issue of whether the world was created would be better advised to search for them in the work of those thinkers who believed that the world was eternal, stable, and hence predictable.

THE ETERNITY OF THE WORLD

According to Aristotle and his followers, it is logically impossible for the world to have been created. For them, the idea of creation was as absurd as the notion that two plus two could equal eighteen. In the *Guide*, the Rambam presented four proofs for the eternity of the world that he attributed to Aristotle, and a further four that he attributed to Aristotle's students. In the Middle Ages, each of these proofs was thought to be a decisive demonstration that the world was eternal. Let us look at Maimonides's discussion of two of these proofs. The first one is from Aristotle:

He [Aristotle] asserts that the matter of the heavens as a whole has no contraries, for circular motion has no contrary, as has been made clear; and there are contraries only in rectilinear motion, as has been demonstrated. He asserts further that in everything that passes away, the cause of its passing away consists in there being contraries in it.

Accordingly, as there are no contraries in the sphere, it is not subject to passing away. Now, what is not subject to passing away is likewise not subject to generation. He thus stated several propositions in an absolute manner and explained them. These propositions are:

> Everything that is subject to generation is subject to passing away.
> Everything that is subject to passing away is subject to generation.
> Everything that has not been generated will not pass away.
> Everything that will not pass away has not been generated. (*Guide*, 2:14)

According to Aristotle, stability is divine, and stasis is a sign of perfection. The material world, in contrast, is always in motion. The only type of motion that is stable (and in this respect resembles rest) is motion in a circle. Circular motion, unlike linear movement, is constant and unchanging. The motion of the spheres is circular, and therefore it partakes in perfection.

Any alteration in motion, according to the Aristotelians, is an indication of decay. Indeed, alteration is not just a sign of decay but also its cause. The perfect, unchanging, and (as people believed then) circular paths of heavenly beings were a sign that they were not subject to degeneration. From the then-accepted fact that heavenly bodies do not decay, philosophers also deduced that they had never come into being. From the perfect motion of the spheres, Aristotle inferred their eternal existence.

Another attempt to prove that the world was not created, one that was highly influential in the Middle Ages, derived the eternity of the world from God's perfection. Although Aristotle did not develop this proof himself, it became part of mainstream Aristotelian thought:

> He asserts—though he does not do so textually—but this is what his opinion comes to—that in his opinion it would be an impossibility that will should change in God or a new volition arise in Him; and that all that exists has been brought into existence, in the state in which it is at present, by God through His volition; but that it was not produced after having been in a state of non-existence. He thinks that just as it is impossible that the deity should become non-existent or that His

essence should undergo a change, it is impossible that volition should undergo a change in Him or a new will arise in Him. Accordingly, it follows necessarily that this being as a whole has never ceased to be as it is at present and will be as it is in the future eternity. (*Guide*, 2:13)

The medieval philosophers understood the word "God" to represent absolute perfection: God is flawless and complete. His absolute perfection precludes any notion of God's developing or fulfilling potential. The notion of "will" indicates a lack of perfection; will suggests an ambition for something that is not; a God who wills is an oxymoron, because if He wills something He is not perfect, and therefore is not God. The assumption that the world was created necessarily assumes that at a certain point in time God revealed a desire to create the world. God's perfection makes the creation of the world an impossibility. As the Rambam expressed it,

> They say: An agent acts at one time and does not act at another only because of the impediments or incentives that may supervene upon him or in him. For the impediments may render necessary the non-accomplishment of a certain action that the agent wishes to accomplish, and on the other hand, the incentives may render necessary a certain wish that the agent did not have before. Now as the Creator, may His name be sublime, has no incentives necessitating the alteration or a will, not hindrances or impediments that supervene and cease to exist, there is no reason in respect of which He should act at one time and not act at another; but on the contrary His action exists, just as His presence does, permanently in actu. (*Guide*, 2:14)

To summarize: the philosophers inferred the eternity of the world based on the perfect motion of the heavenly bodies and also upon the perfection of God.

OBJECTIONS TO THE
IDEA OF THE ETERNITY OF THE WORLD

The Rambam thought there was considerable force in the philosophical arguments for the eternity of the world, yet he was not wholly convinced by them. His goal in the *Guide* was not to refute these arguments but to sow seeds of doubt that would weaken the Aristotelian position that the eternity of the world had been decisively demonstrated. Aristotelians regarded creation as a logical absurdity; the Rambam's aim was to make creation once again a reasonable possibility. Let us look at two of the arguments that the Rambam used to challenge the Aristotelian proofs.

In a famous parable, the Rambam compared humankind to a young man who grew up on a desert island:

> Assume, according to an example we have made, that a man of a most perfect disposition was born and that his mother died after she had suckled him for several months. And the man, alone on an isolated island, took upon himself the entire upbringing of him who was born, until he grew up, became intelligent, and acquired knowledge. Now this child had never seen a woman or a female of one of the species of the other animals. (*Guide*, 2:17)

The parable tells of a man who never learned the most basic facts about how people come into the world. All his life he has encountered only fully grown people; he has never seen a baby being born. Such a man, when asked how human beings come into existence, cannot even conceive of the true explanation—that each originates as a seed implanted in the womb of a woman.

> Accordingly, he puts a question, saying to a man who is with him: how did we come to exist, and in what way were we generated? Thereupon, the man to whom the question was put replied: Every individual among us was generated in the belly of an individual belonging like us to our species, an individual who is female and has such and such a form. Every individual among us was—being small in body—within the belly, was moved and fed there, and grew up little by little—being alive, until it reached such and such a limit in size. Thereupon an opening was opened for him the lower part of the body, from which he issued and came forth. Thereupon he does not cease growing until he becomes such as you see that we are. Now the orphaned child must of necessity put the question: Did every individual among us—when he was little,

contained within a belly, but alive and moving and growing—did he eat, breathe through the mouth and nose, produce excrements? He is answered, "No." Thereupon he indubitably will hasten to set this down as a lie and will draw a demonstration that all these true statements are impossible, drawing inferences from perfect beings that have achieved stability. He will say: If any individual among us were deprived of breath for the fraction of an hour, he would die, and his movements would cease. How then can one conceive that an individual among us could be for months within a thick vessel surrounding him, which is within a body, and yet be alive and in motion? (*Guide*, 2:17)

The process of a thing's *coming into existence* may be very different from the processes of that thing's existence itself. In the Rambam's example, an embryo gestates within its mother's belly, eating and excreting within another body. This is a strange state, unlike what that occurs outside the womb. From observing human life post utero, one cannot infer how people come into being. The fundamental weakness of the Aristotelians was that they looked at the world and derived conclusions about how it came into existence (or how it did not come into existence). It is impossible to derive any conclusions about the world-in-potential from its characteristics as they appear in actuality. The Rambam identified a failure of inductive argument here. Similar to the modern philosophy of science, which points out the problems in attempting to predict the future based on data about the past, the Rambam exposed the pitfalls of trying to describe the primordial past based on observations about the present.

Another of the proofs that the Rambam challenged sought to derive the eternity of the world from God's absolute perfection. The underlying premise of this argument was that "will" is evidence of imperfection and that therefore a perfect God could not have suddenly willed the creation of the world. The Rambam argued that this assumption needed to be reexamined. It is true that human will or desire is typically a response to some lack or need and is aroused by external factors. So, for example, talk about food tends to make the listener feel hungry, and knowledge of social deprivation awakens a desire to do something about it. Human will is affected by our surroundings. However, when we attribute "will" to God, we are talking about something different. Divine will is spontaneous. It is an active will that is not conditioned by the environment. No one can predict God's will, because it is subject to no laws. The fact that God wills something does not show that God is subject to external causes, but rather that God is an independent cause. Since God's will is quite unlike human will, the notion of God's creating the world need not imply any kind of imperfection in God:

It is difficult to resolve this doubt, and the solution is subtle. Hear it. Know that every agent endowed with will, who performs his acts for the sake of something, must of necessity act at a certain time and not act at another time because of impediments or supervening accidents. To take an example: a man, for instance, may wish to have a house, but does not build it because of impediments—if the building materials are not at hand, or if they, being at hand, have not been prepared for receiving the form because of the absence of tools. Sometimes, too, both the materials and tools are at hand, but the man does not build, because he does not wish to build since he can dispense with a shelter. If, however, accidents like heat or cold supervene, he is compelled to seek a shelter, whereupon he will wish to build. It has thus become clear that supervening accidents may change the will and that impediments may oppose the will in such a way that it is not executed. All this, however, only occurs when acts are in the service of something that is external to the essence of the will. If, however the act has no purpose whatever, except to be consequent upon will that will has no need for incentives. And the one who wills is not obliged, even if there are no impediments, to act always. For there is no external end for which he acts and that would render it necessary to act whenever there are no impediments preventing the attainment of the end. For in the case envisaged, the act is consequent upon the will alone.

Somebody might object: all this is correct, but does not the supposition that one wishes at one time and does not wish at another time imply in itself a change? We shall reply to him, "No, for the true reality and the quiddity of will means: to will and not to will. If the will in question belongs to some material being so that some external end is sought thereby, then the will is subject to change because of impediments and supervening accidents. But as for a being separate from matter, its will, which does not exist in any respect for the sake of some other thing, is not subject to change. The fact that it may wish one thing now and another thing tomorrow does not constitute a change in its essence and does not call for another cause; just as the fact that it acts at one time and does not act at another does not constitute a change, as we have explained. (*Guide*, 2:18)

God's will, unlike man's, is spontaneous, self-creating, and not determined by anything external. There can be no explanation for creation except that it was God's will to create the world. This will, uncaused by anything outside of God, is not evidence for any imperfection on God's part. Thus the Aristotelians have no conclusive proof that the world was not created. Their conclusion cannot be logically derived either from the motion of the heavenly bodies or from God's perfection. Their belief that the world is eternal is open to legitimate question.

THE PERPLEXITY OF THE WORLD

Having considered the limitations of both the arguments for creation and the arguments for the eternity of the world, the Rambam proceeded to advance an original set of views in favor of creation. His approach here was an unusual one in his cultural milieu. He did not try to give absolute proofs for creation but rather to show that it was a plausible belief and a more reasonable hypothesis than the theory of the world's eternal existence.

Belief in the eternity of the world rested on a prior assumption that the laws of nature are absolutely binding and that nothing happens in the world that is not subject to these laws. However, the astronomy of the Middle Ages identified a threat to the laws of nature in the form of certain bodies whose motion could not be explained according to the reigning scientific knowledge of the time. The most prominent example of this medieval "uncertainty principle" was the motion of the stars. Aristotelian physics could explain why the heavenly bodies moved; it could even explain why they moved in circles. However, it could not explain the specific direction of movement, or why the heavenly bodies did not move in the opposite direction. The direction and also the speed of these bodies' motion were felt to be islands of non-rationality within an otherwise rational cosmos.[3]

These chaotic "pockets" of existence that were not susceptible to rational explanation could be taken as evidence of another principle in addition to scientific laws: the will of God. If nature contained phenomena that were outside the range of scientific explanation, then it appeared reasonable to believe that God sometimes intervened directly in the world.

Aristotle and his students claimed that there is an absolute order in nature. Epicurus, on the other hand, argued that there is no order in the world whatever. The Rambam's position, based on empirical observation, was that neither of these two opposing sides is entirely correct. There is indeed a wondrous order in the world, but it is not absolute. Conversely, there are indeed pockets of chaos in the cosmos, but the chaos is not absolute either. The Rambam concluded there is a divinely created order in the world but that this order was not absolute; it could not explain all observable phenomena.

Maimonides did not assert his position unequivocally, but he did claim that it was the most reasonable view. Reason cannot determine conclusively which side is right. This kind of uncertainty also characterized the Rambam's conclusions regarding God.

The Necessity of God

The Rambam presented his readers with twin proofs for the existence of God: one was based on the assumption that the world was created, and the other was based on the premise that the world has always existed. Thus he attempted to free theology from dependence on the question of how the world came to be. Whether or not the world was created, God still exists:

> I shall say: the world cannot but be either eternal or created in time. If it is created in time, it undoubtedly has a creator who created it in time. For it is a first intelligible that what has appeared at a certain moment in time has not created itself in time and that its creator is other than itself. Accordingly, the creator who created the world in time is the deity. If, however the world is eternal, it follows necessarily because of this and that proof that there is an existent other than all the bodies to be found in the world; an existent who is not a body and not a force in a body and who is one, permanent and sempiternal; who has no cause and whose becoming subject to change is impossible. Accordingly He is a deity. Thus it has become manifest to you that the proofs for the existence and oneness of the deity and His not being a body ought to be procured from the starting point afforded by the supposition of the eternity of the world, for in this way the demonstration will be perfect, both if the world is eternal and if it is created in time. (*Guide*, 1:71)

The Rambam asserted the certainty of God's existence, even in the absence of a compelling proof for the creation of the world. By means of this dual proof—valid whether the world was created or not, the Rambam immunized God's existence against doubt. Or at least, so it seems at first sight. However, as Warren Zev Harvey has shown, reading between the lines of the *Guide* raises fresh questions.[4]

The proof based on the assumption of creation is straightforward: if the world was created, it cannot have created itself, because then it would have had to exist before its own creation, which is logically absurd. Therefore, if the world was created, it must have had a creator.[5]

The problem here is that although creation requires a creator, it does not necessarily imply the existence of the one God. The Rambam himself cast doubt on the proof of the kalām that purported to connect creation to the unity of God.[6] If the world was created, that means that "something" created it, but that "something" is not necessarily "one," and moreover, the "something" could be a physical entity. This implies that the creator of the Rambam need not be identical to the God of the Rambam.

The proof based on the eternity of the world suffers from the opposite problem. It does indeed demonstrate that God is a unity and that He has no body, but it does not necessarily follow that the world has always existed.

The Rambam could not protect the existence of God from doubt. There is no certainty about His existence, whether one assumes creation or the world's eternity. Maimonides might have rescued his readers from this perplexity by means of a third proof that he adduced, which appeared to rely neither on the assumption that the world was created nor on its eternal existence. This additional demonstration of God's existence was known as the metaphysical proof for God. It had a previous history. It was deployed by Ibn Sina,[7] who preceded Maimonides. However, as Harvey has shown, the Rambam modified the proof. While Ibn Sina's version was purely conceptual, the Rambam's argument depended in part on what we can observe about the world.

> If every existent falls under generation and corruption, then all the existents and every one of them have the possibility of undergoing corruption. Now it is indubitable, as you know, that what is possible with regards to a species must necessarily come about. Thus it follows necessarily that they, I mean all existents, will necessarily undergo corruption. Now, if all of them have undergone corruption, it would be impossible that anything exists, for there would remain no one who could bring anything into existence. Hence it follows necessarily that there would be no existent thing at all. Now we perceive things that are existent. Hence it follows necessarily that if there are, as we perceive, existents subject to generation and corruption, there must be a certain existent that is not subject to generation and corruption. Now in this existent that is not subject to generation and corruption, there is no possibility of corruption at all; rather its existence is necessary, not possible. (*Guide*, 2:1)

The Rambam's proof begins with an answer to a famous philosophical question: What kinds of existents populate the world? The point of this question is to determine whether there are any necessary existents—entities whose existence does not depend on anything external to them. In the first part of this book we saw that, according to the Rambam, there are three kinds of entities: impossible existents, possible existents, and necessary existents. The Rambam asks: If there were possible existents but no necessary existents, could the world exist? His answer was that it could not. From this it follows that if the world exists, then there is some necessary existent that sustains it. Let us try and reconstruct the Rambam's argument.

His proof is based on two central premises:

1. A possible existent is one that could exist and also could not exist. The absence of this thing from the world is a real possibility. For example, my writing desk exists, but it would also be possible for it not to. One may perfectly well imagine the desk being destroyed, for example.[8]

2. In the infinite span of time, anything that is possible will eventually be realized. If there is a possibility, even a remote one that something will happen to a certain object, then on the assumption that time is infinite, that possibility will ultimately be realized at some point in time.

If we join these premises together, we can say that over an infinite span of time, every possible existent will ultimately decay and fall into non-existence. From this it follows that if all of existence is comprised of possible existents then ultimately everything must become extinct. Maimonides's conclusion is that since the world exists, there must be things that are not merely possible but are necessary and which sustain existence, for otherwise everything would ultimately fall into decay and extinction.

This conclusion requires a third assumption, which the Rambam does not state explicitly: that the world exists for an infinite span of time. An infinite amount of time is necessary for all of the infinite possibilities of existence—including the decay and extinction of everything—to be actualized. Therefore, the claim that without a necessary existent everything would have become extinct *depends on the assumption that the world has existed eternally*. Harvey's point is that the metaphysical argument for God's existence, which was meant to be a compelling proof regardless of your view about how the world came into existence, turns out to rely on the assumption of the world's eternity. However, as we have seen, this assumption is open to doubt and therefore the metaphysical proof is not decisive.

The Rambam explicitly articulated an impasse regarding the question of the world's creation. We can now see that he was also implicitly skeptical about proofs for the existence of God. It is not that the Rambam thought that God did not exist; on the contrary, he believed that God's existence is the most reasonable explanation for the universe. But it seems that he was suggesting that we are not dealing here with absolute proofs.[9]

The reader who has navigated all of Maimonides's hidden and revealed assumptions and reached these conclusions may confront an intellectual crisis. After a long, complex, and sometimes dry discussion that extends over many of chapters of the *Guide*, the reader who has successfully followed the arguments recognizes that he does not know how the world came into existence and cannot even have certainty about the existence of God.

12

PERPLEXITY AND GOD

The *Guide for the Perplexed* is a journey toward knowledge of God. Its path to knowing God begins with cleaning up religious language. In the Rambam's view, misunderstanding the language of the Bible is a major cause of misconceptions about God. Scripture entraps its readers with anthropomorphic, physical images of the divine. People forget that these are merely images and not the reality of God.

One of the most startling insights the *Guide* offers is that the Torah, which was supposed to purge human consciousness of idolatry, actually played a role in strengthening a certain kind of idolatrous consciousness, by entrenching in people's minds the anthropomorphic images that it uses. This idea is repeated a number of times in the *Guide*:

> Several groups of people pursued the likening of God to other beings and believed Him to be a body endowed with attributes. Another group raised themselves above this consequence and denied His being a body, but preserved the attributes. All this was rendered necessary by their keeping to the external sense of the revealed books as I shall make clear in later chapters that will deal with these notions. (*Guide*, 1:51)

Misreading of the Holy Scriptures themselves can cause misleading ideas to enter human consciousness.

Freeing Religious Awareness from Language

The Rambam views efforts to describe God in human language as being even worse than idol worship:

[One who believes] that He is a body, or that He is subject to affections; or again that he ascribes to God some deficiency or other. Such a man is indubitably more blameworthy than a worshipper of idols. (*Guide*, 1:36)[1]

Relating to God as a physical being is a serious error in the Rambam's eyes, but it is also a human weakness. People tend to believe in a corporeal God because, to them, existence usually *means* physical existence. If you say to them that God is not physical, it is difficult to understand this statement except as a denial that God exists. It is very hard for humans to free themselves from ingrained patterns of speech. In this case, we are talking about linguistic habits that have become entrenched over many years and that condition the way people think.

A profound change in human consciousness almost always happens gradually. As we saw, the Rambam argued that the Torah sanctioned the offering of sacrifices because it is futile to wage a frontal assault against powerful, long-standing practices. Similarly, the Torah could not destroy in one stroke the human inclination to represent God in human terms. The Torah appropriated anthropocentric language to reach the pagan mentality that conceives of Him as corporeal ("The minds of the multitude were accordingly guided to the belief that He exists by imagining that He is corporeal" [*Guide*, 1:46]).

The same paradigm we used to explain the reasons for the Torah's commandments concerning sacrifices also helps us to understand the issue of anthropomorphic language. The Torah used humanizing language to describe God in order to educate the masses about His existence. The ultimate goal, however, was to enable people to free themselves from the pagan mind-set. The Torah seized the weapons of its intellectual adversary in order to defeat the opposing worldview. However, in the Rambam's view this move had not been wholly successful. When he attempted to explain the pull to conceive of God in physical form, he eschewed psychological explanations and instead identified the cause as literal reading of scripture:

The reasons that led those who believe in the existence of attributes belonging to the Creator to this belief are akin to those that led those who believe in the doctrine of His corporeality to that belief. For he who believes in this doctrine was not led to it by intellectual speculation; he merely followed the external sense of the texts of the Scriptures. This is also the case with regard to the attributes. For inasmuch as the books of the prophets and the revealed books existed, which predicated attributive qualifications of him, may He be exalted, these were taken in their literal sense; and He was believed to possess attributes. (*Guide*, 1:53)[2]

God is beyond language, yet the Torah has no medium other than words to represent God. An ancient Eastern parable tells of a teacher who points his finger at the moon, causing people around him to look at the finger. Similarly, the Torah uses words to gesture at God, who transcends language. So the first task of the *Guide* in paving a way to know God was to free human thought from limiting linguistic habits by reinterpreting traditional, corporeal language applied to the divine.

The Doctrine of Negative Attributes
Part 1 of the *Guide* is dedicated to this task of freeing human consciousness from the misleading effects of religious language. The early chapters of part 1 focus on the ways that language distorts our conception of God. The Rambam's discussion of an exalted God who is absolutely separate from the world reaches its purest expression in the doctrine of negative attributes, which we discussed in chapter 1. Every word that is used to talk about God effectively places God and the world in the same category. Removing God from language expresses His absolute otherness from the world.

But the negation of God-language is not the Rambam's last word about God in the *Guide*. After developing his theory of a God who utterly transcends words, Maimonides surprises his readers with a quite different definition of the divine: God as intellect.

The Rambam's Other God

The Rambam also presents a positive definition of God—God is the intellect that is perfectly united with its knowledge:

> You already know that the following dictum of the philosophers with reference to God, may He be exalted, is generally admitted: the dictum being that He is the intellect as well as the intellectually cognizing subject, and the intellectually cognized object. And that those three notions form, in Him, may He be exalted, one single notion in which there is no multiplicity. We have mentioned this likewise in our great compilation, since this, as we have made clear there, is one of the great foundations of our Law; I mean the fact that He is one only and that no other thing can be added to Him, I mean to say that there is no external thing other than He. (*Guide*, 1:68)

Understanding, according to Aristotle and his interpreters, is the intertwining of intellect with its objects. When a person understands something, his consciousness unites with the things that are understood. However, after a person completes the act of understanding, the gap between consciousness and its object reappears.

When we are speaking about God, however, the gap never reappears. God is the intellect that is always active. God is one with all the objects of God's understanding; it is impossible to make any distinction between God and what God knows. This is not the place for an in-depth exploration of the Aristotelian concept of intellect;[3] nevertheless, it is clear that this theory, which the Rambam appropriates, presents us with an additional way of understanding God; God as intellect, or, in the language of the Middle Ages, "intellect as well as the intellectually cognizing subject, and the intellectually cognized object."

There is a close connection between the Rambam's discussion of God as intellect in part 1, chapter 68 of the *Guide* and in the opening chapter of the book. In chapter 1, Maimonides defines man as intellect; in chapter 68, he defines God as intellect. In chapter 1, he characterizes intellect as divine, as the image of God in man; in chapter 68, he describes the divine intellect by analogy with human processes of understanding. This concept, which has been called "intellectual pantheism,"[4] brings God and humanity very close together; we are essentially intellect, and so is God. The difference is that God's intellect is absolutely united with its knowledge, whereas human intellect is not united in this way with what it knows.

The Rambam gave his readers two different versions of God. The first utterly transcends intellect, while the second *is* intellect. The first is totally beyond language, while the second can be encapsulated in a concise definition. The first is absolutely other, while the second is highly accessible. This glaring contradiction baffled generations of readers, scholars, and interpreters. Throughout history, many attempts have been made to resolve it.[5]

The concept of God as an intellect that is wholly united with its knowledge opened the door to new directions in theology. In his *Ethics*, Spinoza suggested that his radical, pantheistic ideas about the unity of God and the world had Jewish roots. He likely was referring to Maimonides, one of the figures who influenced him most profoundly. Apparently, one should understand Spinoza's interpretation of the *Guide* as follows: the Rambam appropriated the Aristotelian idea that in thought the intellect unites with its objects, but rejected the notion that God thinks Himself.[6] Rather, God thinks the world. That is to say, God, who is the intellect that is united with its knowledge of the world, is essentially God who is united with the world. Maimonides did not say this explicitly. However, taking his words one small step further would push his identification of God with intellect into identification of God with the world and turn Rambam the Aristotelian into a Spinozan.

The two theological options advanced by the *Guide* are at opposite ends of the spectrum of Jewish ideas about God. The first option, God as intellect, is a mere step away from pantheism, the identification of God with the world, while the second option, the doctrine of negative attributes, creates an absolute separation between God and the world.

I do not believe that the pantheistic approach represents the Rambam's true opinion. It seems to me that the dominant approach in the *Guide* is the doctrine of negative attributes. Yet, although the Rambam did not subscribe to the view that identified God with intellect, it was nevertheless important to him to present this view to the reader.

A Confluence of Two Streams in Philosophy

The "two Gods" of the *Guide* reflect the influence of two great philosophical traditions of the Middle Ages: the Aristotelian and Neoplatonic schools. Aristotle conceived God as the intellect that is fully united with its knowledge, whereas the sources for the doctrine of negative attributes may be found in the writings of the third-century Neoplatonic thinker Plotinus, who was influenced by both Plato and Aristotle.

One of the main subjects of Plotinus's thought is the structure of existence. Plotinus argued that the universe has one source, in which everything began and from which everything flows. The source of everything is the One. Plotinus's description of the One echoes the Rambam's concept of God in several respects. As we discussed in part 1, the Rambam believed that the oneness of God is qualitatively different from anything else that we call "one." Anything in our physical reality that appears to us as one can in fact be divided. This is true of everything in the world, whereas God is ultimate, irreducible oneness. Plotinus is the source of this aspect of the Rambam's thought. Indeed, he was not just the source of inspiration for the doctrine of negative attributes; he was also the first to articulate the idea in the form in which the Rambam later presented it.

> From here, one who negates any description of the One and does not give any definition of it, simply assumes its existence, without attributing anything to it (as do those preachers whose praises actually diminish its honor, as their praises are beneath its dignity, because they are incapable of finding fitting words).[7]

To reinforce his position, the Rambam quoted the talmudic story about a prayer leader who used a long string of adjectives to describe God. Like the Talmud, the Rambam harshly attacked the man in the story. Attributing a mass of adjectives to God does not add to His glory; it detracts from it. Silence is the only fitting praise for God. Negative theology, which took its first steps in the writings of Plotinus, reached maturity in the thought of medieval thinkers like Al-Farabi and Ibn Sina, and it was central to Maimonides, who placed it at the center of his thinking.

Much of medieval philosophy derives from Aristotelianism and the Neoplatonic thought originated by Plotinus. Sometimes it is difficult to distinguish between the two, both because Plotinus himself was an important interpreter of Aristotle who integrated Aristotelian ideas into his thought, and also because in the Middle Ages, syntheses of Aristotle and Plotinus emerged. For most of the medieval period, the Neoplatonic stream dominated Jewish thought. However, in the twelfth century the Aristotelian element became more prominent, for example, in the writings of Ibn Daud and, of course, Maimonides. Julius Guttman has demonstrated that the best indicator of whether a philosopher is closer to Aristotle or to Neoplatonism is that thinker's conception of God.[8] Aristotelians tended to identify God as the intellect that thinks itself, whereas the Neoplatonists described God as other and utterly transcendent. Both of these conceptions may be found in the *Guide*. However, the Rambam neither compared nor attempted to integrate these opposing viewpoints. He simply presented them in different parts of his book.

The first part of the *Guide* was constructed with particular care and precision. The chapter about God's transcendence (developing the doctrine of negative attributes) is juxtaposed with two chapters (1 and 68) that talk about God's intimacy with people. The Rambam deliberately set up a tension between discussions of God's distance from us and assertions of God's closeness. Brick by brick, the Rambam built a wall separating God from humanity, only to knock it down in the space of one chapter where he restored the idea of God's intimacy with human beings who are created in God's image.

We have seen that the *Guide* did not resolve the debate between those who believed the world had been created and those who believed the world was eternal; instead, it presented both sides. The Rambam inclined toward the idea of creation, but he did not decisively reject the possibility that the world has existed eternally. Now we see that Maimonides took the same approach to the issue of God. He presented his readers with both a God who is *beyond* intellect and a God who *is* intellect. The Rambam inclined toward the doctrine of negative attributes, but he did not entirely reject the notion of God as intelligence. The arguments that resonated throughout the medieval period between the followers of Aristotle and Plotinus are not decided in the *Guide*, but both sides are represented. The *Guide* served as an arena for the conflict between some of the most influential philosophical ideas of the Middle Ages, and the battle is not brought to a clear conclusion. The reader remains in a state of perplexity.[9]

In his treatment of both of these big questions about the world and God, Maimonides challenged his readers' confidence that there was one, unequivocally correct answer. Rather, he invited his audience to participate in his own intellectual struggles. The *Guide* led its readers to a place of uncertainty. The question is, what is the theological and psychological role of uncertainty in the *Guide*? This will be the subject of the next chapter.

13

THE ROLE OF DOUBT

Maimonides sought to effect a transformation in the consciousness of his readers. He waged a persistent battle against what he identified as one of the greatest threats to spiritual change: the tendency that people have to become overly attached to their own opinions.

In any learning process, people hatch ideas, interpretations, and hypotheses about the subject matter from the outset. The Rambam calls this initial passing of judgment "first thoughts." The thoughts that are born on a preliminary encounter with any area of inquiry tend to be shallow and inaccurate. For example, the Rambam argued that the first thoughts of most people about God are likely to involve the notion of corporeality—God having a physical body.[1] Monotheism, which conceives of God as abstract, is not just a triumph over paganism but also represents liberation from the temptation of first thoughts.

Our thought processes should lead us beyond first impressions. We need to be willing to free ourselves from preconceptions, engage in self-criticism, and, where necessary, change our minds. Opinions can become snares that choke off spiritual growth. People become infatuated with their own thoughts and lock themselves into a limited and limiting framework of ideas.

The instruction to free ourselves from "first thoughts" comes at the opening of the *Guide*. In part 1, chapter 2, the Rambam challenges a certain man who came to him with a textual difficulty in the Bible:

Hear now the intent of our reply. We said: O you who engage in theoretical speculation using the first notions that may occur to you and come to your mind and who consider withal that you understand a book that is the Guide of the first and last men while glancing though it as you would glance through a historical work or a piece of poetry—when in some of your hours of leisure you leave off drinking and copulating: collect yourself and reflect. (*Guide*, 1:2)

This critique is, I suggest, not addressed solely to the man who argued with Maimonides, but to all readers of the *Guide*. The Rambam exhorts us not to get stuck in our first responses to what we read but to be open to moving beyond them. This warning is repeated throughout the *Guide*.

THE ROLE OF DOUBT

Even after we overcome the temptation to surrender to first impressions, other intellectual snares lie in wait for the unwary. The Rambam cites the famous talmudic story of four sages who entered Pardes, the study of esoteric subjects. Of the four who went in, only one, Rabbi Akiva, came out in the same state in which he entered. The other three were harmed by the encounter. Pardes, according to Maimonides, consists of physics and metaphysics—vast, difficult, and esoteric spheres of knowledge—and the *Guide* is the key to understanding them. Despite the centrality of the Pardes story to the Rambam, it is only discussed in one chapter in the *Guide*. In this pivotal section of the book, he offers a novel interpretation of the sin of Elisha Ben Avuya, who turned to heresy as a result of his encounter with the Pardes, and of the greatness of Rabbi Akiva, who emerged unscathed:

You who study my treatise, know that something similar to what happens to sensory apprehensions happens likewise to intellectual apprehensions insofar as they are attached to matter. For when you see with your eye, you apprehend something that is within the power of your sight to apprehend. If, however, your eyes are forced to do something that they are reluctant to do—if they are made to gaze fixedly and are set the task of looking over a great distance, too great for you to see, or if you contemplate very minute writing, or a minute drawing, that is not within your power to apprehend—and if you force your eye, in spite of its reluctance, to find out the true reality of a thing, your eye shall not only be too weak to apprehend that which you are unable to apprehend, but also too weak to apprehend that which is within your power to apprehend. Your eye will grow tired, and you shall not be able to apprehend what you could apprehend before having gazed fixedly, and before having been given this task. A similar discovery is made by anyone engaged in the speculative study of some science with respect to his state of reflection. For if he applies himself to reflection, and sets himself a task requiring his entire attention, he becomes dull and does not then understand even that which it is within his power to understand. (*Guide*, 1:32)

The analogy between thought and vision is an ancient one that appears in many cultures. Plato, for example, likened profound understanding of the Forms to seeing them. The Rambam developed the comparison further.[2] Unlike other parts of the body, which can be strengthened through pushing them to their limits, straining one's eyes weakens them. Trying to see things that are too far away or to read letters that are too small is fatiguing and even potentially harmful. Similarly, straining to apprehend things that are beyond one's grasp can weaken one's intellect to the point that one can no longer understand what used to be comprehensible. According to the Rambam, intellect has limits that cannot really be crossed:

If, on the other hand, you aspire to apprehend things that are beyond your apprehension; or if you hasten to pronounce false things that are beyond your apprehension; or if you hasten to pronounce false assertions the contraries of which have not been demonstrated, or that are possible, though very remotely so—you will have joined Elisha Aḥer.[3] That is, you will not only not be perfect, but will be the most deficient among the deficient; and it shall so fall out that you will be overcome by imaginings and by an inclination toward things defective, evil and wicked—this resulting from the intellect's being preoccupied and its light's being extinguished. In a similar way, various species of delusive imaginings are produced in the sense of sight when the visual spirit is weakened, as in the case of sick people and of such as persist in looking at brilliant or minute objects. (*Guide*, 1:32)

When we try to unravel the great riddles of existence, the dangers of self-deception are great. We tend to convince ourselves that we have arrived at certainty about some metaphysical idea, when in fact no compelling proof is available. We may overlook flaws or gaps in philosophical arguments so as not to undermine our cherished ideas. This self-deception, stemming from people's difficulty in living without certainty, was the principal failing of Elisha Ben Avuya.

In contrast, Maimonides praises those with the strength of character to avoid this trap:

> For if you stay your progress because of a dubious point; if you do not deceive yourself into believing that there is a demonstration with regard to matters that have not been demonstrated; if you do not hasten to reject and categorically pronounce false any assertions whose contraries have not been demonstrated; if, finally, you do not aspire to apprehend that which you are unable to apprehend—you will have achieved human perfection and attained the rank of Rabbi Akiva, peace be upon him, "who entered in peace and went out in peace" when engaged in the discussion of these metaphysical matters. (*Guide*, 1:32)

It is a significant achievement for a person to be in a "place of doubt." The place of doubt is the ground upon which a person stands when he remains unconvinced. Until he encounters decisive arguments, he hesitates to take a firm position on major philosophical questions. Rabbi Akiva's considerable spiritual achievement was his capacity to abide in that place of uncertainty without jumping to hasty conclusions. The greatness of Rabbi Akiva was not in his having reached certainty but in his willingness to live with uncertainty.

In the talmudic story, Rabbi Akiva emerged from Pardes with a vital but enigmatic piece of wisdom: "When you reach the place of pure marble, do not say 'water, water.'"[4] According to the Rambam, the lesson Rabbi Akiva taught here was that when reality is not clear, be careful not to fall for false certainties.

The failing of Elisha Ben Avuya,[5] which appears in the same story, was the converse of Rabbi Akiva's greatness. When Elisha came out of Pardes, it was said of him that he "cut down the saplings." According to the Rambam, Elisha's essential error was self-deception. In this allegorical reading, although Elisha's mistake emerged during a process of intellectual reasoning, it reflected not intellectual weakness but rather a flaw in his character. The error was rooted less in the content of his thoughts than in the emotions that surrounded his intellectual search. His yearning for certainty blinded him to the difference between proof and conjecture.[6] Just as the physical world has its temptations that need to be resisted, so too does the world of philosophy, and foremost among these is the seduction of false certainties.

Maimonides apparently had some concerns about his readers. We may see this from the letter he wrote to one of his students, Rabbi Yosef Bar Yehudah, whose thirst to study philosophy served as the stimulus for the writing of the *Guide*. The Rambam appeared to be taken aback by the strength of his student's ardor to learn, causing him to worry that "maybe the desire of the student will be greater than his comprehension." A large gap between one's yearning for knowledge and one's capacity to understand may prove dangerous. Maimonides expressed concern that his potential readers would fall victim to intellectual desires that outstripped their abilities or their diligence:

> For man has, in his nature, a desire to seek the ends. . . . Now if you were to awaken a man, even though he were the dullest of all people—as one awakens a sleeping individual, and if you were to ask him whether he desired at that moment to have knowledge of the heavenly spheres,

namely what their number is and what their configuration, and what is contained in them, and what the angels are . . . he would undoubtedly answer you in the affirmative. He would have a natural desire to know these things as they are in truth; but he would wish this desire to be allayed, and the knowledge of all this to be achieved by means of one or two words that you would say to him. (*Guide*, 1:34)

Just about anyone whom you would awaken in the middle of the night and ask, "Do you want to know the truth about the great questions of existence?" would say "Yes." The problem is not that people aren't interested in knowing the truth but that they want to know it too fast. Aristotle said that "all men by nature desire to know."[7] The Rambam understood that this desire could drive men to extraordinary achievements, but he was also well aware that it could lead to intellectual superficiality. People want learning, but too often they are unwilling to put in the hard work necessary to attain it. They jump to conclusions and dogmatically declare that have arrived at the truth, rather than suspending judgment and remaining in a state of uncertainty until patient research and well-founded arguments yield real knowledge.[8]

METHODOLOGICAL SKEPTICISM VERSUS ESSENTIALIST SKEPTICISM

The Rambam's efforts to persuade his readers to reserve judgment in their consideration of philosophical issues raise an interesting question. Is this a kind of methodological skepticism, or does it reflect a deeper skepticism about the nature of truth?

Methodological skepticism assumes that the intellectual journey can indeed lead to an encounter with absolute truth. Doubt is a condition for eventually reaching truth, not a substitute for it. If you immediately commit to your first impressions or initial hypotheses about a subject, you may well close off possibilities for intellectual growth and ultimately prevent yourself from reaching truth. On the other hand, if you question your first impressions and continue to develop along your path of intellectual inquiry, you can reach a more mature understanding of the big philosophical issues. The great example of this in the history of philosophy was Descartes.[9] Beginning by doubting everything, Descartes identified one point, his own existence, that was immune to skepticism, and based on that he developed proofs for the existence of God and the world.

The more radical possibility is that the Rambam is advancing not methodological doubt but rather a more thoroughgoing skepticism. It is not that he is telling us to reject false certainties so that we may ultimately reach the truth. Perhaps absolute truth is unreachable. At the end of the journey, there are no definitive answers, only more questions. The intellectual path is endless, because there is no ultimate truth accessible to the human mind. This possibility is clearly addressed in the passage concerning Rabbi Akiva:

> If, finally, you do not aspire to apprehend that which you are unable to apprehend—you will have achieved human perfection and attained the rank of Rabbi Akiva, peace be upon him, "who entered in peace and went out in peace" when engaged in the discussion of these metaphysical matters. (*Guide*, 1:32)

The Rambam interpreted the state of peace in which Rabbi Akiva entered and left Pardes as the achievement of a level of human perfection. Rabbi Akiva's acknowledgment of what he could not know and his willingness to remain in a state of uncertainty are not described as *conditions* for reaching the truth and attaining perfection; rather, these characteristics are constitutive of perfection itself. In this section Rambam is doubtful as to whether the philosophical journey could achieve absolute knowledge. Uncertainty, then, is not merely a means but also the end.

However, other passages cause us to hesitate before reaching this conclusion. For example, at the end of the same chapter, Rambam writes:

> Do not criticize the terms applied to the intellect in this chapter and others. For the purpose here is to guide toward the intended notion and

not to investigate the truth of the essence of the intellect; for other chapters are dedicated to give a precise account of this subject. (*Guide*, 1:32)

In this chapter's final lines, the Rambam advised his readers about how it should be read. He acknowledged that it left the reader with an impression that metaphysical certainty is unreachable. But he asked his readers not to overemphasize this aspect of the chapter. The point of the chapter was "to guide toward the intended notion," not "to investigate the truth of the essence of the intellect." If the reader arrived at the over-hasty conclusion that Maimonides was a relativist and a skeptic, the author counseled him to think again. He enjoined us to remain in a state of uncertainty about the possibility of ultimate philosophical truth.

There is only one place where the *Guide* describes the mind of the person who succeeds on the intellectual journey and is able to reach true knowledge of God. This description appears as part of the best-known parable of the *Guide*—the king in his palace. In this parable, the Rambam compared true intellectual achievement to entry into the innermost chambers of the king's habitation. The spiritual climax of this journey was arriving in the throne room of the king himself. The intellectual level of the one who reached that place is described as follows:

> He, however, who has achieved demonstration, to the extent that it is possible, of everything that may be demonstrated; and who has ascertained in divine matters, to the extent that it is possible, everything that may be ascertained; and who has come close to certainty in those matters in which one can only come close to it—has come to be with the ruler in the inner part of the habitation. (*Guide*, 3:51)

This supreme level included the ability to know when we cannot reach certainty but may only "come close to it." Plato understood philosophy as being the move from approximate understanding to knowledge. When a person has emerged from the cave and meditates upon the Forms, he attains absolute knowledge. For the Rambam, philosophy takes us in the opposite direction. The more exalted the truth that we are trying to grasp, the less are we able to attain certainty. Philosophy brings us to a place where we know that we only approximately understand. Whether in the orchards of the Pardes or in the innermost chambers of the king, the seeker finds more questions than answers.

In another place, the Rambam wrote that the nearer the subject matter draws to metaphysics, the greater human perplexity becomes:

> The things about which there is this perplexity are very numerous in divine matters, few in matters pertaining to natural sciences, and non-existent in matters pertaining to mathematics. (*Guide*, 1:31)

This is not a relativistic position that would cast doubt on everything just because at the far end of the intellectual spectrum there are riddles that are insoluble. Maimonides argued that one may indeed *approach* certainty. We are fated to live in the space between the *eros* that yearns for absolute knowledge and the limits of our minds, which can approach that knowledge but never reach it.

Only now can we properly understand the conclusions that should be drawn from our discussions about some of the fundamental issues of the *Guide*. For example, the debate about the creation of the world brings the reader to a place of uncertainty; doubt in relation to how the world came to be reflects an intellectual modesty and clarity that counters self-deception. The Rambam taught us how the sages of the kalām stumbled by attributing an illusory certainty to their arguments in favor of creation. The Aristotelians stumbled in the same way by assuming that their proofs on the opposite side were absolutely compelling, when they were not; also the arguments between the Neo-Aristotelians and Neoplatonists about the nature of God (whether He is an "intelligence" or completely indescribable) ran into the problem of dogmatism. We saw that the combatants on the intellectual battlefields of the Middle Ages were not exactly modest in their mode of argument, and they frequently failed to distinguish between persuasive conjectures and absolute proofs. They fell into the same trap as Elisha Ben Avuya and became overly attached to their own theories.

In all of these areas, the Rambam tried to break down the dogmatism of the Middle Ages and to present his readers with diverse and sometimes contradictory views on the great questions about God and the world. He sought to raise his readers to the level of Rabbi Akiva, teaching them to stand in a place of doubt and to learn to live without certainty.

The Rambam grew up in Andalusia, Spain, in a tranquil and prosperous age. Jews coexisted peacefully with their Arab neighbors, and Maimonides lived in a relatively tolerant and open environment. The idyll was shattered by the invasion of a fanatical Muslim sect, the Almohads, who forced the inhabitants of the area to convert to Islam. This outburst of religious zealotry forced the young Moses to embark with his family on a life of wandering that was formative. His life story was one of running from tyranny, but the drama of his intellectual life was not one of escape; it was about struggle and resistance. The *Guide* is a struggle against tyrannies of the mind, not only those imposed by extreme religious movements, but also those formed out of our own hasty preconceptions.

14

HALAKHAH AND DOGMATISM

In the previous chapter, we saw how philosophy requires a willing-ness to live with uncertainty. This conclusion led us to reconsider the role of *halakhah*. Now we will look at another perspective on the purpose of the mitzvot, building on our discussion in part 2. We will examine how *halakhah* trains us for a life of study and research that does not necessarily lead to certainty. In other words, we will ask how *halakhah* forms non-dogmatic personalities.

The *Guide* opened its discussion of the reasons for mitzvot with the assertion, "The Law as a whole aims for two things: the welfare of the soul and the welfare of the body." Welfare of the soul is defined as follows: "As for the welfare of the soul, it consists in the multi-tude's acquiring correct opinions corresponding to their respective capacity." In other words, welfare of the soul means working toward intellectual perfection. Welfare of the body is described as having two parts: "one thing is for them to abolish their wrong-doing toward each other. . . . The second thing consists in the acquisition by every human individual of qualities that are useful for life in society so that affairs of the city may be well-ordered" (*Guide*, 3:29).

Working to perfect society and the characters of the people who comprise it are necessary conditions for philosophy to flourish. However, the moral perfection of the philosopher himself is a vital precondition for his philosophical achievements.

In one of the early chapters of the *Guide*, the Rambam wrote that in addition to intellectual study, the would-be philosopher must also focus on training his personality.

> We say that a man should not hasten too much to accede to this great and sublime matter at the first try, without having made his soul undergo training in the sciences and the different kinds of knowledge, having truly improved his character, and having extinguished the desires and cravings engendered in him by his imagination. (*Guide*, 1:5)

It is not just our thoughts that need honing for the study of metaphysics; we must refine our personalities too. Elsewhere, the Rambam wrote that intellectual achievement requires mental equanimity. Similarly, in his introduction to *Avot*, he spoke of the walls that separate man and God. Among the barriers that block contact between human beings and God, he included certain intellectual weaknesses alongside defects of personality:

> Among the prophets, there were those who saw God through many layers of separation, and others who beheld God through very few barriers, according to the degree of their closeness to Him and the level of their prophecy—up to the level of Moses, our teacher about whom it was said that he beheld God behind one, transparent veil. (Introduction to *Avot*, chapter 7)

In this metaphor, the fewer barriers there are between a person and God, the higher is his spiritual level, and the closer he is to realizing his inherent intellectual potential. Conversely, of course, the more barriers there are separating the person from God, the lower his level: what then are the barriers that keep us from knowing God?

> Among them are defects such as foolishness, stupidity and difficult of comprehension. . . . [T]here are also character defects, such as lust, pride and anger. . . . [T]hese are the barriers that separate between a person and God, may He be exalted. (Introduction to *Avot*, chapter 7)

Our success or failure in grasping the great metaphysical truths depends not only on our mental powers but also on our moral level.

These claims are not easy to reconcile with the Rambam's taxonomy of the human soul, in which the intellectual and moral sides of a person are not synonymous.[1] Moreover—and this is the point that I wish to explore—the notion that there is a link between moral and intellectual achievement does not square well with common sense. The smartest kid in the class is not always the nicest. Life experience does not support the idea that there is a necessary connection between character and intellect.

On the Causal Connections between Perfection of Character and Perfection of the Intellect

Now that we are equipped with conclusions from the previous chapter about the level of Rabbi Akiva and the temptations that await a person in Pardes, we are in a better position to understand the relationship between the level of our characters and the quality of our thinking. Pursuit of the higher branches of knowledge not only entails intellectual challenges but also requires dealing with the psychological demands of entering the palace of secrets.

Most people tend to push away ideas that they are not used to. Someone who is not capable of freeing himself from his preconceived notions will stick firmly by them even when the secrets of existence are revealed to him. Consequently, he is likely to have only a distorted apprehension of what is revealed. (Similarly, a passionate commitment to a certain political position often makes it difficult to listen to opposing views and to acknowledge that there may be anything of value in them. People resort to stereotyping of rival ideologies and dismiss the possibility that they could learn anything interesting or new from their opponents.) The Rambam taught that people become over-attached to familiar ideas. This is the reason, for example, not to teach the secret names of God to people who are not on the right moral level:

Blameworthy people started learning the name having twelve letters and through this corrupted beliefs. This happens whenever anyone who is not a perfect man comes to know that something is not as he had imagined it to be in the first place. The sages therefore made a secret of this name likewise, and taught it only to the discreet among the priests. (*Guide*, 1:62)

When such people are exposed to new ideas, they do not change their minds but instead try to twist what they are being told so that it conforms to what they already know. This causes them to fall into the same intellectual traps again and again:

For whenever a man finds himself inclining . . . toward lusts and plea-sures, or preferring anger and fury, giving the upper hand to his irascible faculty and letting go its reins, he shall be at fault and stumble wherever he goes. For he will seek opinions that help him in that toward which his nature inclines. I have drawn your attention to this in order that you should not be deceived. (*Guide*, 2:23)

One who is still in thrall to his passions will be ruled by them even when he is studying metaphysics. His thoughts and opinions will remain slaves to his desires.

Herein lies the importance of our discussion about the sin of Elisha Ben Avuya and the greatness of Rabbi Akiva. Pitfalls await the spiritual seeker who tries to enter the realm of esoteric knowledge. The most dangerous of them is the seduction of illusory certainty. Those who venture into Pardes need to know how to rein in their thirst for knowledge and be willing to remain in a state of uncer-tainty. This capacity requires considerable character training. We saw earlier that we need to able to subdue our physical lusts before we can enter Pardes; in addition, we must be able to control our intellectual desires in order to emerge whole and undamaged.

Philosophers with flawed characters are all too likely to reach con-clusions that reflect and justify their own negative personality traits. Rather than liberating themselves and others from preconceptions they merely perpetuate preexisting attitudes. Therefore, the Rambam described two types of training for a philosophical life; one to perfect the mind, and the other to improve character. The course of intellectual preparation begins with learning logic and mathematics, which lead to studying physics and astronomy. Only then is one ready to enter the "Holy of Holies"—metaphysics. This requires spiritual training. The seeker must work to develop the intellectual modesty and self-restraint that will help him to avoid dogmatism and false certainties.

The Mitzvot as a Cure for Dogmatism

How are we to embark on this program of spiritual training? The first step[2] can be found in some brief remarks that the Rambam makes in *Hilkhot Yesodei HaTorah* ("Laws of Foundations of the Torah"). The first four chapters of that book deal with physics and metaphysics. Then, at the end of chapter 4, the Rambam wrote:

> These four chapters deal with five *mitzvot* which the earlier sages termed "Pardes," as in the talmudic story "Four Entered Pardes." Even though the four were great sages in Israel, not all of them had the intellectual strength to know and understand properly what they found in Pardes. So I say, that one should not enter Pardes unless one has first filled one's belly with bread and meat—"bread and meat" means an understanding of what is allowed and what is forbidden. (*MT, Hilkhot Yesodei HaTorah*, 3:14)

According to this passage, the failure of the great sages of Israel who were harmed by their foray into Pardes was primarily an intellectual one: they did not have "the intellectual strength to know and understand properly." The Rambam prescribes studying *halakhah* as a prophylactic against these dangers. I would suggest he is less interested in the intellectual training that halakhic study entails and more concerned with its effect on our temperament. "The debates of Abbaye and Rava," as he characterized in-depth study of the halakhic sources later in the same passage, "settle a person's mind at the start of his path." The study and practice of *halakhah* can confer the restraint and self-disciple that help one focus on intense intellectual study and resist the temptations that distract from the final goal.[3]

How does this process of spiritual training work? We saw the answer in our discussion of the reasons for the commandments. The Rambam viewed mitzvot as a continuous education in delayed gratification. They train the soul in self-restraint and moderation of the appetites. This is the central goal of *halakhah*.

We must be trained to resist not only physical temptations but also intellectual ones. While logic and mathematics train the intellect for metaphysics, *halakhah* prepares the personality. It inculcates the self-restraint that protects the philosopher from jumping to hasty conclusions and allows him to live with doubt. The ideal halakhic man will be able to plumb the great mysteries of existence without taking refuge in premature certainty.

This idea is particularly striking in the light of the way the Rambam presented the *halakhah* in the *Mishneh Torah*. He set out his halakhic conclusions without argument, without citing dissenting views, and usually without giving reasons. How can it be that the *halakhah*, which he presented in such a decisive and confident style, can defend us from dogmatism?

The *Guide* does indeed attempt to protect us from dogmatic certainty. However, the alternative the Rambam offers to such illusions is not absolute skepticism. Recall his description of the excellent individual who is worthy of entering the precincts of the king's palace:

> He, however, who has achieved demonstration, to the extent that it is possible, of everything that may be demonstrated; and who has ascertained in divine matters, to the extent that it is possible, everything that may be ascertained; and who has come close to certainty in those matters in which one can only come close to it. (*Guide*, 3:51)

One who reaches this high level knows how to distinguish between what is certain and what is almost certain, and to make his peace with the inability to always be sure. The Rambam offers his readers a new goal: a life that can come close to the ultimate truths. The *Guide* describes the goal, but the *Mishneh Torah* trains us to strive to reach it.

15

THE CRISIS OF REASON

"All men by nature desire to know." This principle, with which Aristotle opened his *Metaphysics*, echoes throughout *The Guide for the Perplexed*. Knowledge, according to the Rambam, is more than the highest desire of human beings. It is also the true purpose of their life. However, not all items of knowledge are equal in this respect. Some are irrelevant to reaching my goals, such as knowing the exact height and weight of my desk. On the other hand, there is knowledge of a more difficult and complex kind, the attainment of which is critical to the meaning of my life. This knowledge is a higher rung on the metaphysical ladder of existence.

To grasp the significance of this idea in the Rambam's thought, we need to first understand how medieval thinkers conceived of existence. At the center of the cosmos stood the Earth. However, its central place did not imply a preeminent importance. On the contrary, the Earth was made of the four physical elements that were at the very bottom of the metaphysical ladder of existence. Above the Earth were the spheres, which, according to medieval cosmology, were made of invisible matter. Resting on the spheres were the stars, which were believed to move in circular orbits.[1] In the Middle Ages there were arguments about the number of the spheres, but there was widespread agreement about their essential nature. The spheres were thought to be living entities endowed with both intelligence and desire. Indeed, the movement of the spheres was believed to be caused by their yearning for metaphysical knowledge. Above the spheres were the separate intelligences. These were pure forms, devoid of material substance, to which the spheres were believed to aspire. Each sphere had a corresponding separate intelligence that it desired to know. Above it all was the unmoved mover, God, the summit of all existence. God was the cause of the motion of all the heavenly bodies, because all of them desired to know Him.

The medieval cosmos was alive. When man looked up at the night sky he saw beings that were suffused with intelligence and desire. To the modern mind, this picture of existence seems very strange. Modernity "killed" the cosmos and reconceived it as inanimate rather than alive. We no longer see the stars as intelligent beings, but as lumps of dumb matter moving through space. This is one reason for modern man's sense of loneliness and alienation. The universe that was once full of life, intelligence and desire has fallen silent.

There is a further philosophical significance to the prevailing medieval model of existence. The force that was believed to cause the motion of the heavenly bodies was their thirst for knowledge. You might say that philosophy, literally the love of wisdom, is what moved the whole universe. So when people do philosophy, they are participating in this universal cosmic yearning for knowledge.

In sum, human intellectual progress was a journey from knowing objects that were on a lower metaphysical level to grasping things on ever more exalted metaphysical planes: from understanding the earthly world of the four elements to knowledge of the spheres, the separate intellects (non-physical entities whose existence was assumed in medieval metaphysics to explain the cosmic motion of the spheres), and ultimately knowledge of God.

Did Maimonides accept this classical picture of the cosmos? He sought to remove God from the confines of language and understanding. We have seen how the God beyond words and thought was inaccessible even to the greatest of the prophets, Moses. If we then take away God as a potential object of human understanding, we are left with the separate intelligences as the highest level of knowledge to which we may aspire.

Out of all the separate intelligences, the one that is most relevant to our discussion is the "active intellect," the intelligence whose influence causes our physical world of the four elements to function. But can we ever know the "active intellect"? The Rambam's view about this is unclear. He scattered oblique hints about the question throughout the *Guide*. His ambivalence provided fertile soil for many debates over the centuries about what he really thought.

One of the most convincing and carefully argued positions on this issue was developed by Shlomo Pines, a great twentieth-century Maimonides scholar. He based his view both on textual proofs from the *Guide* and also on comparisons with other philosophical texts in Maimonides's oeuvre. Pines argued that, according to the Rambam, it is impossible to know the separate intellects. One of Pines's most convincing proof texts is a passage in which Maimonides declared that he was uncertain as to whether the separate intellects exist. Aristotle inferred their existence from the movements of the spheres; their perfectly circular motion could only be understood as evidence that they were moved by the separate intellects. The Rambam viewed this inference as weak:

> Know that the opinions held by Aristotle regarding the causes of the motions of the spheres from which opinions he deduced the existence of separate intellects—**are simple assertions for which no demonstration has been made**, yet they are, of all the opinions put forward on the subject, those that are exposed to the smallest number of doubts. (*Guide*, 2:3)

Not only were proofs for the existence of the separate intellects unconvincing, but the Rambam also cast doubt on whether we could know them even if they did exist.[2]

The limits of what reason could know contract still further. If the Rambam believed that God lay beyond the boundaries of human understanding and that the separate intellects were also outside those borders, then only the heavenly spheres remained as suitable supernal objects of human understanding. But Maimonides raised serious questions about even our ability to know these. In part 2, chapter 24 of the *Guide*, he elaborated on some of the most vexing problems in medieval cosmology and showed that the prevalent medieval vision of the universe, based on Aristotelian foundations and elaborated by Ptolemy, faced a serious crisis. There was a split between astronomy and physics. Astronomers described the movements of the heavenly bodies based on observation, but their findings could not be reconciled with the basic laws of physics:

> See now how all these things are remote from natural speculation! All this will become clear to you if you consider the distances and dimensions, known to you, of every sphere and star, as well as the evaluation of all of them by means of half the diameter of the earth so that everything calculated according to one and the same proportion and the eccentricity of every sphere is not in relation to the sphere itself. (*Guide*, 2:24)[3]

Maimonides saw the conflict between astronomy and physics as evidence of essential shortcomings of the human mind. He believed that the stars and heavenly spheres were not accessible to our intellects and that most of Aristotle's doctrines on this were therefore not relevant:

> All that Aristotle states about that which is beneath the sphere of the moon is in accordance with reasoning. . . . However, regarding all that is in the heavens, man grasps nothing but a small measure of what is mathematical. (*Guide*, 2:24)

Aristotle's teachings, which the Rambam termed "the pinnacle of human reasoning,"[4] turn out to be unreliable regarding the sphere of existence that is beneath the moon.[5] Reason must know its limits:

> It [i.e., knowledge of the heavens] is a matter the knowledge of which cannot be reached by human intellects. And to fatigue the minds by notions that cannot be grasped by them and for the grasp of which they

have no instrument, is a defect in one's inborn disposition, or some sort of temptation. (*Guide*, 2:24)

This is a radical statement in the context of medieval philosophy—and also against the background of Maimonides's thinking.[6] The same Rambam who urged his readers to study the heavenly bodies, the stars, and the spheres as the fingerprints of God also wrote that the project of understanding the heavens could yield, at best, a very small degree of success. In his conclusion to this chapter, the Rambam sent a barbed message to anyone who thought that he had solved the crisis in medieval astronomy and physics:

> That is the end of what I have to say about this question. It is possible that someone else may find a demonstration by means of which the true reality of what is obscure for me will become clear to him. The extreme predilection that I have for investigating the truth is evidenced by the fact that I have repeatedly reported my **perplexity** regarding these matters as well as by the fact that I have not heard, nor do I know a demonstration as to anything concerning them. (*Guide*, 2:24)

The author of the *Guide* admitted his perplexity about issues that lay at the heart of his book and of philosophy.[7] The proofs for the existence of God relied on the movement of the spheres, and the proofs for the existence of the separate intellects were based on the circular motion of the heavenly bodies. Maimonides built an intellectual edifice upon the movement of the stars, and then, in a single chapter, he demolished the foundations of the whole project. The stars were placed outside the purview of reason. Out of all the cosmos, only the earthly world of the four elements remained accessible to our intellects.

To my mind, this is the central conclusion of the *Guide*: Maimonides, more than any other Jewish thinker, placed knowledge and understanding at the summit of our religious aspirations. Yet he was more skeptical than any other classical Jewish thinker about our capacity to acquire certain knowledge. How could someone who made reason so central to religious life also believe that the intellect is so limited?

We have seen a series of contradictions in the *Guide* about some of the biggest philosophical questions, such as whether the world was created and about the nature of God. Generations of scholars have puzzled over these riddles. To me, however, the greatest contradiction of the *Guide* concerns perplexity itself. Why did this book, which ultimately teaches that reliable answers to the great questions is unattainable, exhort readers to seek those answers? Why does the *Guide* take us on an ultimately futile journey? Before we grapple with this question, let us broaden it, for the crisis of astronomy and the perplexity of reason are symptoms of a broader collapse of authority, as we will see in the following chapter.

16

THE CRISIS OF
TRADITION

A venerable tradition of Jewish philosophy preceded the Rambam. Jewish philosophy began with Philo of Alexandria and reawakened in the Middle Ages in the work of Isaac Israeli, Rabbi Sa'adiah Gaon, Rabbi Yehudah Halevi, and Rabbi Abraham Ibn Ezra. Each of these figures offered a body of systematic Jewish thought about major philosophical questions. Maimonides, however, did not view himself as part of this tradition. In the introduction to part 3 of the *Guide*, he wrote that in the distant past there had been a tradition of Jewish philosophy but that it had died out and no longer existed in his time:

> This is the reason why the knowledge of this matter has ceased to exist in the religious community so that nothing great or small remains of it. And it had to happen like this, for this knowledge was only transmitted from one to another and has never been set down in writing.

Not only did Maimonides disclaim a connection with the tradition of medieval Jewish philosophy that preceded him, he denied its very existence. The Rambam did not call philosophy the thoughts of Rabbenu Bachya Ibn Pakuda, Yehudah Halevi, and Ibn Ezra. In matters of *halakhah* the Rambam viewed himself as an heir to the Sephardi halakhic tradition. In philosophy, on the other hand, he saw himself as an orphan.

Maimonides believed that the ancient philosophical knowledge that was once in the possession of the Jewish people had been lost but that it could be recovered through a careful and sensitive reading of the hints to that knowledge in the Bible and Rabbinic writings. However, the Rambam was at times sharply critical of the level of scientific and philosophical knowledge displayed by the sages of the Talmud. In his discussion of the doctrine of negative attributes, Maimonides cited a talmudic story and remarked that it was very insightful from a philosophical point of view. He added, however, the following comment: "You also know their famous dictum— would that all dicta were like it" (*Guide*, 1:59)—in other words, would that other talmudic sayings and stories displayed a similar philosophical acumen.

Throughout the *Guide*, the Rambam pointed out scientific and philosophical errors in the Talmud. He did not feel the need to reinterpret talmudic writings so that they would conform to scientific truth. Maimonides did not sacrifice his intellectual honesty for the sake of presenting the rabbis of the Talmud as profound scientists:[1]

> There is the fact that I always hear from all those who had some smattering of the science of astronomy, that what the sages, may their memory be blessed, have said regarding distances was exaggerated. . . . Do not ask of me to show that everything they have said regarding astronomical matters conforms to the way things really are. For at that time, mathematics was imperfect. (*Guide*, 3:14)

That the Rambam did not identify with any extant Jewish scientific or philosophical tradition was no accident. Throughout the *Guide* he reflected on the weakness and inadequacy of human intellect, in part because of the tendency to give excessive respect to old and established ideas. The more venerable a view, the more reliable many took it to be. In his letter to the sages of Montpellier, he attacked astrology and those who believed in it, arguing that one reason for its wide acceptance was the influence of ancient astrological books: "It is a great and evil sickness that people think that if a thing is written in a book then it is true, and all the more so if the book is very old."[2] Old books can have a seductive aura that obscures our critical faculties. When the Rambam tried to explain why there was a Jewish magical tradition, he found that ancient books about magic were largely to blame:

> Thereupon, these lies invented by the first wicked and ignorant man were written down and transmitted to good, pious and foolish men who lacked the scales by means of which they could know the true from the false. These people accordingly made a secret of these writings, and the latter were found in the belongings left behind them, so that they were thought to be correct. To sum it up, *A fool believes everything* (Prov. 14:15). (*Guide*, 1:62)

Those who subscribed to ancient, popular folk beliefs were the target of frequent criticism in the *Guide*. Their error consisted not just in believing in ideas simply because they were old and popular but also in extrapolating from what was supposedly widely known to areas that were less familiar. This kind of process leads to comparing God to man and the metaphysical realms with concrete, physical existence. In the most blatant form of this mistake, human physical characteristics are attributed to God. Those with more highly developed imaginations ascribe to God only human spiritual qualities, and those who were on a higher level yet managed to separate God from the realm of human attributes while still attempting to speak about Him using human language. It is very difficult for us to entirely transcend the physical plane of reality that we are accustomed to: "The multitude cannot at first conceive of any existence save that of a body alone; thus that which is not a body nor existent in a body does not exist in their opinion" (*Guide*, 1:26).

Those who fall into this error have two options: denial of God, or belief in a God who is physical:

> For the multitude perceive nothing apart from bodies as having a firmly established existence and as being indubitably true, for anything that is

not a body, but subsists in a body is existent; but its existence is more deficient than that of a body, as it requires a body in order to exist. That, however, which is neither a body nor in a body is not an existent thing in any respect, according to man's initial representation, particularly from the point of view of the imagination. (*Guide*, 1:46)

According to popular belief, matter is the only thing that is deemed to exist. There is nothing existing that is not physical:

They thought that God has a man's form, I mean his shape and configuration . . . and deemed that if they abandoned this belief . . . they would even make the deity nothing at all, unless they thought that God was a body provided with a face and a hand like them. (*Guide*, 1:1)

The need to give God a physical shape stems from mental attachment to concrete existence. Since people do not encounter beings without physical form in their day-to-day experience, they conclude that such beings cannot exist:

Now every such essence is of necessity endowed with attributes. For we do not ever find an essence of a body that while existing is divested of everything and is without an attribute. This imagination being pursued, it was thought that He, may He be exalted, is similarly composed of various notions, namely His essence, and the notions that are superadded to His essence. Several groups of people pursued the likening of God to other beings, and believed Him to be a body endowed with attributes. Another group raised themselves above this consequence and denied His being a body, but preserved His attributes. All this was rendered necessary by their keeping to the external sense of the revealed books. (*Guide*, 1:51)

Anthropomorphic representation of God is a consequence of copying familiar ways of thinking onto unfamiliar subjects. Just as people prefer to stick with food that they like rather than trying new things, and live in areas where they feel comfortable rather than venturing into unfamiliar neighborhoods, so people tend to remain in familiar furrows of thought rather than exploring new intellectual pastures.[3]

The Rambam challenged both individuals and communities on this issue. Just because a person has believed something for a long time does not mean that he needs to continue thinking it. Similarly, the fact that a culture has followed a certain course in the past does not mean that it must do so in the future. Reason can emancipate a man both from himself and from worn-out intellectual traditions.

CRITICIZING THE ARISTOTELIAN TRADITION

However, even after freeing himself from limiting intellectual habits and traditions, was not the Rambam himself imprisoned by his commitment to a particular philosophical school, that is, the Greek tradition? We have seen him criticizing Jewish thought with tools from Aristotelian science and philosophy. Many have believed that while the Rambam used Aristotle to criticize, he did not criticize Aristotle. Aristotle was the yardstick the Rambam used to measure all other opinions, but Aristotle himself was not to be judged. Did Maimonides merely exchange one set of dogmatic opinions for another?

The *Guide* shows, however, that Maimonides did not regard the Aristotelian tradition as infallible. At the heart of the Rambam's criticism of the Aristotelian tradition lay the accusation that the authoritarian style of this school as it had developed in the Middle Ages did not liberate thought but rather limited it.

> Though I know that many men imbued with a partisan spirit will tax me because of this statement, either with having but little comprehension of their argument or with deliberately deviating from it, yet shall I not because of that, refrain from saying what I in my inadequacy have apprehended and understood. . . . Everything that Aristotle has said about all that exists from beneath the sphere of the moon to the center of the earth is indubitable correct, and no one will deviate from it unless he does not understand it or unless he has preconceived opinions that he wishes to defend or that lead him to a denial of a thing that is manifest. On the other hand, everything that Aristotle expounds with regard to the sphere of the moon and that which is above it is, excepting certain things, is something analogous to guessing and conjecturing. All the

more does this apply to what he says about the order of the intellects, and to some of the opinions regarding the divine that he believes; for the latter contain grave incongruities and perversities that manifestly and clearly appear as such to all nations, that propagate evil, and that he cannot demonstrate. (*Guide*, 2:22)

The Rambam was describing the power of the Aristotelian consensus in the Middle Ages. Neo-Aristotelian zealots were blind to significant problems in Aristotle's thought. According to the Rambam, we should judge a philosophical argument based on its content, rather on the name of the person who makes it. Aristotle's prestige did not render his thought immune to error.

Indeed, the Rambam believed that Aristotle's thought was full of errors. Aristotle's God was described in terms of His positive attributes, whereas the dominant strand of the *Guide* ruled out any attempt to speak about God. Aristotle believed that there were separate intellects and that the heavenly spheres moved in perfect circles, whereas Maimonides saw that this was an inaccurate description of the universe. He believed that Aristotle's cosmology only held true for the space below the sphere of the moon:

All that Aristotle states about that which is beneath the sphere of the moon is in accordance with reasoning; these are things that have a known cause, that follow one upon the other, and that, concerning which it is clear and manifest at what point wisdom and natural providence are effective, However, regarding all that is in the heavens, man grasps nothing but a small measure of what is mathematical. (*Guide*, 2:24)

Limiting the writ of Aristotelian doctrine to the lowest sphere of existence underlies the Rambam's appeal to his readers to emancipate themselves from philosophical traditions. For him, the very idea of a philosophical tradition was an oxymoron; if thought is constrained by authority then it is not philosophy.

The Rambam contended that both religious thought and the Aristotelian philosophy of the Middle Ages fell into the trap of extrapolating from the familiar to the strange. He identified two illegitimate ways in which the Aristotelians did this:

1. The Rambam believed that the world above the sphere of the moon was not accessible to human reason, in contrast to what lies beneath the sphere of the moon, which may be understood. Maimonides assumed that the universe above the sphere of the moon was quite different from the terrestrial world. Aristotelians, on the other hand, derived inferences about the upper worlds from their conclusions about the lower world that we inhabit. They painted the universe in familiar colors, without taking into account the immense physical and cognitive distance that separates us from the stars.

2. As part of his strategy to sow doubt about Aristotelian proofs for the eternity of the world, the Rambam articulated the "Parable of the Island," which questioned our ability to infer any reliable information about how an object came into being from what we observe about the object's present existence. Looking at a person, for example, will not tell you anything about how babies come into the world. Similarly, reflecting on the world cannot teach us how it came to exist. Our inability to live with insoluble riddles drives us to extrapolate from what we know to areas where we have no experience.

Aristotelian philosophy, Maimonides believed, fell into the same traps as religious thought. Over time, philosophy turned into dogmatism and, instead of freeing man, imprisoned him in unproven and questionable beliefs. Maimonides was not an Aristotelian. Although he adopted many of Aristotle's principles in the *Guide*, he was also harshly critical of Aristotelian dogmatism. Maimonides departed substantially both from the tradition of Jewish thought and also from Aristotelianism. He attempted to liberate the reader from the mistakes of both systems.

Often rebels eventually become authorities themselves. Did the Rambam attempt to emulate this pattern? Having undermined the major sources of authority in medieval philosophy, did he try to establish his own thought as a new source of intellectual authority? No, he did not. In the *Guide*, the Rambam's challenge to authority is directed as much at himself as toward other thinkers. He was open about his own perplexities and admitted that he knew no more about the universe above the sphere of the moon than the Neo-Aristotelians whom he attacked. The difference between him and them was that they thought that they knew, whereas Maimonides knew that he didn't know. Maimonides wrote in his letters that the way to establish authority was to advance a clear and unequivocal system. That is what he accomplished so masterfully in the *Mishneh Torah*. But the *Guide* did not offer an orderly, systematic body of thought. Instead, it presented an apparently disorganized work open to multiple interpretations. Whether in the areas of creation, prophecy, providence, the commandments, or the nature of God, there was not one important claim made in the *Guide* that Maimonides did not also call into question by advancing a counterclaim. He offered thesis and antithesis, theory and then criticism of the theory. The *Guide* is an antiauthoritarian book, undermining even its own authority. Unlike the *Mishneh Torah*, in which the Rambam successfully propounded normative *halakhah*, the *Guide* leaves the reader without binding intellectual norms. Taking the two books together, the Rambam gave the reader certainty about how to act but a wide area of freedom regarding what to think.

By keeping his readers from treating tradition as an authoritative source of knowledge about the most exalted issues of philosophy, the Rambam made reason the primary authority in those matters. But here is the problem: Maimonides did not have great faith in reason either. True, he believed in it more than he believed in anything else as a reliable guide and tool in philosophy, but he saw it as limited. He thought that we could not know God, or the separate intellects, or the heavenly spheres. The *Guide* attacked claims to absolute authority made by philosophical traditions and at the same time undermined uncompromising faith in reason. It left its readers without firm theological ground beneath their feet.

This conclusion forces us to return to what is, in my view, the central question about the *Guide*: How can this book, which sets up knowledge as the goal of human life, also determine that we cannot know the great truths of existence? How could this thinker, who urged his students to acquire knowledge, also be so skeptical about our ability to know?

Human reason is bound to suffer bruising encounters with its own limits. Yet the goal of the *Guide* is not some kind of hopeless Sisyphean failure. The disappointment with philosophy's failure to reach all of its aspirations is not the end of the journey. Rather, I would argue, Rambam saw this disappointment as a springboard to higher spiritual achievements.

The Rambam did not dictate to his readers the steps that might help them to move beyond perplexity. He suggested a number of paths that they might take, but he left it to his readers to choose among them. The end of the *Guide* is open. In the next two chapters I will discuss the paths that lead beyond perplexity.

17

FROM PERPLEXITY TO MYSTICISM AND POLITICS

In his introduction to *The Guide for the Perplexed*, the Rambam compares his book to "a key permitting one to enter places the gates to which were locked." But this does not imply that the *Guide* contains answers to all of the secrets. Once "these gates are opened, and these places are entered into," readers must continue the journey on their own. Two of the gates that the *Guide* may open are mysticism and political action.

FROM PERPLEXITY TO MYSTICISM
There is only one place in the *Guide* where the Rambam advised his readers on how to take the steps of consciousness that lay beyond philosophy. This move has been termed "post-intellectual contemplation,"[1] the process that a person may embark upon after reaching the summit of understanding. The Rambam writes:

> Let us now return to the subject of this chapter, which is to confirm men in their intention to set their thought to work on God alone after they have achieved knowledge of Him, as we have explained. This is the worship peculiar to those who have apprehended the true realities; the more they think of Him and of being with Him, the more their worship increases. (*Guide*, 3:51)

After a person has reached the highest possible levels of intellectual understanding, he does not abandon philosophy but rather becomes entirely absorbed in it. He should contemplate the concepts he has grasped and focus all of his consciousness on them. This important chapter of the *Guide* expressed the traditional, mystical desire for consciousness to dissolve into an all-encompassing awareness of God. How does this kind of contemplation result from philosophical investigation?

The Rambam instructed the thinker to focus his awareness entirely on God, who had been understood after long intellectual effort. The problem with this suggestion, however, is that, according to Maimonides, it is impossible to understand anything about God.[2] We should take the Rambam at his word: he was urging us to devote our thoughts entirely to reflecting upon the God of the doctrine of negative attributes, about whom nothing may be said. The spiritually developed person concentrates on emptying his concept of God's physical characteristics and, ultimately, of any characteristics whatsoever. Consciousness that is focused on a contentless notion of God is a contemplation of nothingness. The Rambam was describing here an advanced state of meditative awareness in which the mind is emptied. Such a state of consciousness can only be achieved through a degree of separation from the world:

> The Torah has made it clear that this last worship to which we have drawn attention in this chapter can only be engaged in after apprehension has been achieved; it says: *To love the Lord your God, and to serve Him with all your heart and with all your soul* (Deut. 11:13). Now we have made it clear several times that love is proportionate to apprehension. After love comes this worship to which attention has also been drawn by the sages, may their memory be blessed, who said: this is the worship of the heart. In my opinion, it consists in setting thought on the first intelligible and in devoting oneself exclusively to this as far as this is within one's capacity. Therefore you will find that David exhorted Solomon and fortified him in these two things, I mean his endeavor

to worship Him after apprehension has been achieved. He said: *And thou, Solomon, my son, know thou the God of thy father and serve Him, and so on. If thou seek Him, He will be found of thee, and so on* (1 Chron. 28:9). The exhortation always refers to intellectual apprehensions, not to imagination; for thought concerning imaginings is not called knowledge but *that which cometh into your mind* (Ezek. 20:32). Thus it is clear that after apprehension, total devotion to Him and the employment of intellectual thought in constantly loving Him should be aimed at. Mostly this is achieved in solitude and isolation. Hence every excellent man stays frequently in solitude and does not meet anyone unless it is necessary. (*Guide*, 3:51)

With his doctrine of negative attributes, the Rambam tried to liberate God from language. He urged his readers to free their consciousness of God from language and contemplate Him without words. He was not speaking of an infantile preverbal state but rather of an advanced, mystical postverbal consciousness. Thought breaks through its limits by focusing on the nothingness of God. The Rambam thus bypassed the intellectual systems that had been found wanting: he did not suggest contemplating the heavenly spheres or the active intellect, but rather meditating on God. A formless, contentless divinity can free human consciousness from the narrow confines of concepts and language. This kind of mystical awareness is born not from an abandonment of reason but from an attempt to bring the findings of reason to full consciousness.

The ecstatic, mystical interpretation of the end of the *Guide* has been very popular through the centuries, yet it is almost entirely lacking in any explanation of the meditative techniques that are meant to bring one to this state of consciousness. The Rambam hinted at a kind of mystical awareness that the philosopher may reach, but he barely offered any practical exercises that might help him to reach it. Over the generations, some commentators on the *Guide* chose the mystical path and filled this gap with techniques that they imported from other cultural contexts. The most notable of these was the Rambam's son, Abraham Ben Maimon, who actualized his father's teaching by means of exercises from the Sufi tradition, among other sources. Another striking example was Abraham Abulafia, who offered all those who wished to achieve the ultimate goal of the *Guide* mystical, meditative techniques to bring one to a state of unity with the divine nothingness.[3]

FROM PERPLEXITY TO POLITICS

In addition to mysticism, the *Guide* offered a different option, not of hermit-like ecstatic contemplation, but rather intense involvement with society. This possibility emerges most strongly at the very end of the book.

The final chapter of the *Guide* is built around a midrash that Maimonides elaborates on, based on the following verses from the book of Jeremiah:

> Let not the wise man glory in his wisdom, neither let the mighty man glory in his might, let not the rich man glory in his riches, but let him glory only in this: that he understands and knows Me, for I am God who does lovingkindness, judgment and righteousness in the world; for in these things I delight, says the Lord. (Jer. 9:23–24)

These verses express a movement toward a final level of perfection that is not satisfied with intellectual understanding. A person rises through the levels of wisdom, might, and riches, arriving at understanding of God: "that he understands and knows Me." Surprisingly, Jeremiah did not stop there, but continued: "for I am God who does lovingkindness, judgment and righteousness in the world; for in these things I delight, says the Lord." Jeremiah was describing a movement toward intellectual perfection and then beyond—to social and political action.

The final lines of the *Guide* take on a new meaning in the light of Maimonides's statements about the limits and limitations of reason. One of the paths out of perplexity that he proposed was a transition from philosophy to politics. Someone who understands that philosophical perfection is unattainable may choose to redirect his energies toward the perfection of society.

There is a similarity here with Plato's philosopher-king, who returns to the cave in order to lead those who remain in darkness toward the light of truth. So too, Maimonides's philosopher, having reached the heights of intellectual inquiry, devotes himself to the well-being of his society. Both are called to move from a life of contemplation to a mission of perfecting the world. However, I would suggest that there is a profound difference between Maimonides's philosopher and that of Plato. The Platonic philosopher, who emerges from the cave and is able to contemplate the true reality of the Forms has fully realized his *eros*—his desire for knowledge. Maimonides's thinker, on the other hand, does not completely satisfy his passionate intellectual desire. He is forced to realize that he cannot fully grasp the most exalted metaphysical subjects. His passion for social improvement is a transfer of unsatisfied intellectual desire onto the political realm. The intellectual search for God ignites an inner passion that philosophy alone is unable to satisfy. This passion is the fuel that drove prophets and philosophers to make the leap from individual quest to collective, social action.

The Rambam indeed saw himself as a guide for the perplexed, but a guide who took his readers only so far. He led them to the limits of philosophy, to the point where they encountered insoluble problems, and then he pointed out a number of paths upon which they could continue alone beyond perplexity.

In this chapter we have discussed the paths of ecstatic mysticism and of political action; in the following chapter we will look at a third option: transforming intellectual perplexity into spiritual liberation.

18

THERAPEUTIC PERPLEXITY

From the dawn of philosophy there have been thinkers who have maintained that knowledge is redemptive. The Rambam, I would argue, believed that knowing the limits of our knowledge is what redeems. He did not place this idea at the end of the *Guide* as a kind of final and definitive resolution of perplexity, but rather alluded it throughout his writings. It is this therapeutic role of intellectual perplexity that makes the *Guide* especially relevant to skeptical, questioning readers today.

LOVE AND AWE

For the Rambam, the ultimate spiritual goals to which we aspire include not just original thoughts but also new feelings. The highest religious experiences are marked by an outpouring of two lofty emotions: love and awe. Attaining these feelings is a positive commandment:

> It is a positive commandment to love and fear the honored and awesome God, as it says, *you shall love the Lord your God and you shall fear God.* (*MT*, *Hilkhot Yesodei HaTorah*, 2:2)

The Rambam was well aware of the absurdity of presuming to command emotions. Our feelings are mostly involuntary. We cannot turn them on or off at will. If we could, then the world would be a far less romantic place. The drama of countless novels, movies, and plays flows from the fact that love is not subject to human decision. How, then, can it be commanded?

Although we cannot activate these emotions directly, we can arouse them indirectly. By way of analogy, I cannot will my heart to beat faster, but I can choose to engage in vigorous exercise that will result in my pulse rate rising. Similarly, the Rambam believed that while we cannot spontaneously engender love, we may cultivate habits that will give rise to feelings of love:

> What is the way to love and fear Him? When a person meditates on God's wondrous actions and creations, and sees His infinite, unfathomable wisdom, he will immediately love, praise and glorify Him and with a great desire will yearn to know God's great name, as David said, *My soul thirsts for God, the living God* (Ps. 42:3). (*MT, Hilkhot Yesodei Ha-Torah*, 2:2)

Profound study of nature and the cosmos can bring us to a powerful sense of amazement at the vastness of the universe and the astonishing wisdom that is contained in it. It is not that this sense of wonder brings us to love of God; it is the *essence* of love of God. Maimonides reinterpreted the most elemental religious feelings. Love of God is the emotion that resonates throughout a person's being when he encounters nature. And this feeling awakens another emotion that is no less intense—awe of God:

> When he thinks about those things, he will immediately be afraid and will know that he is a small, lowly creature made of dust and that his intellect is slight compared to the Pure of Knowledge, as David said, *When I behold Your heavens . . . what is man that you have been mindful of Him?* (Ps. 8:4–5). (*MT, Hilkhot Yesodei HaTorah*, 2:2)

Being aware of the vastness of the universe gives rise to a sense of our smallness, of humility. A person should be aware of how tiny, marginal, and utterly insignificant he is in the face of the immensity of the cosmos. It is not that this awareness brings us to awe of God; it is the *essence* of awe of God. This is a paradoxical kind of religious experience that simultaneously elicits contrasting emotions. The more a person studies science, the more these feelings are aroused and deepened. As Maimonides put it in the *Guide*, "love is proportional to the level of our understanding" (3:51).

People speak of "intellectual types" and "emotional types." These cultural understandings reflect a current in Western thought which holds that in order to achieve a profound, emotional grasp of reality we need to abandon reason and strive for a state of "mystical simplicity."[1] Another common perception is that an active rational, intellectual life creates people who are desiccated and cut off from their emotions. A Bratslaver Hassid once told me that he could always tell people who studied the *Guide*. Most of them, he said, were pale and lifeless.

This *halakhah* from the *Mishneh Torah* breaks down such artificial distinctions between feeling and intellect. The Rambam thought that the strongest emotional experiences arise from profound study. The scientist and the philosopher are not cut off from emotion. Powerful feelings of love and awe burn within them.

It is interesting to note that these twin emotions emerging from scientific study are described in a remarkably similar way by one of the greatest modern scientists, Albert Einstein. In his book *The World as I See It*, Einstein described the religious sensibility of great scientists:

> The scientist's religious feeling takes the form of a rapturous amazement at the harmony of natural law, which reveals an intelligence of such superiority that, compared with it, all the systematic thinking and acting of human beings is an utterly insignificant reflection.[2]

The amazement that the Rambam describes at the wisdom of creation that is strikingly akin to Einstein's astonishment at "the harmony of natural law." Similarly, Einstein echoes Maimonides's sense of man's smallness and insignificance: "One who understands this will know that all man's wisdom and intellect are no more than a dim, insignificant flickering."[3]

Love and Awe: Another Perspective

However, further investigation of the Rambam's view shows that words like "wonder" and "smallness" do not fully capture his understanding of the complex religious emotions of love and awe.

> He will love, praise and glorify Him and with a great desire will yearn to know God's great name. (*MT, Hilkhot Yesodei HaTorah,* 2:2)

Enfolded within the experience of wonder is a great desire for knowledge. Love of God is not only an outcome of knowledge. It also arouses a thirst for additional knowledge. But what kind of knowledge awakens such a powerful yearning?

A related question flows from the way in which the Rambam described fear of God:

> He will immediately be afraid and will know that he is a small, lowly creature made of dust and that his intellect is slight compared to the Pure of Knowledge. (*MT, Hilkhot Yesodei HaTorah,* 2:2)

According to the Aristotelian concept that the Rambam adopted, there is no gap between a person and the objects of his understanding.[4] In this view, knowledge is something that enlarges us as we absorb new ideas. However, in the passage above the Rambam describes the experience of knowledge as one that leads to a sense of smallness ("he will know that he is a small, lowly creature"). What kind of learning causes us to feel so small?

These two questions share a single, surprising answer that is hinted to at the end of this *halakhah*: "his intellect is slight compared to the Pure of Knowledge." This is not an experience of physical smallness, but rather of intellectual insignificance. A person feels intellectual smallness when he does not understand. This *halakhah*, I propose, describes an experience of not understanding. When a person experiences this sense of wonder in the face of a universe that is infinitely greater than his capacity to grasp, he feels the immensity of this gap, and then he understands that he does understand. This is a kind of knowledge that does not quench the thirst for knowledge but arouses a desire for more.

Love and awe arise not just from our understanding of the world, but also from the failures of our understanding to grasp more than we do. The intellectual perplexity that results from reading the *Guide*, which leads some to pursue ecstatic mysticism and others to a life of social action, brings all its serious students to love and awe of God. One who sets out to know God will inevitably come up against the limits of reason. When he meets a metaphysical brick wall that intellect cannot breach, he confronts the limits of his humanity and realizes his smallness in the face of the immensity of the cosmos. This evokes love and awe.

Perplexity leads us to a sense that the world exceeds our understanding. You might compare it to two men who have spent their whole life on a deserted island standing on the seashore and gazing off into the distance. One of them believes that human powers of vision are unlimited and assumes that the place beyond which he cannot see is actually the end of the world. The other, more modest, understands that the visible horizon may not be the end of the world, that reality might extend further than he can see.

Similarly, a certain kind of rationalist believes that the limits of understanding mark the limits of the universe. In the *Guide*, Maimonides attempts to free his readers from such a notion. Beyond our senses, intellect, and imagination, there are planes of existence that we cannot grasp. Encountering the limits of reason engenders a sense of mystery.

There are two kinds of thought that cannot reconcile themselves with this notion that there may be whole areas of existence beyond what we know: folk theology and atheism. Folk theology maintains that there is a God but that He is part of the world that we ordinarily know. Atheism, on the other hand, asserts that there is no God, that there is only the world that we know. Both of these approaches shrink reality to fit the bounds of what is knowable. Maimonides, by contrast, asserted that God exists but that we cannot know God. He posited a world beyond what we can grasp that is not accessible to human intellect.

The encounter with the borders of reason is the key to Maimonides's therapeutic philosophy: there is something profoundly healing about recognizing our intellectual limits; it undermines self-centeredness.

EGOCENTRICITY

The belief that we are at the center of the world is responsible for many of our psychological, political, and theological problems. Maimonides's understanding of the problem of evil, as we saw in part 1, was that it stemmed from the widespread but mistaken human assumption that the world exists to serve us. But the world does not work like that, and the dissonance between our expectations and reality leads to regular frustration and despair. Freedom from this self-centered attitude can lead to a healthier awareness that the world is not designed to meet our every need or want and that many outcomes that we had previously called "evil" were the result of our own unrealistic expectations.

The traditional belief in providence posits that God watches over the life of every human being. For the believer, God redeems each of us from our cosmic loneliness and gives us a sense of absolute self-worth. The Rambam, as we saw, reframed the concept of providence; providence is not God's constant interest in every person, but rather a spiritual achievement of one who seeks God. Similarly, he reconceived prophecy so that it was no longer a result of God's deciding to be involved in human life, but primarily an initiative of human beings who decide to live their whole life as an endeavor to come closer to God. Throughout the *Guide*, God, not man, is placed at the center.

The Guide for the Perplexed is a redemptive book. It belongs to an ancient tradition that affirmed the existence of a body of knowledge, the understanding and internalization of which can liberate us from the pains and sorrows of the world. However, unlike Gnosticism, Epicureanism, Spinozism, and certain schools of Kabbalah, for the Rambam the most liberating knowledge is the knowledge that we do not know.

The *Guide* informs us that it does not communicate its teachings fully. It gives us the chapter headings and leaves its readers to understand the rest of the message from their own intellectual resources. The reader becomes a partner in the construction of the book. The Rambam called on his readers not just to understand what he had written but also to uncover meanings that were not explicitly stated. A reader is invited to not only interpret the *Guide* but also to continue and extend its teaching based on his sense of the hidden, internal logic of the book. Therefore, any extensive reading of the *Guide* has an element of midrash to it. This chapter is my midrash on the *Guide*, which says, in essence, that the goal of knowledge is to encounter the limits of knowledge. The full realization of this intellectual project will bring us to a life of awe and wonder in which we are aware that there is mystery at the heart of the world, making us no longer able to see ourselves as the center or purpose of creation.[5]

REDEMPTIVE PERPLEXITY

The Western cultural and philosophical climate of the second half of the twentieth century was, in general, characterized by radical skepticism. Man lost faith in his ability to make objective ethical judgments or to advance universally valid scientific theories. Objective truth no longer existed; there were only narratives. There were many versions of this attitude, which is often referred to as postmodernism. Some saw the assertion that a statement is objectively true as an attempt to achieve power and control. Others viewed "truth" as no more than a compliment that was paid to dignify certain opinions. For others, the word "truth" expressed nothing except the advantage gained by using the word. The second half of the twentieth century was indeed an era of perplexity.

The Rambam would have understood the sense that it is difficult to reach the truth. For him though, the encounter with the limits of reason did not engender frustration, cynicism, and despair, but rather awakened love and awe. The *Guide*'s profound treatment of fundamental questions in Jewish philosophy made the Rambam a seminal teacher for many generations of students. However, it is the central issue of the book—the challenge of living with perplexity—that makes the book especially relevant in the postmodern era.

The Rambam's perfect man was not one who reached certainty, but rather one who could, without self-deception, distinguish between proofs that were compelling and proofs that were almost, but not entirely, compelling:

> For if you stay your progress because of a dubious point; if you do not deceive yourself into believing that there is a demonstration with regard to matters that have not been demonstrated; if you do not hasten to reject and to categorically pronounce false any assertions whose contraries have not been demonstrated; if finally you do not aspire to apprehend that which you are not able to apprehend—you will have reached human perfection. (*Guide*, 1:32)[6]

Let us go back to the parable of the palace, in which the Rambam depicted the spiritual hero at advanced stages on the path to perfection. The hero is described as almost—but not quite—reaching certainty:

> He, however, who has achieved demonstration to the extent that it is possible, of everything that may be demonstrated; and who has ascertained in divine matters to the extent that that is possible, everything that may be ascertained; and who has come close to certainty in those matters in which one can only come close to it—has come to be with the ruler in the inner part of his habitation. (*Guide*, 3:51)[7]

The Rambam's hero lives with the knowledge of being close to the truth, but without jumping to precipitous conclusions. The *Guide* itself is an example of philosophy done in this spirit. We have seen how the Rambam asserted certain positions, for example, on the creation of the world, not because they were irrefutably proven to be true but because the balance of probabilities was in their favor.

The driving quest of philosophy, from Plato through Descartes and into the modern era, was for absolute certainty. However, the greater the ambition, the more easily it could be undermined, and the more painful was its eventual disappointment. One small doubt was enough to destroy a proof that claimed to be absolute. The modern history of ideas is a progression from seeking complete certainty to surrendering to total skepticism, from the philosophers' claim that they had found the truth to the postmodernist claim that there is no truth. The seeds of radical skepticism may be found in the radical certainty that philosophy sought throughout the ages. If your faith depends on absolute certainty, then its absence will destroy your faith absolutely.

The radical skepticism that has become the received wisdom in our era of perplexity is not entirely new. In ancient Greece there were already thinkers such as Protagoras and Pyrrho who espoused similar notions. Postmodernism is a new version of old ideas; its novelty is cultural rather than philosophical. An idea that used to be on the periphery of the intellectual conversation became central—not because stronger philosophical arguments for skepticism were discovered, but because of the terrible history of the last century.

The twentieth century was the culmination of modernism. Ideas that were born in the eighteenth and nineteenth centuries evolved into extreme ideologies, and the results were Fascism, Nazism, and Stalinist communism. In the first half of the twentieth century, humanity fell victim to absolute certainties. As Karl Popper put it, "The attempt to make heaven on earth invariably produces hell." From Auschwitz to the Siberian gulags, the grotesque failures of modernity were clear. This was a story of people who, with total certainty about what was good, ended up doing an immense amount of evil.

Postmodernism in philosophy was a reaction to the atrocities of the twentieth century. Certainty about good and evil gave way to skepticism about the concepts of good and evil themselves. Vaulting ideologies that tried to encompass everything were traded in for modest narratives that were content to explain just a little. Anyone who speaks of certainty today is suspect. The Western world has turned to skepticism in the hope that this will save us from a repetition of the twentieth century's catastrophes. Postmodernism is above all post-trauma.

However, there is a high price to pay for radical skepticism. It shackles the curiosity of humankind. If there is no truth, then there is no point in seeking it. Reading ancient books, studying diverse religions, and learning about profound philosophies is motivated by an urge to find the truth. If truth were to disappear there is a danger that the search would also. In practice, there are two extremes that snuff out the desire for knowledge: dogmatism and radical skepticism. Dogmatism asserts that the search is unnecessary because we already have the truth. Radical skepticism says the search is pointless because there is no truth.

Two conditions, then, are necessary for a real philosophical conversation: belief that there is truth, and an absence of certainty about it. The Rambam tried to create a new intellectual archetype: the man whose beliefs did not depend on absolute knowledge, who was prepared to live without self-deception by ideas that fell short of certainty. By releasing us from the need for certainty, the Rambam also shielded us from radical doubt. It is this possibility which, after the failures of modernism and postmodernism, makes *The Guide for the Perplexed* more relevant today than ever.

CONCLUSION

The Purpose of Life

The reader who makes his way through the storm of ideas that the Rambam unleashed in the *Guide*, who successfully negotiates complex discussions about religious language, proofs for the existence of God, dilemmas around the question of creation, and debates about prophecy, providence, the problem of evil, and the reasons for the commandments, finds himself at the end of the book in a discussion about the purpose of life.

What is the true purpose of life? In part 3 of the *Guide*, Maimonides presents three possibilities: in chapter 51, mystical contemplation; in chapter 52, stronger dedication to *halakhah*; and in chapter 54, a life of social and political action. Which path does the *Guide* direct its readers to follow? Each has supporters who claim that theirs is *the* true path that Maimonides advocates. Some have argued that meditative contemplation leading to mystical ecstasy is the true goal of life for the Rambam.[1] Others have claimed that a stronger commitment to *halakhah* is the purpose he advocates.[2] Still others have insisted that he believes engagement in social and political life is the ultimate purpose.[3]

In the end the issue remains open. Maimonides does not proclaim that any one of these options is superior to the others. He walks with his readers to the border of the promised land—a whole, fulfilled life—but does not enter it with us. Like Moses the son of Amram, he remains behind, looking down from the mountain, enabling his readers to make their own way onward.

NOTES

INTRODUCTION

1. Moses Maimonides, *The Guide of the Perplexed*, trans. Shlomo Pines (Chicago: University of Chicago Press, 1963), 16. Maimonides wrote the *Guide* in Arabic for his student Joseph Ibn Aknin, who was struggling to reconcile traditional belief with Aristotelian science. In response to a written request for a Hebrew translation from the Jewish community of Lunel, the Rambam assured them that while he had no time for such an undertaking, the accomplished translator Shmuel Ibn Tibbon was working on it. Indeed, Ibn Tibbon consulted Maimonides while he drafted the Hebrew version. In 1190, this famed Provençal translator and linguist presented his Hebrew translation of the *Guide*. Most of the later translations were based on Ibn Tibbon's work, which is considered highly accurate. For example, the sixteenth century saw both Latin and Italian versions of the *Guide*, both using Ibn Tibbon as their source. Later, German and Hungarian versions came out. An English translation by the Princeton-educated Methodist minister James Townley of the section in part 3 on the reasons for the commandments was published in 1827. A year after the debut of the Ibn Tibbon translation, the Spanish poet Yehuda Alharizi completed his own Hebrew translation. While considered both more lyrical and accessible than Ibn Tibbon's, the Alharizi version never gained the same recognition. The Rambam's son, Abraham, wrote that it contained inaccuracies. The scholar Solomon Munk returned to the original Arabic for his French translation and the first critical edition of the *Guide* (1856). Munk used manuscripts he had copied from the Bodleian Library, Oxford, and incomplete manuscripts from the Bibliothèque nationale, Paris. Michael Friedlander produced the first English translation of the whole of the *Guide* based on the original Arabic in 1881. In 1963, Israel Prize laureate Shlomo Pines introduced a new English translation based on the Arabic. The Pines version is considered authoritative, and it spurred a flurry of academic interest in Maimonides in North America. In 1972, Yosef Kapach produced a new Hebrew translation. Professor Michael Schwarz of Tel Aviv University

released his own Hebrew translation in 1997. The Hebrew version of this book used the Schwarz translation. The English version uses the Pines translation.

2. For a summary of the history of interpretation of the *Guide*, see Aviezer Ravitsky, "Sitrei Torato Shel Moreh Hanevukhim" [Secrets of the teaching of *The Guide for the Perplexed*], in *Al Daat Hamakom: Mehkarim B'hagut Hayehudit Ub'toldoteheh* [Studies in Jewish thought and its history] (Jerusalem: Keter Press, 1991), 142–82.

Part 1
1. The God of Maimonides

1. See, e.g., the surveys published by the Interdisciplinary Center, Herzliya, http://www.midgam.com/results/articles/article.asp?articleId=33.

2. Moshe Halbertal, *Maimonides: Life and Thought, trans. Joel Linsider* (Princeton: Princeton University Press, 2014), 2.

3. See, e.g., *Guide*, part 1, chapter 26 [hereafter cited in the form 1:26]: "To speak at length of this matter would be superfluous, were it not for the notions to which the minds of the multitude are accustomed. For this reason, it behooves to explain the matter to those whose souls grasp at human perfection and, by dint of expatiating a little on the point in question just as we have done, to put an end to the fantasies that come to them from the age of infancy."

4. I have chosen to use the proofs from the *Mishneh Torah*, as they are stated there more clearly than in the *Guide*. Translations from the *Mishneh Torah* are by Yedidya Sinclair.

5. See *Mishneh Torah, Hilkhot Yesodei HaTorah*, 3; see also *Guide*, 2:1: "it is impossible that He should be two or more, because of the impossibility of a multitude of separate things that have no physical form."

6. See the introduction to part 2 of the *Guide*, premise 12.

7. See *Guide*, 2:1.

8. For example, "One thing I ask of the Lord . . . to gaze upon the beauty of the Lord" (Ps. 27:4); "My soul thirsts . . . O when will I come to appear before God!" (Ps. 42:3). Translations of biblical passages are from the JPS Tanakh.

9. See, e.g., Moshe Halbertal, *Concealment and Revelation: Esotericism in Jewish Thought and Its Philosophical Implications*, trans. Jackie Feldman (Princeton: Princeton University Press, 2007).

10. The most prominent source of this idea is in the thought of Plotinus. See my discussion in chapter 12, "Perplexity and God."

11. *Guide*, 1:56.

12. See, e.g., Hermann Cohen, *Religion of Reason: Out of the Sources of Judaism*, trans. Simon Kaplan (New York: Oxford University Press, 1995); and Yehezkel Kaufmann, *Toldot Haemunah Hayisraelit* [History of the religion of Israel] (Tel Aviv: Dvir Press, 1952), 2:227.

13. Today, more than a few Bible scholars disagree with the unequivocal distinctions made by Kaufman and claim that the biblical text is richer and more multifaceted than Kaufman allowed. One of the most interesting voices in this discussion is Yisrael Knohl, who argues that in Leviticus one may find an almost Maimonidean version of monotheism. Knohl, *The Sanctuary of Silence* (Minneapolis: Fortress Press, 1995).

14. Warren Zev Harvey, "Maimonides' Avicennianism," *Maimonidean Studies* 5 (2008): 107–19.

15. Some modern interpreters of the Rambam have argued that there is no essential theological difference between negating tens of attributes of God and negating hundreds of divine attributes. Either way, we cannot say anything about God. To my mind, this claim empties of all meaning the doctrine of negative attributes and undermines the theology that the Rambam constructed upon it. However, from various hints that the Rambam gives, it appears that he thought that human consciousness could represent God but that such representations could not be given verbal expression. Description of God through negation does have a function in refining how we think about God: "As for the negative attributes, they are those that must be used in order to conduct the mind toward that which must be believed with regard to Him, may He be exalted" (*Guide*, 1:58). The doctrine of negative attributes frees our thoughts about God from language, enabling a purer mental representation of God. According to this mode, the doctrine of negative attributes is a move from theology to cognitive praxis. For discussion of this see Eyal Bar Eytan, "Moreh Derekh l'yediyat Ha'elohim: Al Ha'megama Ha'hiyuvit shel Ha'teologia Hashelilit B'sefer *Moreh Hanevukhim*" (Guide to Knowing God: On the Positive Aspects of Negative Theology in Maimonides' *Guide for the Perplexed*) (unpublished PhD diss., Hebrew University of Jerusalem, 2001).

16. Maimonides writes at the beginning of the *Guide* that his intention is "to explain the meanings of words that appear in the books of the prophets." In the introduction to part 3 he explains his purpose a little differently as being "to explain what can be explained of the Account of the Beginning and the Account of the Chariot." For an attempt to address this tension, see Steven Harvey, "Maimonides in the Sultan's Palace," in *Perspectives on Maimonides: Philosophical and Historical Studies*, ed. Joel Kramer (Oxford: Oxford University Press, 1994), 47–75.

2. PROPHECY

1. A full articulation of this view may be found in Yehudah Halevi's *Sefer Hakuzari* [Book of the Kuzari] (Tel Aviv: Dvir, 1994), 1:40–43. It should be noted that when Maimonides sketches out the popular view of prophecy, he does not include all of the motifs that appear in Halevi's theory of prophecy.

2. See, e.g., *Guide*, 1:7.

3. The possibility of this sort of miraculous involvement in the prophetic event elicited astonishment from generations of "radical interpreters" of the *Guide*, who believed that Maimonides's true, esoteric teaching in the *Guide* was essentially Aristotelian. The concept of radical interpretation in the context of the *Guide* was popularized by Ravitsky in *Sitrei*, 143–46.

4. From Maimonides, *Ha'hakdama L'masekhet Avot* [Introduction to *Avot*], in *Hakdamot Harambam Laperush Hamishnah* [The Rambam's introductions to the commentary on the Mishnah] (Jerusalem: Mossad Harav Kook, 1961), 168.

5. Aristotle, *Nicomachean Ethics*, trans. Terence Irwin (Indianapolis: Hackett, 1985).

6. Maimonides, *Ha'hakdama L'masekhet Avot*, 159.

7. Maimonides, *Ha'hakdama L'masekhet Avot*, 159.

8. Maimonides, *Ha'hakdama L'masekhet Avot*, 159.

9. See *Guide*, 1:34.

10. See *Guide*, 2:36.

11. Maimonides, *Hakdama L'perek Helek* [Introduction to chapter *Helek*], in *Hakdamot*, 115.

12. The metaphor of "overflow" is taken from Plotinus. We will explore it in chapter 12.

13. "The Works of Creation" is a name for the first chapter of Genesis, in which the world is created. Maimonides understood the "Work of Creation" as containing the laws of physics.

14. "The Works of the Chariot" refers to the first chapter of Ezekiel and contains the secrets of metaphysics, according to Maimonides.

15. *Otzar Ha'geonim* (Jerusalem: Hebrew University Press, 1932), vol. 4, Tractate *Hagigah*, 31.

16. As Yaakov Levinger has shown, this idea is rooted in the thought of Ibn Sina. Ibn Sina understood the prophetic event to be a kind of arousal a nondiscursive faculty of intuition. According to Levinger, Maimonides adopted this notion but substituted for intuition the faculty of divination, which, because it works very quickly, appears intuitive. Levinger, *Harambam K'filosof V'khposek* [Maimonides as philosopher and legal decisor] (Jerusalem: Mossad Bialik, 1990), 34–35.

17. See Barry S. Kogan, "What Can We Know and When Can We Know It? Maimonides on the Active Intelligence and Human Cognition," in *Moses Maimonides and His Time*, ed. E. L. Ormsby (Washington DC: Catholic University of America Press, 1989), 121–37.

18. One may note that this prophetic quality is reminiscent of what the Rabbinic sages termed the ability to "predict what will result" ("ro'eh et ha'nolad"). See, e.g., Babylonian Talmud [hereafter BT] *Tamid*, 32a. Rashi, in his commentary to BT *Pesachim*, 9b, sees this quality as a type of prophetic ability.

19. Avraham Nouriel, "Mishalim V'lo Nitparesh Shehem Mishal *B'moreh Hanevukhim*" [Parables that are not interpreted as parables in the *Guide for the Perplexed*], *Da'at* 25 (1990): 85–91.

20. See, e.g., Warren Zev Harvey, "Miriam the Prophetess and the Seventh Principle of the *Guide for the Perplexed*," in *At the Mouth of the Well: Studies in Jewish Thought and the Philosophy of Halakhah Presented to Gerald Blidstein*, ed. Uri Ehrlich, Hayim Kreisel, and Daniel Y. Lasker (Beer Sheva: Ben Gurion University Press, 2008), 183–94.

21. *Guide*, 1:54.

3. PROVIDENCE

1. *Igeret Harambam L'rabi Yefet bar Eliyahu Hadayan* [Letter to R. Yaphet Bar Eliyahu the Judge], in *Igrot Harambam* [Letters of the Rambam], ed. Yitzhak Shilat (Jerusalem: Shilat Publications, 1987), 1:311.

2. *Miscellany of Hebrew Literature*, trans. Dr. H. Adler (London: N. Trubner, 1872), 1:223.

3. *Guide*, 3:16.

4. Maimonides also proposed a metaphysical approach to evil in *Guide*, 3:10. There he makes the classic argument that evil is absence of God and therefore God cannot create evil, just as it is impossible to create darkness. This claim has ancient roots; see Plato, *The Republic*, trans. G. M. A. Grube (Indianapolis: Hackett, 1974).

5. This is a recurring theme in Maimonides's writings; see, e.g., "Hanhagat Habriyut: Igeret Ha'refua Miiharambam z"l L'melekh Yishmael" [Healthy behavior: A medical letter from the Rambam *z'l* to the Ishmaelite king"], trans. Moshe Ibn Tibbon, edited from the manuscript by Zisman Montner in *Medical Writings* (Jerusalem: Mossad Harav Kook, 1957); *Ha'hakdama L'masekhet Avot*, 281; *MT*, *Hilkhot De-ot*, chapter 4; George Geimm, *The Doctrine of the Buddha* (Cambridge UK: Cambridge University Press, 1926), 3.

6. Geimm, *Doctrine of the Buddha*, 3.

7. One of the most important Western exponents of the view that the pursuit of happiness can be self-defeating was the German philosopher Arthur Schopenhauer; see Schopenhauer, *The World as Will and Representation* (New York: Dover, 1966).

8. Geimm, *Doctrine of the Buddha*, 264–71.

9. See Immanuel Kant, *Critique of Pure Reason*, trans. Norman Kemp Smith (London: Macmillan, 1929).

10. There have been many versions of this proof. For an important and relatively recent discussion of the question, see Richard Taylor, *Metaphysics* (Englewood Cliffs NJ: Prentice-Hall, 1974), 112–14.

11. See, e.g., the Ramban's commentary on Genesis 1:1, 11:28, 46:15; Exodus 13:16, 6:2; and Leviticus 26:11.

12. The Rambam also presented an additional approach, which we do not examine in depth here, that of the Mu'atzila. According to this view, everything that happens

in the world flows from a divine decision. God knows everything. God's providence governs all creatures, and God is infallible, always doing good and never evil. Man has free will, and God rewards or punishes every human choice according to what we deserve.

13. For a discussion of Moses Ibn Tibbon's treatment of the questions of evil and providence, see Halbertal, *Maimonides*, 340.

14. *Guide*, 1:1.

4. REDEMPTION

1. There is a wide range of opinions within the different streams of Kabbalah regarding the nature of the *sefirot* and the question of which ones are in contact with the lower worlds and which are never revealed. On this see, e.g., Haviva Pedaya, *Ha'rambam: Hitalut Zman Mahzori V'text Kadosh* [The Rambam: The elevation of cyclical time and the holy text] (Tel Aviv: Am Oved, 2003), 135–42; and Moshe Idel, *Absorbing Perfections: Kabbalah and Interpretation* (New Haven: Yale University Press, 2002), 26–111.

2. In addition to redemption, providence, and prophecy, the Rambam also offered a new perspective on the mitzvot, which we will explore in part 2, and on the idea of creation, which we will examine in part 3.

3. It is possible that the Rambam is basing his view here on a midrash (*Shemot Rabbah*, 36:3) according to which the light of Torah saves from harm one who learns it. The *midrash* interprets "The path of the righteous is like radiant sunlight, ever brightening until noon. The way of the wicked is all darkness; they do not know what will make them stumble" (Prov. 4:18–19) as follows: "This is like someone who is standing in darkness and has a torch in his hand, so he can see a stone in front of him and doesn't stumble on it; he sees a pit in front of him, and does not fall into it, because of the light in his hand." The midrash compares wisdom to a light that prevents one from coming to harm.

4. *Guide*, 3:18.

5. Aviezer Ravitsky, "Kfi Koah Ha'adam: Yemot Ha'mashiah B'mishnat Harambam" [According to human ability: The Messianic Era in the thought of the Rambam], in *Al Daat Hamakom*, 74–104.

6. In the light of this analysis, I propose accepting at face value the Rambam's assertion that the decree of poverty was a consequence of the primal sin of eating from the Tree of Knowledge in the Garden of Eden, which was itself the result of imagination overcoming need. This entails rejecting Sarah Klein Braslavy's allegorical interpretation. See Klein Braslavy, "Peirush Ha'rambam La'sipurim al Adam B'farshat Bereishit" [Maimonides' interpretation of the Adam stories in Genesis], in *Prakim B'torat Haadam shel Harambam* [A study in Maimonides's anthropology] (Jerusalem: Reuven Publishing, 1986), 118–21.

7. For further discussion of this reversal, see Aviezer Ravitsky, "Kfi Koah Ha'adam," 77.

8. *Guide*, 2:40 and 3:27.

9. BT *Niddah*, 68a.

10. See, e.g., the Ramban on the Torah, commentary to Deuteronomy, 31:6.

11. This idea also has roots on the Talmud: "The lifetime of the world is 6000 years; 2000 years of chaos, 2000 years of Torah and 2000 years of the messianic era." BT *Sanhedrin*, 97a.

12. See Gershom Scholem, *On the Kabbalah and Its Symbolism*, trans. Ralph Manheim (New York: Schocken, 1969), 72–77.

13. Carlyle was the most prominent exponent of the view that history is primarily the story of "great men" who created the major events of history and were not dependent on external forces. See Carlyle, *On Heroes, Hero Worship, and the Heroic in History* (London: James Fraser, 1841).

14. This is the view of Marxist historians. See Nathan Rothenstreich, "Ha'yahid Ve'hahistoria" [The individual and history], in *Ha'ishiyut V'dora: Kovetz shel Hartzaot Shehushmeu B'khenes Ha'shimini L'iyun B'historia* [Personalities in their generation: Collected lectures from the Eighth Conference for the Study of History] (Jerusalem: Israeli Historical Society, 1964), 15–38; also Tzvi Ya'avetz, "Deot Shonot al Mekoma shel Ha'ishiut Ba'historia" [Different opinions on the role of personality in history], in *Historia V'ruah Ha'zman: Az V'ata* [History and the spirit of the age: Then and now] (Tel Aviv: Dvir, 2002), 45–57.

15. On this distinction see Ravitsky, "Kfi Koah Haadam," 75–87; and Ravitsky, "Harambam: Ezoteriut V'hinukh Filosofi" [Maimonides: Esotericism and philosophical education]," *Da'at* 53 (2004): 43–62.

16. See Menachem Lorberbaum's distinction between messianism and utopianism in the Rambam's writings in *Politics and the Limits of Law: Secularizing the Political in Medieval Jewish Thought* (Stanford: Stanford University Press, 2001).

17. This is one of the central claims of Popper's monumental work *The Open Society and Its Enemies* (London: Routledge, 1945).

5. EMPOWERING HUMANITY

1. Richard Dawkins, *The God Delusion* (New York: Mariner Books, 2008); Christopher Hitchens, *God Is Not Great: How Religion Poisons Everything* (New York: Twelve, 2009).

2. Dawkins, *The God Delusion*, 31.

3. Terry Eagleton, "Lunging, Flailing, Mispunching," *London Review of Books*, October 19, 2006, 32.

4. Karen Armstrong, *The Case for God* (New York: Anchor, 2010).

5. Armstrong, *The Case for God*, 11.

6. MT, *Hilkhot Teshuvah*, 10:3.

7. A good deal has been written about this. See, e.g., Moshe Halbertal, *Mahapeikhot Parshaniot B'hithavutan* [Interpretative revolutions in the making] (Jerusalem: Magnes Press, 1997).

8. See Halbertal, *Maimonides*, 313–21.

CONCLUSION

1. For more on religious experience in Maimonides's thought, see chapter 18.

Part 2
6. IS THE TORAH DIVINE?

1. See, e.g., Karen Armstrong, *A History of God* (New York: Ballantine, 1993), 357.

2. See the discussion of prophecy in chapter 2.

3. This chapter is a central one in the *Guide*, as can be seen from the number of other chapters that refer to it. See *Guide*, 1:8, 1:15, 1:16, 1:21, 1:38, and 3:54.

4. For a detailed study of *Guide*, 1:54, see Chana Kasher, "Peirushei Harambam L'sipur Nikrat Hatzur" [Maimonides' interpretations of the story in the cleft in the rock], *Da'at* 35 (1995): 29–36.

5. *Eudaemonia* is the Greek term that denotes both success and a person's full, human flourishing.

6. However, he made some significant changes to Aristotelian ethics in adopting the concept of the golden mean. On this see Marvin Fox, "The Doctrine of the Mean: Aristotle and Maimonides," in *Studies in Jewish Religion and History Presented to Alexander Altmann on the Occasion of His Seventieth Birthday*, ed. S. Stein and R. Loewe (Tuscaloosa: University of Alabama Press, 1979), 93.

7. Aristotle, *Nicomachean Ethics*, 2.1.

8. Aristotle also hints at this view. For a broader discussion of this point see Fox, "The Doctrine of the Mean," 100.

9. This point has been the subject of some controversy. According to Lorberbaum, *Guide*, 1:54, deals with the development of Moshe's political leadership and not with the creation of law. I am inclined to agree with Eliezer Goldman and Warren Zev Harvey, who argue that the chapter also reflects the process of the birth of the Torah's laws. It seems to me that at the root of this argument is a more fundamental disagreement about the relationship between leadership and law. According to Lorberbaum, the Rambam believed that leadership is prior to law and therefore the leader can transgress the law when law is blocking effective leadership. See Lorberbaum, *Politics and the Limits of Law*. For Harvey, on the other hand, law is a central tool of leadership and, other than in exceptional cases, it cannot be overridden. For Harvey, *Guide*, 1:54, describes the origins of the Torah's law, which went hand in hand with Moses's leadership, whereas for Lorberbaum, who wished to separate law and leadership, the chapter is about the development of Moses's wisdom as a leader.

My discussion here is based on the assumption that law is also a central subject of this chapter and, I believe, lends further support to that view. Goldman, "Ha'avoda Ha'meyuhedet B'mesigei Ha'amitot: Hearot Parshaniot *La'moreh Ha'nevukhim*, Helek Gimel, Perakim 51–54" [The special work in apprehending truths Interpretative notes on *Guide for the Perplexed*, 3:51–54], *Sefer Ha'shanah shel Universitat Bar Ilan* 6 (1966): 287–313; and Warren Zev Harvey, "Harambam al Klaliut Hahok V'tafkid Hashofet" [The Rambam on the generality of law and the role of the judge], in *Din V'yosher B'Torat Ha'mishpat shel Ha'rambam* [Law and reasoning in the Rambam's legal thought], ed. Hanina Ben-Menachem and Berachyahu Lifshitz (Jerusalem: ha'Makhon le'heker ha'mishpat ha'Ivri, 2004), 253–71.

10. The purpose of all that exists beneath the sphere of the moon is to supply the needs of human beings, as the Rambam explains: "Know that the ancients did wonderfully wise work and verified everything in existence has a purpose, and nothing there is nothing that exists for no reason. . . . [A]s a rule, everything that exists beneath the sphere of the moon exists solely for the purposes of man; of all kinds of living things, some exist to be man's food and some for his other needs" (*Peirush Al Ha'mishnah*).

11. I expand on this point in chapter 7.

12. It should be noted that the Rambam does in fact give reasons for some of the details of the sacrifices. On this problem see Chana Kasher, "Omanut Ha'ketiva B'moreh Ha'nevukhim" [The art of writing in the *Guide for the Perplexed*], *Da'at* 37 (1996): 63–106; and Josef Stern, *Problems and Parables of Law: Maimonides and Nachmanides on Reasons for the Commandments* (Albany: State University of New York Press, 1998).

13. See Michael Tzvi Nehorai, "Torat Hamitzvot shel Harambam" [The Rambam's teaching on the commandments], *Da'at* 13 (1984): 32–33.

14. *Guide*, 2:4.

15. On this see Amos Funkenstein, "Tefisato Hahistorit V'hameshihit shel Harambam" [Maimonides' conception of history and messianism], in *Tadmit V'todaah Historit B'yahadut Ub'svivatah Hatarbutit* [Historical consciousness in Judaism and its cultural surroundings] (Tel Aviv: Am Oved, 1991), 121–23.

16. On this see Alvin J. Reines, "Maimonides's Concept of Mosaic Prophecy," HUCA 40–41 (1969–70): 169–206.

17. The Torah's practical answer to this problem is *Hora'at Sha'ah*, a temporary injunction. See Shalom Rosenberg, "Al Derekh Harov" [The way of the majority], *Shnaton Hamishpat Haivri* 14–15 (1988–89): 190–91. Compare Levinger, *Harambam K'filosof V'khposek*.

18. Compare Aristotle, *Nicomachean Ethics*, book 5.

19. See *MT*, *Hilkhot Yesodei HaTorah*, chapter 2.

20. According to the Rambam, God is above language, so when the Torah attributes speech to God it is referring to God's will or thought. *Guide*, 1:65.

21. This is similar to an idea in the thought of Philo of Alexandria. In Philo's view, there is a profound accord between the laws of nature and the laws of the Torah. See Mireille Hadas-Lebel, *Philon Ha'alexandroni: Bein Yahadut L'helenism* [Philo of Alexandria: Between Judaism and Hellenism] (Tel Aviv: Yediot Books, 2006), 135–40. See also Shlomo Pines, "Hashvaot bein Hahuka Hadatit L'vein Harefua eitzel Al Farabi V'eitzel Harambam" [Comparisons between religious law and medicine in Al-Farabi and Maimonides], *Jewish Law Annual* 14–15 (1988–89): 171–75.

7. REASONS FOR THE COMMANDMENTS

1. For a classic, scholarly discussion of the kabbalistic *sefirot* see Gershom Scholem, *Major Trends in Jewish Mysticism* (New York: Schocken, 1941), 205–43.
2. See Moshe Idel, *Kabbalah: New Perspectives* (New Haven: Yale University Press, 1988), 173–99.
3. On Maimonides's approach to this in other writings, see chapter 4 in this volume.
4. We should qualify this claim by pointing out that immediately afterward the Rambam lowers the reader's expectations by limiting the discussion to understanding the general reasons for the commandments:

> What everyone endowed with a sound intellect ought to believe about the commandments is what I shall set forth to you: The generalities of the commandments necessarily have a cause and have been given because of a certain utility; their details are that in regards to which it was said of the commandments that they that they were given merely for the sake of commanding something. (*Guide*, 3:26)

There is a further lowering of expectations in the Rambam's claim that although the commandments work to perfect our personalities, they do not work equally well for all types of people:

> Among the things that you likewise ought to know is that the Law does not pay attention to isolated cases. The Law was not given with a view to things that are rare. For in everything that it wishes to bring about, be it an opinion, or a moral habit, or a useful work, it is directed only toward the things that happen in the majority of cases and pays no attention to what happens rarely, or to the damage occurring to the unique human being because of this way of determination and because of the legal character of the governance. (*Guide*, 3:34)

The mitzvot work to perfect human beings, but they cannot always take account of exceptional cases. Indeed, they may even cause damage in the case of extraordinary individuals.

5. See, e.g., Yehezkel Kaufmann, *Toldot Ha'emuna Ha'yisraelit: Mimei Kedem ad Sof Bayit Sheini* [The religion of Israel: From its beginnings to the end of the Second Temple] (Tel Aviv: Mossad Bialik, 1937), 1:1–32.

6. Abraham's conclusions as they are described in the first chapter of *Hilkhot Avodat Kokhavim* of the *Mishneh Torah* are quite different from those attributed to him in the *Guide*. In the former, Maimonides appears to represent Abraham as proving the existence of God based on the eternal existence of the world, whereas in the latter, Abraham's meditation on the cosmos leads him to conclude that the world was created. *Guide*, 3:29.

7. According to Maimonides, one of the essential features of pagan idolaters is that they were enslaved to their sensory experience. The Rambam describes Abraham, in contrast, as a free man, a wandering spirit not bound to sensory experience. See part 3 of this volume on the importance of freeing oneself from preconceptions.

8. The Rambam declared flatly that Christianity was idolatrous; see MT, *Hilkhot Avodat Kokhavim*, 9:4, in the uncensored Shabtei Frankel edition (Jerusalem: Frankel, 2001). The Rambam's position on Christianity was no doubt influenced by his strong opposition to any kind of visual representation of God (see chapter 1). Less uncompromising views on Christianity held by Jewish authorities of the Middle Ages include the opinion of Tosafot that Christianity should be considered an idolatrous religion for Jews but not for Christians (see, e.g., Tosafot BT *Sanhedrin* 63a) and the opinion of Menachem Ha-Meiri that Christians were not idolatrous, but are rather *[umot] ha-gedurot be-darkei ha-datot*, that is, people who are bound by the ethical laws of a religion; see, e.g. *Beit ha-Bechirah* on BT *Avodah Zarah* 26a. See also Lawrence J. Kaplan, "Maimonides on the Singularity of the Jewish People," *Da'at* 15 (1985): v–xxvii.

9. Maimonides, *Igeret Teiman* [Epistle to Yemen], in *Igrot Harambam*, 1:120.

10. Medieval Jewish thinkers tended to view Jesus as the founder of Christianity. See Avigdor Shinan, *Oto Ha'ish: Yehudim Misaprim al Yeshu* [That man: Jews talk about Jesus] (Tel Aviv: Yediot Books, 1999). Maimonides appears to have anticipated modern scholarship's distinction between Christianity and Jesus.

11. Another example of this dynamic is the persistence of monotheism within the tribe of Levi during the Egyptian exile. According to the schematic history of MT, *Hilkhot Avodat Kokhavim*, chapter 1, the tribe of Levi alone kept the faith during the exile. One might think that this example shows how an idea can persist even without commandments. In fact, however, it serves as an additional illustration that rituals preserve ideas, rather than the opposite. According to Maimonides in MT, *Hilkhot Issurei Bi'ah*, 13:2, the tribe of Levi alone continued the rite of circumcision in Egypt. The fact that they also preserved monotheistic faith is no coincidence. In *Guide*, 3:49, Maimonides argues that the main reason for the commandment of circumcision is to create a framework of commitment to the monotheistic idea.

12. This is based upon a book that Maimonides translated called *Nabataean Agriculture*, which describes Sabian practices in some detail. Though they are mentioned three times in the Koran, there is considerable scholarly debate over who the Sabians were or when and where they lived.

13. *Guide*, 3:37.

14. It is possible that within Maimonides's attack on Sabian religion there is also a concealed polemic against Abraham Ibn Ezra and Yehudah Halevi for their astrological-magical explanations of some of the mitzvot. On this possibility, see Halbertal, *Maimonides*, 347.

15. BT *Bava Batra*, 25a.

16. It is interesting to note that this approach is employed today in biblical scholarship, for example, in Binyamin Uffenheimer's contention that the Bible introduces idolatrous myths and motifs into the text in order to confront them more effectively. Uffenheimer, "Hitmodedut Ha'mikra" [The struggle of scripture], in *Or L'ya'akov* [A light to Jacob], ed. Y. Hoffman and P. Polak (Jerusalem: Mossad Bialik, 1997), 17–35. In a similar vein, Yisrael Knohl claims, following Cassuto, that the showbread in the Sanctuary were adopted from the world of idolatry so as to dispel the pagan-magical associations that were attached to displaying the bread. See Knohl, *Mikdash Ha'Dmama: Iyun B'rovadei Ha'yitzira Ha'cohanit Sheba'torah* [The sanctuary of silence: A study in the literary layers of the priestly Torah] (Jerusalem: Magnus Press, 1993), 127–31. It is also interesting that the Rambam admitted: "I do not know the reason for having bread on the table (in the sanctuary) always" (*Guide*, 3:45). Knohl offers an answer to what the Rambam did not know, in a Maimonidean spirit.

17. I discuss this question extensively in part 3.

18. See also *Guide*, 3:43.

19. See Halevi, *Sefer Ha'Kuzari*, 1:76.

20. See Rabbenu Bachya Ibn Pakuda, *Duties of the Heart* (New York: Feldheim, 1996), introduction.

21. For more on Yom Kippur, see *Guide*, 3:43.

22. The Rambam's approach to this in the *Mishneh Torah* is a little different. See *Hilkhot Teshuvah*, 1:6.

23. There is a tension within the Rambam's writings over whether some personality types have characteristics that block them from developing certain other traits. In the *Mishneh Torah, Hilkhot Teshuvah*, chapter 2, the Rambam writes that although some people are born with deep-rooted negative characteristics, they may overcome them. This contradicts his stance in the *Guide*, 1:34. One may ask whether the Rambam changed his psychological view over the course of his life. On this possibility, see Hannah Kasher, "*Moreh Ha'nevukhim*: Yetzirat Mofet or Kitvei Kodesh?" ["*The Guide for the Perplexed*: Great book or holy text?"], *Da'at* 32–33 (1994): 73–83.

24. The distinction between praxis and virtues of character is taken from Aristotle's *Nicomachean Ethics*, 2.1: "Virtue, then, is of two sorts, virtue of thought and virtue of character . . . virtue of character (i.e. of *ethos*) results from habit (*ethos*); hence its name, 'ethical,' varied slightly from '*ethos*.'"

25. According to Eliezer Schweid, the main difference between Aristotle's and Maimonides's ethical systems lies in how they understand the purpose of achieving moral perfection. See Schweid, *Ha'rambam V'hug Hashpaato* [The Rambam and his circle of influence], ed. Dan Oryan (Jerusalem: Akadamon Press, 1982), 68.

8. MAN AND THE TORAH

1. Yeshayahu Leibowitz, *The Faith of Maimonides* (New York: Lambda, 1989).
2. Yeshayahu Leibowitz, "Religious Praxis: The Meaning of Halakhah," in *Judaism, Human Values and the Jewish State* (Cambridge: Harvard University Press, 1995), 3–29.
3. Rabbenu Bachya Ibn Pakudah, *Gate of Unity*, chapter 6, p. 59.
4. I heard this orally from Aviezer Ravitsky.
5. William James, *The Varieties of Religious Experience* (New York: Macmillan, 1961), 42.
6. James, *Varieties*, 59.
7. The emotions of "love" and "awe" that are described in *Guide*, 3:52, flow from dedication to Torah and would appear to be somewhat different from the feelings of "love" and "awe" that are aroused through contemplation of nature. I discuss this in part 3, particularly in chapter 18.

9. THE UNIVERSALITY OF THE TORAH

1. See, e.g., *MT*, *Hilkhot Nizkei Mamon*, 5:5.
2. For a recent scholarly perspective on this question, see Halbertal, *Maimonides*, 197–228.

Part 3

10. CONTRADICTIONS

1. Yair Lorberbaum, "On Contradictions, Rationality, Dialectics and Esotericism in Maimonides' *Guide for the Perplexed*," *Review of Metaphysics* 55 (June 2002): 711–50.

11. THE CREATION OF THE WORLD

1. The dedicatory epistle of the *Guide* asks what status we should give to their arguments. The Rambam writes there to his student Rabbi Joseph, son of Rabbi Judah: "You . . . asked me to make clear to you certain things pertaining to divine matters, to inform you of the intentions of the *Mutakallimun* in this respect, and to let you know whether their methods were demonstrative, and if not, to what art they belonged. As I also saw, you had already acquired some smattering of this subject from people other than myself; you were perplexed, as stupefaction has come over you."
2. It also appears in medieval Jewish literature. See, e.g., Rabbi Saadiah Gaon's *Book of Beliefs and Opinions* and Rabbenu Bachya Ibn Pakuda's *Duties of the Heart*.

3. See *Guide*, 2:19.

4. W. Z. Harvey, "Maimonides' Avicennianism," 107–9.

5. See *Guide*, 2:2.

6. *Guide*, 1:75–76.

7. Herbert A. Davidson, *Proofs for Eternity, Creation and Existence of God in Medieval Islamic and Jewish Philosophy* (New York: Oxford University Press, 1987), 309.

8. In a letter to Shmuel Ibn Tibbon, the Rambam explains the idea that a possibility becomes a certainty over an infinite span of time. See *Igrot Harambam*, 2:548.

9. In *Guide*, 2:1, the Rambam presented additional proofs for the existence of God. It is open to question whether he considered these proofs decisive.

12. PERPLEXITY AND GOD

1. See also *MT, Hilkhot Teshuvah*, 3:7.

2. See also *Guide*, 1:51.

3. See Aristotle, *Metaphysics*, book 11, sec. 9.

4. Moshe Idel, *Studies in Ecstatic Kabbalah* (Albany: State University of New York Press, 1988), 1–33.

5. For more on this contradiction, see Shlomo Pines, "The Limitations of Human Knowledge in Al-Farabi, Ibn Bajja and Maimonides," in *Studies in Medieval Jewish History and Literature*, ed. Isadore Twersky (Cambridge: Harvard University Press, 1979), 82–102.

6. For an important discussion of this idea, see Warren Zev Harvey, "A Portrait of Spinoza as a Maimonidean," *Journal of the History of Philosophy* 19, no. 2 (1981): 164–65.

7. Plotinus, *Fifth Ennead, The Enneads: Abridged Edition*, ed. John Dillon, trans. Stephen MacKenna (New York: Penguin Books, 1991).

8. Julius Guttman, *Ha'filosophia shel HaYehadut*[The philosophy of Judaism] (Jerusalem: Magnus Press, 1951), 127–28.

9. As discussed, I claim that the *Guide* does not contradict itself in order to advance one opinion and reject another as much Maimonidean scholarship claims, but rather in order to present the different alternatives without deciding firmly between them. See Marvin Fox, "The Many-Sided Maimonides," in *Interpreting Maimonides: Studies in Methodology, Metaphysics, and Moral Philosophy* (Chicago: University of Chicago Press, 1995), 3–25.

13. THE ROLE OF DOUBT

1. *Guide*, 1:26.

2. See his explanations of the Hebrew words for "look" and "see" in *Guide*, 1:4.

3. Elisha Ben Avuya was also known as Elisha Ahe; see BT *Hagigah* 15a.

4. BT *Hagigah*, 14b.

5. See BT *Hagigah* 15a. On the possibility that the Rambam based his image of Elisha Ben Avuya on Islamic sources, see Sarah Stroumsa, "Elisha Ben Avuya and Muslim Heretics in Maimonides' Writings," *Maimonidean Studies* 3 (1995): 173–93.

6. It would appear that behind the Rambam's idea here is the Aristotelian distinction between decisive and dialectical proof; the former confers certainty, while the latter only approaches certainty. See Arthur Hyman, "Demonstrative, Dialectical, and Sophistic Arguments in the Philosophy of Moses Maimonides," in *Maimonides and His Time*, ed. E. L. Ormsky (Washington DC: Catholic University of America, 1989), 35–51.

7. Aristotle, *Metaphysics*, I:I.

8. Elsewhere the Rambam writes about how upsetting the balance between desire and apprehension can damage understanding: "Moreover, every perfect man—after his intellect has attained the cognition of whatever in its nature can be grasped—when longing for another apprehension beyond that which has been achieved, cannot but have his faculty of apprehension deceived or destroyed" (*Guide*, I:21). Elisha Ben Avuya is not the only figure in whom the Rambam diagnosed this imbalance. Maimonides also attributed the sin of the elders of the People of Israel, who wished to ascend Mount Sinai, to a lack of intellectual restraint. The Rambam demands patience of those who would come to know God: "He should not make categorical affirmations in favor of the first opinion that occurs to him and should not, from the outset, strain and impel his thoughts toward the apprehension of the deity; he rather should feel awe and refrain and hold back until he gradually elevates himself" (*Guide*, I:5). A similar understanding of the sin of the elders may be found in MT, *Hilkhot Meilah*, 8:8.

9. René Descartes, *Thoughts on First Philosophy* (Oxford: Oxford University Press, 2008).

14. *HALAKHAH* AND DOGMATISM

1. The question is, why is a well-balanced personality, and not just a well-balanced society, necessary for philosophical achievement? The question is sharpened if we consider Maimonides's Aristotelian taxonomy of the soul, according to which the soul has five components: "The nutritive part, is the physical component and is connected to the art of medicine; the emotional part is the component responsible for the five senses . . . sight, hearing, taste, smell and touch; the imaginative part recalls sensory impressions after they have passed from the sense that perceived them; the appetitive part is the component with which a person desires something or is repelled by it; the intellectual part is the power that understands, reflects and acquires wisdom" (*Ha'hakdama L'masekhet Avot*, chapter 1).

According to the Rambam, ethical characteristics are acquired through the appetitive part of the soul: "Ethical qualities may be found in the appetitive part alone" (*Ha'hakdama L'masekhet Avot*, chapter 2). This implies that the intellectual and ethical domains are located in two different parts of the soul. A person may know what is good without being a good person. Whereas intellectual improvement requires study, ethical improvement is achieved by habituation to ethical behavior. But if there is such a clear dichotomy between the intellect and ethical character, why is ethical perfection a necessary precondition for intellectual achievement according to the Rambam? There are plenty of distinguished intellectuals who are not necessarily paragons of righteousness.

2. Julius Guttmann, *Daat v'mada: Kovetz Maamarim V'hartzaot* [Religion and science: Collected articles and lectures] (Jerusalem: Magnus Press, 1956), 95.

3. *MT, Hilkhot Yesodei HaTorah,* 4:13.

15. THE CRISIS OF REASON

1. For a detailed description of the structure of the spheres, see *Guide*, 1:72.

2. We may infer this from, among other things, the doubt that the Rambam casts on our ability to prove the eternity of the soul. He mocked one of his theological opponents for basing a proof of the soul's eternity on the assumption that the soul is eternal: "Now this is a wondrous method, for it makes clear a hidden matter by something even more hidden. To this, the proverb well known among the Syrians may truthfully be applied: Your guarantee needs another guarantee. It is as if he already possessed a demonstration of the permanence of souls, and as if he knew in what form they last and what thing it is that lasts, so that he could make use thereof for drawing inferences" (*Guide*, 1:73).

Knowledge of the separate intelligences would ground belief in the eternity of the soul (for they could enable the soul to continue without a body), but if we are not convinced of the eternity of the soul, this indicates that we are not persuaded of the existence of separate intelligences either.

3. One of the contradictions between medieval physics and astronomy arises over the direction of movement of the spheres. According to Aristotle, the existence of a vacuum is a logical contradiction, because it implies the existence of a nonexistent. Therefore, he thought that there could not be any space between the heavenly spheres; they must be touching. Consequently, the larger spheres move the smaller spheres, and therefore they must be moving in the same direction. However, astronomical observation showed that this is not the case:

> Even more incongruous and dubious is the fact that in all cases in which one of two spheres is inside the other and adheres to it on every side, while the centers of the two are different, the smaller sphere can move inside the bigger one without the latter being in motion, whereas the bigger sphere cannot move upon any axis whatever without the smaller one being in motion. For whenever the bigger sphere moves, it necessarily, by means of its movement, sets the smaller one in motion, except in the case in which its motion is on an axis passing through the two centers. From the demonstrative premise and from the demonstrated fact

that vacuum does not exist and from the assumptions regarding eccentricity, it follows necessarily that when the higher sphere is in motion it must move the sphere beneath it with the same motion and around its own center. Now we do not find that this is so. We find rather that neither of the two spheres, the containing and the contained, is set in motion by the movement of the other nor does it move around the other's center or poles, but that each of them has its own particular motion. Hence necessity obliges the belief that between every two spheres there are bodies other than those of the spheres. Now if this be so, how many obscure points remain? (*Guide*, 2:24)

Such contradictions between medieval scientific theory and observation spurred the development of new, complicated astronomical and physical theories that the Rambam found unconvincing. Maimonides was one of the earliest figures in the history of science to identify the insoluble problems of medieval astronomy and physics. In this respect he was a precursor of Kepler, Copernicus. and Galileo, who solved the problems by demolishing the medieval, geocentric foundations of science.

4. See the letter to Rabbi Shmuel Ibn Tibbon's about translating the *Guide* in *Igrot Harambam*, 2:553.

5. See *Guide*, 2:22.

6. The first Hebrew translator of the *Guide*, Rabbi Shmuel Ibn Tibbon, expressed surprise at the Rambam's skepticism about what may be known of the natural world and added marginal notes opining that parts of Maimonides's text must be "missing." See Warren Zev Harvey, "Maimonides' Critical Epistemology and *Guide* 2:24," *Aleph* 8 (2008): 213–35.

7. There is another substantial admission of perplexity in part 1 of the *Guide*: "The things about which there is this perplexity are very numerous in divine matters, few in matters pertaining to natural science, and non-existent in matters pertaining to mathematics" (1:31), That is to say, the more elevated the body of knowledge, the more perplexity there is about it.

16. The Crisis of Tradition

1. See Yair Lorberbaum, *Tmurot B'yahaso shel Ha'rambam L'midrashot Hazal* [On Maimonides's relationship to rabbinic *Midrash*], *Tarbiz* 78 (2009): 203–30.

2. *Igeret el Hokhmei Montpellier* [Letter to the sages of Montpellier], in *Igrot Harambam*, 2:475–76.

3. See *Guide*, 1:31.

17. Mysticism and Politics

1. On this, see D. R. Blumenthal, "Maimonides, Prayer, Worship and Mysticism," in *Approaches to Judaism in Medieval Times*, ed. D. R. Blumenthal, vol. 3 (Atlanta: Scholars Press, 1988), 1–14.

2. The Rambam himself here refers his readers to his discussion of negative attributes: "as we explained when we spoke of attributes" (*Guide*, 3:51).

3. Elliot Wolfson, *Abraham Abulafia, Kabbalist and Prophet: Hermeneutics, Theosophy, and Theurgy* (Los Angeles: Cherub Press, 2000), 38–52; Moshe Idel, *The Mystical Experience in Abraham Abulafia* (Binghamton: SUNY Press, 1988).

18. THERAPEUTIC PERPLEXITY

1. The Rambam criticizes the approach that sets up not knowing as a goal of life and sees spiritual virtue in ignorance. His purpose is not to extol ignorance but to point out that there are limits to the powers of reason.

2. Albert Einstein, *The World as I See It* (New York: Philosophical Library, 1949), 29.

3. Einstein, *The World as I See It*, 29.

4. *Guide*, 1:68.

5. The most prominent modern exponent of this approach to Judaism was Rabbi Abraham Joshua Heschel. In my view, Heschel gave the fullest articulation of the religiosity of the *Guide* and the *Mishneh Torah*. See, e.g., his book *God in Search of Man* (New York: Farrar, Strauss and Giroux, 1976).

6. Note that the Rambam also warns against the opposite intellectual sin of skepticism toward opinions that have been decisively proved to be true; see *Guide*, 1:59.

7. On different types of proof in the *Guide*, see Arthur Hyman, "Demonstrative, Dialectical and Sophistic Arguments in the Philosophy of Moses Maimonides," in Ormsky, *Maimonides and His Time*, 35–51.

CONCLUSION

1. See, e.g., S. Harvey, "Maimonides in the Sultan's Palace."

2. See, e.g., David Hartman, *Torah and Philosophic Quest* (Philadelphia: Jewish Publication Society, 1976).

3. The possibilities that the Rambam presents regarding the ideal life are reflected in a profound disagreement between the medieval Islamic thinkers Ibn Bajja, who believed that the highest human fulfillment consisted in separation from society and devotion to study, and Al-Farabi, who thought that the ultimate fulfillment of philosophy was involvement in society and politics. See Pines, "The Limitations of Human Knowledge."

INDEX

nature, order and chaos in, 180–81; not made for human beings, 143–45; perfection/unchangingness of God and, 175–76, 178–80; Shabbat commandment and, 129–30; unity/oneness of God and, 171–74. *See also* eternity of the world; Garden of Eden crisis of reason, 213–18

David (brother of Maimonides), death of, 41, 63
Dawkins, Richard, *The God Delusion,* 81–82
Day of Atonement (Yom Kippur), 116, 132, 159
decisive versus dialectical proof, 261n6
deism, 1
Descartes, René, 201, 243
desire, refocusing, 83; *eros* (sexual desire), conservation of, 83–85; imbalance between apprehension and desire, 261n8; prophecy and, 27–28, 39; providence and the experience of evil, 48, 50–51, 52; redemption and, 67, 68–69, 71, 79. *See also entries at* love
details in Torah, arbitrariness of, 109–10
dialectical versus decisive proof, 261n6
dietary laws, 136
differences between people, 69–72
distancing commandments, 125–27
divination, 31–32
divinity of Torah, 94, 98
dogmatism: Aristotelianism, Maimonides's critique of, 223–25; authoritativeness, Maimonides seeking to avoid, 225–27; doubt counteracting, 203–4; *halakhah* as means of avoiding, 205–11; mitzvot as cure for, 209–11
doubt, 195–204; "first thoughts," freeing oneself from, 195–96; as intellectual sin, 264n6; methodological versus essentialist, 200–204; postmodernism and, xxi, 241–44; role of, 196–200
dreams, prophecy and, 27–28, 30

Eagleton, Terry, 81–82
economic well-being, reason, and redemption, 67–68, 77–78, 79
egocentrism. *See* anthropocentrism

Egypt: exodus from, 58, 74; Maimonides as physician to sultan in, 41–42; Saladin's conquest of, 48
Einstein, Albert, *The World as I See It,* 237
ekrasia, 135–36
Emden, Jacob, xv
Enosh, religion of, 119–20, 122
Epicurus and Epicureanism, 53, 181, 241
"Epistle to Yemen" (Maimonides), 73, 76, 123
eros (sexual desire), conservation of, 83–85
essentialist versus methodological skepticism, 200–204
eternity of the soul, 262n2
eternity of the world: arguments for, 174–76; existence of God and, 181–85; objections to, 176–80; Torah interpretation and, 87
eudaemonia, 254n5
evil. *See* providence and the problem of evil
existence, medieval understanding of structure of, 213–18
existence of God, 3–15; created/eternal world and, 181–85; doctrine of negative attributes and, 5, 9–15, 82–83, 249n15; immateriality, 6–8; language, God beyond, 9–10; metaphysical proof of, 11–13, 183–85; Mount Sinai, revelation on, 34; unchangingness, 8–9, 14; unity/oneness, 4–9
exodus from Egypt, 58, 74
Ezekiel (prophet), 28, 31, 86

Al-Farabi, 193, 256n21, 264n3
first fruits, 136
"first thoughts," freeing oneself from, 195–96
the Flood, 14, 99
folk beliefs and folk theology, 221, 239
Footnote (film, 2012), xv
formative mitzvot, 129–33
"foundation of foundations," 4–9
Freudian dream theory, 30
Friedlander, Michael, 247n1

Galileo, 263n3
Garden of Eden: nature of sin in, 99; poverty as consequence of sin in, 252n6; as utopian society, 78–79

Gnosticism, 241

God, xx, 1–92; Aristotelianism and Neo-platonism on, 7, 9, 88, 192–94; as author of Torah, 98; balanced personality as imitation of, 107; conservation of *eros* and, 83–85; desire to know, 99–101; evil as absence of, 251n4; hidden and revealed faces of, 65; immateriality/incorporeal-ity of, 3, 6–8, 85, 87, 88, 171–74, 183; as intellect/as transcending intellect, 190–94; interpretation of Bible and, 85–89; language, limitations of, 9–10, 187–89, 193, 231, 255n20; militant atheism on, 81–82; nature as revelation of, 92; negative attributes of, 5, 9–15, 82–83, 189, 192, 193, 231, 249n15, 264n2; palace parable about closeness to, 95–97; physical representation of, 3, 6–8, 85, 87, 88, 187, 221–23, 257n8; reason and intellect, identification in, 164; religion, as greatest threat to, 1, 14–15; religious hero, new concept of, 38–39, 91; Thirteen Attributes of, 102–3; unchangingness/perfection of, 8–9, 14, 65, 175–76, 178–80; unity/oneness of, 4–9, 171–74, 182–83; universality of, 153–56. *See also* existence of God; love of God; prophecy; providence and the problem of evil; redemption

"Golden Mean" (middle way), 24, 104–7, 254n6

Goldman, Eliezer, 254n9

gradual development, principle of, 108–9

The Guide for the Perplexed (Maimonides), xiii–xxi; American readers of, xvii; audience for, 165–66; authoritativeness, seeking to avoid, 225–27; authorship of, xv; Christianity influenced by, xiv, xviii; contradictions and concealment of knowledge in, xvii–xix; dating of, xviii; dedicatory epistle, 259n1; on God, xx, 1–92; Israeli secular culture and, xv–xvii; midrashic nature of reading, 241; *Mishneh Torah* compared, xv, xx, 155–56, 169, 226; perplexity in, xxi, 165–245; personal cir-cumstances of Maimonides when writing,

41–42; purpose of life in, 245; radical interpretation of, 23, 250n3; reason for composing, 15, 247n1, 249n16; structure of, xx; on Torah, xx, 93–64; translations and editions of, 247n1. *See also* contradictions and concealment of knowledge in *Guide*; God; perplexity; Torah

Guttman, Julius, 193

Ha'hakdama L'masekhet Avot (Introduction to *Avot*; Maimonides), 105, 135, 149, 206, 250n4, 251n5, 261n1

Hai Gaon, 29

halakhah and the law: Abraham and, 160; balanced personality, development of, 160, 205–7; divine law and human law, dif-ferentiation of, 36; dogmatism, as means of avoiding, 205–11; for Israel and "the new Jew," xvi; leadership and law, relationship between, 254n9; Maimonides's *Mishneh Torah* concerned with, xv, 169, 210; nature, changes to law of, 74; non-Jews and, 156–58; palace parable and, 95–97, 158, 161, 210; philosophy versus, 156, 158, 167–68; prophecy and, 35, 38; purpose of life in *Guide* and, 245; redemption, Messianic era, and Torah law, 75–78; spiritual great-ness distinguished from, 97, 158, 160–61; utopian anarchy, with no need for, 69–72; welfare of soul and body as aim of, 205. *See also* commandments

Halevi, Yehudah, 154, 219, 249n1, 258n14

happiness, 50, 251n7

Harvey, Warren Zev, 182, 254n9

hechalot literature, 29

Hegel, Georg Friedrich Wilhelm, 77

hero, religious, new concept of, 38–39, 91

Herzl, Theodor, 76

Heschel, Rabbi Abraham Joshua, 264n5

history, Maimonides's views on, 76–77

Hitchens, Christopher, *God Is Not Great*, 81

Holy of Holies, xvii, 128, 159, 160, 209

Hora'at Sha'ah, 255n17

huqqim, 116–17

Ibn Bajja, 264n3

Ibn Daud, 193
Ibn Ezra, Abraham, 219, 258n14
Ibn Pakuda, Rabbenu Bachya, 38, 130, 144, 219, 259n2
Ibn Sina, 183, 193, 250n16
Ibn Tibbon, Shmuel: Hebrew translation of *Guide* by, 247n1, 263n6; letters from Maimonides to, 42, 260n8, 263n4; on providence, 59–61
ideal life and ideal society: economic well-being and reason, 67–68; *halakhah,* as aim of, 205; Ibn Bajja versus Al-Farabi on, 264n3; peace and reason, 68–69; as primary quests of *Guide,* xxi, 245; utopian anarchy, concept of, 69–72. *See also* balanced personality, development of; political theory in *Guide*
idolatry: appropriative commandments and, 127–29, 258n16; of Christianity, 123, 124, 142, 257n8; distancing commandments and, 126–27; emergence of religions and, 120, 123, 124, 125; Maimonides's struggle against, 3, 11; physical representations of God, Maimonides resisting, 3, 6–8, 85, 87, 88, 187, 221–23, 257n8; Torah and idolatrous consciousness, 187
ignorance, 264n1
imagination, and prophecy, 25–26, 26–27, 29, 37
immateriality/incorporeality of God, 3, 6–8, 85, 87, 88, 171–74, 183
intellect. *See* reason and intellect
intellectual pantheism, 190–92
interpretation of Bible, 85–89
Isaac, binding of *(Akedah),* 32, 142
Isaiah (prophet), 28, 66, 74, 86
Islam: Almohad invasion of Spain, 48, 204; Ash'ariyya, 55; kalām and Mutakallimun, 171–74, 182, 203; Mu'atzila, 251n12; Sabians in Koran, 257n12; Saladin's conquest of Egypt, 48; Sufism, 232; sultan, Maimonides as physician to, 41–42
Israeli, Isaac, 219
Israeli secular culture and *The Guide for the Perplexed,* xv–xvii

Jacob wrestling with angel, 32
James, William, *The Varieties of Religious Experience,* 148, 149, 150
Jeremiah (prophet), 44, 86, 232
Jesus: distinguished from Christianity, 257n10; religion of, without commandments, 122–24
Jews and Judaism: Chosen People, 153–54; exodus from Egypt, 58, 74; in Messianic era, 65–66, 73–79; philosophical tradition of Jews, Maimonides on, 219–23
Job, 44, 51–52, 62, 157–58, 169
Joseph Ibn Aknin (Yosef Bar Yehudah), 199, 247n1, 259n1
Jubilee, 75, 158

Kabbalah, xviii, 9, 65, 75, 114–15, 151, 241, 252n1
kalām and Mutakallimun, 171–74, 182, 203
Kant, Immanuel, 93, 130, 251n9
Kapach, Yosef, 247n1
kashrut, 136
Kaufman, Yehezkiel, 249n13
Kepler, Johannes, 263n3
Knohl, Yisrael, 249n13, 258n16
knowledge, love of, 83–85, 200, 213–14, 233, 239
Korach, rebellion of, 44

language, God as beyond, 9–10, 187–89, 193, 231, 255n20
law. *See* commandments; *halakhah* and the law; Torah
Leibowitz, Yeshayahu, 139–42, 146
Levi, tribe of, 158–59, 257n11
Levinger, Yaakov, 250n16
linen and wool, mixing, 116, 126
Lorberbaum, Yair, 170
Lorberbaum, Menachem, 253n16, 254n9
love: *eros* (sexual desire), conservation of, 83–85; of knowledge, 83–85, 200, 213–14, 233, 239. *See also* desire, refocusing
love of God: Abraham as model for, 141–42; *eros* and, 84; evil, overcoming, 61–63; motivation for fulfilling mitzvot and, 78, 145–51; nature, study of, 76, 259n7; as

love of God (*continued*)
primary purpose of mitzvot and Torah, 139–42; as religious experience, 259n7; therapeutic perplexity and cultivating feelings of, 235–40

magic, 221

Maimonides: authoritativeness, seeking to avoid, 225–27; childhood flight from Spain, 47–48, 204; death of brother David, 41, 63; "Epistle to Yemen," 73, 76, 123; *Ha'hakdama L'masekhet Avot* (Introduction to *Avot*), 105, 135, 149, 206, 250n4, 251n5, 261n1; on history, 76–77; Ibn Tibbon, letters to, 42, 260n8, 263n4; knowledge recovered by, xvii–xviii; Montpelier, letter to sages of, 220; physical representations of God resisted by, 3, 6–8, 85, 87, 88, 257n8; as physician to sultan, 41–42; *Shmoneh Perakin (The Eight Chapters)*, 134; significance of, xiv–xv. See also *Guide for the Perplexed*; *Mishneh Torah*

Marx, Groucho, 164

Marx, Karl, and Marxism, 77, 253n14

Menachem Ha-Meiri, 257n8

Messianic era, 65–66, 73–79

metaphysical proof, 11–13, 183–85

methodological versus essentialist skepticism, 200–204

"middle way" (Golden Mean), 24, 104–7, 254n6

midrashim: commandments and, 121, 132; *Guide* and, 241; interpretation of Bible and, 87, 88; on knowledge of God, 100; postmodernism and, xxi; prophecy and, 33; redemption and, 73; on Torah, 112, 252n3

miracles, 20–21, 54–56, 58, 74, 86, 92, 132, 171

Mishnah, 29, 140, 141

Mishneh Torah (Maimonides): Abraham in, 257n6; on commandments, 131, 141, 142, 147, 209; on conservation of *eros*, 84; on emergence of religions, 119, 120, 121, 123, 124; on evil due to bad habits, 48; existence of God in, 4, 248n4; *Guide* compared, xv,

xx, 155–56, 169, 226; *halakhah* addressed in, xv, 169, 210; on immateriality of God, 6, 7, 8; on love and awe, 235, 236, 237, 238; on miracles, 74; on non-Jews, 155–58; on prophecy, 17, 31, 34; on redemption and Messianic era, 65, 67, 73–78; on sin of the elders at Mount Sinai, 261n8; structure of, xviii; on tribe of Levi, 158–59, 257n11; on unchangingness of God, 8, 9; on unity/oneness of God, 4, 5, 6, 8, 9, 248n5; on universality of spiritual excellence, 158–61

mishpatim, 116–17

mitzvot. *See* commandments

monotheism, 11, 119, 122, 142, 257n11

Montpelier, letter to sages of, 220

moon, things existing beneath sphere of, 216, 224, 255n10

moral perfection: causal connections between perfection of character and intellect, 207–9, 261n1; observance of commandments and, 130–31; of philosophers, 205–7; of prophets, 24–25

Moses: authorship of Torah and, 98; commandment-based religion of, 124–25; desire to know God, 99–101; exodus from Egypt and, 58; history changed by, 77; political wisdom of, 101; prophecy of, 34–37, 98; providence and, 44; spiritual equanimity of, 101–4

Mother Teresa, 10

motions of the spheres, 7, 11, 215–18, 262n3

Mount Moriah, 127–28

Mount Sinai, revelation on, 33–34, 98, 261n8

Mu'atzila, 251n12

Munk, Solomon, 247n1

Muslims. *See* Islam

Mutakallimun and kalām, 171–74, 182, 203

mysticism, 9, 28–29, 169, 229–32, 245

Nabataean Agriculture, 257n12

nature: changes to law of, 74, 76; general utility versus individual damage in, 111; God revealed in, 92; imitating balance and equilibrium of, 106–7; love of God and study of, 76, 259n7; mitzvah, contemplation of nature as, 112; not created for human beings, 143–45; order and chaos in, 180–81; political wisdom gained from, 101, 107; spiritual equanimity derived from, 101–4; symmetry of Torah imitating balance of, 111–12; Torah as imitation of, 107–8

necessary existents, 12–13, 184

negative attributes, doctrine of, 5, 9–15, 82–83, 189, 192, 193, 231, 249n15, 264n2

Neo-Aristotelians, 88, 203, 224, 226

Neoplatonism, 192–94, 203

Nietzsche, Frederick, 91

Noahide Laws, 160

non-Jews, 154–58

Nouriel, Avraham, 32

oath asking readers not to explain *Guide,* xviii–xix

old books, seductive aura of, 220–21

oneness/unity of God, 4–9, 171–74, 182–83

ontology, 11–12

paganism: exodus from Egypt and, 58; God in, 11, 18, 58; monotheism versus, 195; nature and, 11; Sabians and Sabian religion, 125–27, 146, 257n12, 258n14; sensory experience and, 257n7; Torah and commandments, 113, 115, 119, 125–27, 128, 129, 188, 258n16

palace parable, 95–97, 158, 161, 202, 210, 242

Pardes, 196, 199, 201, 203, 207, 208, 209

Paul (disciple of Jesus), 130

peace, reason, and redemption, 68–69, 77

perfection: intellectual, 117–19, 133–34, 207–9, 261n1; unchangingness of God, 8–9, 14, 65, 175–76, 178–80. *See also* moral perfection

perplexity, xxi, 165–245; audience of *Guide* and, 165–66; crisis of reason and, 213–18; in divine matters versus natural science and mathematics, 263n7; God as beyond language, 9–10, 187–89, 193, 255n20; God as intellect/as transcending intellect, 190–94; Jewish philosophical tradition,

Maimonides on, 219–23; mysticism as way beyond, 229–32; politics as way beyond, 232–33. *See also* contradictions and concealment of knowledge in *Guide;* creation; dogmatism; doubt; therapeutic perplexity

personality and character. *See* balanced personality, development of

Philo of Alexandria, 219, 256n21

philosophy: authoritativeness, Maimonides seeking to avoid, 225–27; doubt and, 202–4; *halakhah* versus, 156, 158, 167–68; Jewish philosophical tradition, Maimonides on, 219–23; moral perfection of philosopher, 205–7; postmodernist, xxi, 241–44. *See also specific philosophers and philosophical schools*

physical representations of God, Maimonides resisting, 3, 6–8, 85, 87, 88, 187, 221–23, 257n8

physics, laws of: Aristotelian, 181; astronomical observation and, 216–17, 262n3; creation and, 250n13; eternal nature of, 74; God not limited by, 56; in *Mishneh Torah,* 209; Moses's desire to grasp, 100, 101; motions of the spheres, 7, 11, 215–18, 262n3; Pardes and, 196; prophecy and, 28; providence and, 56, 57; study of, 209

Pines, Shlomo, 215, 247n1

Plato, 84–85, 105, 192, 197, 202, 233, 243, 251n4

Plotinus, 192–94, 248n10, 250n12

political theory in *Guide:* conservation of *eros* and, 85; dogmatism and political commitment, 207; egocentrism, problem of, 240; ideal society, interest in conditions for creating, xxi; law and leadership, relationship between, 254n9; nature, political wisdom gained from, 101, 107; perplexity, politics as way beyond, 232–33, 245; providence and, 47; redemption and, 69–70, 71, 72, 74, 76, 77, 78–79; Torah and, 101, 107, 117, 118, 121, 158

Popper, Karl, 79, 243

postmodernism and doubt, xxi, 241–44

potentiality and actualization, 19–20

proofs: decisive versus dialectical, 261n6; dogmatism regarding, 203–4. *See also* existence of God

prophecy, 17–39; biblical stories interpreted as prophetic visions, 32–33, 38; characteristics of prophets, 24–26, 36, 83; desire, refocusing, 27–28, 39; divination (discerning the future), 31–32; experience of, 26–31; *halakhah* and, 35, 38; hero, new concept of, 38–39; Ibn Sina on, 250n16; imagination and, 25–26, 26–27, 29, 37; mitzvot compared, 116; of Moses, 34–37, 98; Mount Sinai, revelation on, 33–34, 98; naturalized yet requiring God's involvement, 20–23; Rashi on, 250n18; reason and intellect in, 26–27, 29, 37–38; traditional and philosophical views of, 17–21; universality of, 154–55; visions, 27, 28–29, 32–33

Protagoras, 243

providence and the problem of evil, 41–63; anthropocentrism, avoidance of, 45, 51, 240; biblical and talmudic understandings of, 43–44; defining and categorizing evil, 45–48, 251n4; denial of existence of evil, 44; denial of existence of providence, 52; desire, refocusing, 48, 50–51, 52; different opinions about, 52–57, 251n4, 251n12; emotional need versus intellectual honesty and, 42–43; human responsibility and, 45–49; Job and, 44, 51–52, 62; love of God and experience of, 61–63; mitzvot compared, 116; personal circumstances of Maimonides and, 41–42, 62–63; reason and intellect, role of, 56–61, 83; suffering of human soul and, 49–52; theodicy, 44, 49; therapeutic approach to, 49, 51, 58; universality of, 155

psychological suffering of human soul, 49–52

Ptolemy, 216

Pyrrho, 243

radical interpretation of *Guide*, 23, 250n3
radical skepticism of modern world, xxi, 241–44

the Rambam (acronym for Rabbi Moses Ben Maimon). *See* Maimonides

Rashi, 250n18

Rava and Abbaye, debates of, 209–10

Ravitsky, Aviezer, 146

reason and intellect: active intellect, 26, 215, 231; causal connections between perfection of character and intellect, 207–9, 261n1; commandments, intellectual perfection through, 117–19, 133–34; contradictions within, 168; crisis of reason, 213–18; differences between people and, 71–72; economic well-being and, 67–68; God as intellect/as transcending intellect, 190–94; identification of God and human essence in, 164, 190–92; light metaphor for, 252n3; limitations of, 197–200, 213–18, 226, 261n8; love of knowledge, 83–85, 200, 213–14, 233, 239; Messianic era and, 66; peace and, 68–69; philosopher, intellectual perfection of, 205–7; prophecy and, 26–27, 29, 37–38; providence and, 56–61, 83; redemption brought about by, 66, 77–79, 83; tensions in *Guide* between Jewish tradition and, 167–68; Torah and, 37–38

redemption, 65–79; desire, refocusing, 67, 68–69, 71, 79; economic well-being and, 67–68, 77–78, 79; marginal place in *Guide*, 65–67; Messianic era, 65–66, 73–79; nature, alteration of laws of, 74, 76; peace and, 68–69, 77; reason and intellect bringing about, 66, 77–79, 83; therapeutic perplexity and, 241–44; Torah laws and, 75–78; unchanging perfection of God, tension with, 65; utopian anarchy, concept of, 69–72; utopian society, unattainability of, 78–79

religion: of Abraham, 120–22, 124, 125, 257nn6–7; apophatic approach to, 82; atheism on, 81–82, 93; emergence of, 119–25; of Enosh, 119–20, 122; experience of, 92, 148–51, 163; God as greatest threat to, 1, 14–15; as infantilizing, 93; James's definition of, 148; of Jesus, 122–24; of Moses, 124–25; nature and experience of, 92; of

Torah (*continued*)
117–18; universality of, 153–61. *See also*
commandments
Tosafot, 257n8
Tower of Babel, 99
Townley, James, 247n1
trees, restrictions on eating fruit from, 126

Uffenheimer, Binyamin, 258n16
uncertainty principle, 181
unchangingness/perfection of God, 8–9, 14,
65, 175–76, 178–80
unity/oneness of God, 4–9, 171–74, 182–83
universality of God and Torah, 153–61
utopian anarchy, concept of, 69–72

utopian society, unattainability of, 78–79

visions, 27, 28–29, 32–33

wool and linen, mixing, 116, 126
world: medieval understanding of cosmos,
213–18. *See also* creation; eternity of the
world

Yom Kippur (Day of Atonement), 116, 132,
159
Yosef Bar Yehudah (Joseph Ibn Aknin), 199,
247n1, 259n1

Zechariah (prophet), 31